D0272332

CLOUGH: THE AUTOBIOGRAPHY

The AUTOBIOGRAPHY

WITH JOHN SADLER

PARTRIDGE PRESS

LONDON · NEW YORK · TORONTO · SYDNEY · AUCKLAND

TRANSWORLD PUBLISHERS LTD
61–63 Uxbridge Road, London W5 5SA

TRANSWORLD PUBLISHERS (AUSTRALIA) PTY LTD
15–25 Helles Avenue, Moorebank, NSW 2170

TRANSWORLD PUBLISHERS (NZ) LTD
3 William Pickering Drive, Albany, Auckland

Published 1994 by Partridge Press
a division of Transworld Publishers Ltd
Copyright © Brian Clough 1994

Reprinted 1994 (four times)

The right of Brian Clough to be identified
as the author of this work has been asserted in accordance
with sections 77 and 78 of the Copyright Designs and
Patents Act 1988.

A catalogue record for this book is available
from the British Library.
ISBN 185225 1980

This book is sold subject to the Standard
Conditions of Sale of Net Books and may
not be resold in the UK below the net
price fixed by the publishers for the book.

All rights reserved. No part of this publication may
be reproduced, stored in a retrieval system, or
transmitted in any form or by any means,
electronic, mechanical, photocopying, recording,
or otherwise, without the prior permission of
the publishers.

Typeset in 11/15pt Century Old Style by
Falcon Graphic Art Ltd,
Wallington, Surrey
Printed and bound in Great Britain by
Mackays of Chatham PLC, Chatham, Kent

For Peter

Still miss you badly. You once said: 'When you get shot of me there won't be as much laughter in your life.' You were right.

ACKNOWLEDGEMENTS

I should like to thank the following for their help and patience: Barbara, Jo Sadler, Wendy Lawrence, Colin Lawrence, Ron Fenton, Adam Sisman and Gerald Mortimer.

They are all good friends. Most of all I should like to acknowledge the help of John Sadler, without whom this book could not have been written.

CONTENTS

CLOUGH: THE AUTOBIOGRAPHY

1
THE MANGLE

I'm a bighead, not a figurehead.

IF EVER I'M FEELING A BIT UPPITY, WHENEVER I GET ON MY HIGH horse, I go and take another look at my dear Mam's mangle that has pride of place in the dining-room at my home in Quarndon.

It had stood for a dozen years or so in our Joe's garage before being beautifully restored. Now it serves as a reminder of the days when I learned what life was all about. On top of it is the casket holding the scroll to my Freedom of the City of Nottingham. My whole life is there in one small part of one room.

The mangle has the greatest significance. It is the symbol of my beginnings. I spent my formative years mangling the sheets for my Mam Sarah. My wife, Barbara, berates me to this day because she believes I wasted my education. I never managed to progress further than a secondary-modern school, no O levels, no A levels, but that mangle taught me more than any teacher in any classroom.

My values stemmed from the family. Anything I have achieved in life has been rooted in my upbringing. Some might have thought No. 11 Valley Road, Middlesbrough, the end of the terrace, was just another council house, but to me it was heaven. Growing up in a hard-working, often hard-up home I was as happy as a pig in the proverbial. I absolutely adored that red-brick house, with its lovely wooden gate and the garden round the side where Dad grew his rhubarb and his sprouts. Council houses had big rooms in those days, so we didn't live like sardines even though we slept three to a bed.

The first memory I have is of running down the alley for my dinner. Now we call it lunch, but it was dinner to us then. I can still recall the lovely, welcoming smell that greeted me as I skipped round the corner.

Mam had eight of us to feed, eight pairs of shoes to clean every night. Joe, my eldest brother, was head of the family, as he still is today. After him came sister Doreen, brothers Des and Bill, me, Gerald, little sister Deanna, and Barry. Another sister, Betty, had died before I arrived. I was born on the first day of spring, 21 March 1935.

Dad, Joseph, seemed to work all the hours God sent. A sugar boiler originally and then manager at Garnett's sweet factory, near Middlesbrough's football ground, Ayresome Park, Dad was obsessed with football and footballers. The great Middlesbrough players of the time, men like Wilf Mannion and George Hardwick, would go to the factory and Dad would give them sweets. Nowadays footballers get cars and too much money. The pendulum has swung the other way and swung too far.

We didn't see that much of Dad. He was off to work by seven-thirty and not home until six or so. But Mam was always there. She ran the house, as most women did in those days. She made my childhood warm and cosy and safe – the most precious gift parents can give their offspring. The smell of liver and onions and the thought of dumplings, always crispy, and then her own rice pudding with nutmeg on the top to follow . . .

Dinner was always on the table and we had to be there to eat it. On time, on the dot. It was the equivalent of a crime to let the dinner go cold. She put it down, piping hot, always with the warning, 'Eat it from around the edges where it's cooler.' I've never forgotten that.

Afterwards there would be Mam's rice pudding, made with Carnation milk. Everything we did, the way we lived, the way the house was run, was controlled by Mam, because she was the one who did the work and the organising. When I look back now to those early days of sheer contentment one factor stands out above all others. My mother was there. All the time, when we got out of bed in the mornings, raced home from school for dinner, again in the afternoon and after playing cricket or football on Clairville Common or Albert Park, she was there.

It's not the fashion to say this nowadays, but a woman's job is to be there. If she is going to have children, she has to look after them. It is not the only part of her job, but it is the most important part. Women who choose to stay at home and raise their families make one of the most valuable contributions to society as far as I am concerned. It is a source of intense annoyance to me when people talk of such women as 'only' housewives. As if it is not a proper job – when in reality it is the toughest and most worthwhile job of all. To come home to an empty house must be petrifying for a small child. I remain certain that the character and disposition of children is established during those formative years. Women today have broader interests and involvements, but I will always be grateful for the security and peace of mind the Clough clan gained from Mam always being there and making our home the best place to be.

She turned that little house into a palace. The front step was scrubbed regularly. I remember how she was so proud of her net curtains and the fact that she managed to keep the same stair carpet for thirty years. Sunday was the only day of the week we were allowed into what we called 'the other room' – that's where the piano was kept and that was the day the whole family gathered round while Mam played and we sang along, songs like 'Come on to my house – I'm going to give you everything'. And she did.

She wouldn't let Dad smoke in that room. He was a Woodbine man and she'd say, 'Dad, if you want to smoke – get out.' No questions, he'd just go out. If he ever dared to do the washing-up with a fag on she would ask, 'Are you dropping ash in that sink?' That had the same effect – he'd go and smoke outside.

Sunday was special but not necessarily popular. Not with me, because Mam would drag us all to the Anglican church where she somehow found the time to scrub their steps as well, every Thursday. All we boys in Fair Isle jumpers looked forward to the walk back when we were allowed an ice-cream. If you were clumsy the blob fell off your cornet and there would be tears but no replacement. Mine never fell off!

There was no playing on Sundays. We wore our Sunday best and that was it. Mam took us to the early service so that she could be home in time to get the dinner ready. We were not allowed out to play on wet days either. The roofs of neighbouring houses were the guide. 'You're not going out until the slates are dry,' she would say – and the message was clearly understood.

There was discipline in our house because, with eight of us, there had to be. I remember my parents arguing and shouting at times but it didn't upset me. We all got out of the way. Mam and Dad didn't swear, but she did get annoyed when he walked into the house with his Woodbine going. She would shout 'Out' and out he'd go.

Dad had our respect, too. He was a calm, gentle, lovely man but he wasn't in charge of that family – Mam was. He'd go to work on his bike, taking his sandwiches in a carrier bag strung on the handlebars. We looked forward to Dad coming in because we didn't have as much time with him as with our Mam. Once we were told 'Dad's coming home', we'd stop messing about and settle down. There was no television, we were brought up on the wireless, gramophone and piano.

Sport – cricket and football – was everything to me from those very early days. My early memories are full of football talk around the house, of Dad standing on the terraces at Ayresome Park, of the occasional precious new pair of boots. I used to practise all the time, and soon I knew that I was better than the others. You don't know you're learning in those lovely, innocent, childhood days in the park or beneath the lamp-post, you're just kicking a ball. The more natural talent you have, the easier it comes to you. Just think how good I might have been if we'd had a school team! But there wasn't one at Marton Grove, not in the junior section, only games lessons for practice. And only after the 'long march'. On Tuesdays we were assembled for the walk, half a mile or more, to another local school, a snobby one. Any school that had a pitch, at that time, was regarded as snobby. A whole column of us walked two-by-two, as if instructed by Noah himself. By the time we reached the pitch we were knackered. But I was out of the classroom, all that mattered to a lad who was besotted, consumed by football.

Academically I was thick. School wasn't bad, but I was.

In many ways I was a disgrace, such was my lack of interest in everything other than games. All I wanted in the early days at school was to get out into the open air. I'm not sure school taught me that Columbus discovered America, I learned that in later life. Some people might wish he never had, because if they are the leading lights in this world, my God, they leave a lot to be desired.

Some weekends Dad would bike to the factory and I can still feel that warm glow when I recall his invitation: 'If you want to come, son, you walk up there.' I ran the entire mile and a half and was never out of breath. As you might imagine, the sweet factory was an Aladdin's Cave to one so young. We were allowed a quarter of sweets on those occasions, but I stole much more. I used to pinch as a kid: apples, pears, and sometimes stamps from Woolworths. I don't know why, because I gave the stamps away.

I still shudder at the thought of the day, the only day, I played truant. What makes a lad skip school? Fear, maybe? Perhaps it was a history lesson or geography lesson I didn't fancy, I can't recall exactly, but I vividly remember a scary feeling inside when I decided to do a bunk and spend the afternoon in Albert Park, tadpoling in the stream. I fell in. I was terrified of Mam and Dad finding out. I was wet through up to the waist of my shorts and my sandals were squeaking, but somehow I managed to talk my way out of trouble and they never discovered the truth.

The only time I embarrassed them was when a Woolworths girl who used to live opposite us caught me nicking stamps and blabbed to Mam. I didn't exactly look forward to Dad returning from work that night because I had to confess. I wasn't allowed out again until the next day and that, to me, was purgatory. All I ever wanted was to get out and run around and play with a ball – mainly cricket. I really wanted to be a cricketer. Believe it or not, cricket was my first love. I would genuinely have swapped the dream of a winning goal at Wembley for a century against the Australians at Lord's. I wanted to be Len Hutton. I spent long, idyllic summers believing I could be just like him. Hutton was, of course, a Yorkshireman, and since I was Yorkshire through and through, he was my boyhood hero. I was to meet him, indeed, to sit alongside him, at a match years later, and he was such a let-down. He bored me to tears.

In my school days, though, he was the sporting figure I idolised. Someone else for whom I have the greatest respect and admiration is Geoffrey Boycott, who became a close family friend. Unlike many, Geoffrey did not slip down the batting order as he got older. He spent his entire career going first to face that hard, shiny, dangerous new ball – even at forty years of age – and never shirked it. Now he is among the most accomplished of cricket's commentators.

I still take delight, though, in reminding him of the day I got him out, caught-and-bowled, at Lord's in a charity match with the Taverners. He will say he spooned it back deliberately, but don't you believe it. He couldn't read my wrong-'un.

Winters were just as wonderful as the summer days when the sun shone. I was always outside with a pal called Wogger Gibson who had been to Borstal: I never found out why and wasn't bothered enough to ask. He was a couple of years older than me. Mam would warn: 'You keep away from him,' but he was always around and, like me, not put off by the cold.

One of the highlights was to wee in the snow. We've all done it, haven't we? When you come out of the house and into the cold you want to wee. I was the best in the neighbourhood at spelling my name. To be fair, though, I only used to write 'Brian' because whenever I attempted 'Clough' I always soaked my shoes.

Winter meant Christmas and we believed in Father Christmas at our house because it never crossed our minds that our Mam or

Dad would tell us any lies. It was a stocking each, not a pillowcase as in some houses – Mam and Dad couldn't afford to fill one of those. Oh, that sense of wonder and excitement as we woke on Christmas morning and the stocking arrived as if by magic! A tangerine, an apple and a packet of sweets. Some nuts and, at the very bottom, a two-shilling piece or the old half-crown. Dad used to go to the bank to make sure the coins were shiny, new ones.

They couldn't afford to give us lavish presents, although I do remember Dad giving me a fort with soldiers and indians. Everything was shared, and the others joined in when I played with it on the stairs. Mostly, though, play was with a ball. Summer meant cricket, and tennis in Albert Park with my first racket that was the pride and joy of my life and which my eldest son, Simon, still possesses to this day. Winter meant football through the darker nights. Many an FA Cup Final was played beneath street lamps.

My first physical training was 'doing the messages', the errands we shared for Mam. I used to run everywhere. When I fetched a couple of stones of spuds, for instance, I split them into two bags. Running hard with a bag in each hand created an excellent sense of balance. They said that was one of my gifts as a player, years later – always balanced. I suppose there were times when the young Clough actually walked, apart from to church on Sunday mornings and reluctantly into a history lesson, but I don't remember many. It was run, run, run.

A man on a bike came down Valley Road so regularly you could set your watch by him if you had one. I never knew his name, he was just a bloke on his way home from work, but I'd run with him for as far as I could. I'd be about ten years old and he once asked me if I was using him as a pacemaker. I hadn't a clue what he was talking about but I suppose I was doing exactly that. He was somebody to run with or against –

just another opportunity, another challenge, another chance to run. Maybe he was the reason why I eventually won the school marathon.

I ran to fetch the herrings from the bloke who came round once a week with his horse and cart. I ran for the pease-pudding and faggots. Now that little task needed balance, because I had to take a dish: if I spilled any on the way back I'd get a clip from anyone who was handy. Our Joe used to clip me on occasions – elder brothers did in those days.

The back-kitchen was the nerve centre of the Clough operation. It was where Mam did the cooking and the washing and cleaned all those bloody shoes and suffered her persistent headaches, from which she found relief with a couple of aspirins and the request, 'Draw the curtains a while, son. I'll rest a little.' I suppose it was what we'd call a migraine, these days. It worried me to see her in any kind of distress.

It pleased me to see her smile. I remember how much she used to look forward to her weekly night out at the local cinema and theatre, the Empire and Palladium. That was her way out of the back-kitchen, her break from looking after eight of us. Everybody has to get the hell out of it sooner or later. I have to, even now.

Every year Mam and Dad somehow scraped together enough money to take us all for a two-week holiday in Blackpool. What joy and adventure the youngsters of today are missing as they sit indoors mucking about with computer games and videos!

Such an upbringing relied heavily on discipline and routine. The boys had to be cleaned up when we came in muddy and bedraggled from the latest 'cup tie' in the park. We 'did' for one another. Knees and feet had to be washed in the kitchen sink. Eventually we were all warm and clean – you had to be when you slept three to a bed and possessed two sets of clothes, one for school and Sundays and the other, with holes in, for everything else. Little wonder we weren't allowed out to play unless the slates were dry.

When I got home I was expected to help mangle the sheets, so that it was all done before Dad got home at six. He would nearly always ask, 'What have you been doing all day?'

Mam was not one to be impressed by relatively unimportant things. She was never carried away by my later success in football and so-called fame as a manager but I know it pleased her when they made me Head Boy of Marton Grove. Thick, but Head Boy all the same and, before you ask, no, I was not a stroppy one. If I caught the late-comers I didn't clout them but just reminded them of the importance of being on time. I had been caught out arriving at ten past nine once myself, and I was ashamed and embarrassed. Mam had done her bit. She had got me up, fed me and thrown me out with the rest as usual.

It was a Monday – it must have been because Mondays were murder. It was school again, after the sheer bliss of the weekend at home, and I didn't want to go. It was washing day and Mam was always up earlier than in the rest of the week. If it was a good drying day she'd be out there in her little woollen hat pegging the sheets before nine o'clock. The only time my mother ever bragged was when she said, 'Mrs Fisher, next door, never has her washing out until after ten o'clock in the morning.' Mam was always on time and yet there I was, turning up at school at ten past nine.

Becoming Head Boy – that still makes me as proud as my OBE, my Honorary Degree, or my Freedom of Nottingham. Thick, but Head Boy – I think one of the senior teachers with an interest in sport brought some influence to bear. The school gave me a cap for being Head Boy – England only gave me two, years later, for being the best goal-scorer around!

Yet I was never Mam's favourite son – that was our Bill, who once won a teapot in a 'lovely baby' contest. She used to say that Bill was a big lad, and gave him 'seconds' at dinner. He always got more food than any of us. Why? Because he won the teapot and later went to grammar school. He is the most placid and charming of men and now lives in the Lake District. But I remember to this day how he once humiliated me. One of my pals had told him that I'd failed my Eleven Plus; Bill came home on his bike, walked into the house and blurted it out for everyone to hear. I was feeling bad enough without that.

I was the one out of the family who did least well at school. Although I was to go on and 'make it' in terms of fame and fortune, the surviving members of the family know that if ever I'm in danger of getting uppity they only need to tell me to walk into my dining-room.

And take one more look at Mam's mangle.

2

FINDING MY FEET

Get that f**king ball over to me. I'm here to put
it in the net, not you.

WHEN I WAS A KID GROWING UP IN THE NORTH-EAST, FOOTBALL WAS
a religion. It was in the blood. Even today, the game generates
more passion among the folk of that region than anywhere else
in the country. In the eyes of the Geordies, Wear-siders and
Teessiders, England finishes at Middlesbrough. There is nothing
of any importance or significance beyond Ayresome Park. The
North-East is the most passionately parochial place I have ever

known: perfect for a starry-eyed youngster born with a burning desire to put the ball in the net.

Sport wasn't just an activity, a release from the thought of schoolwork, or a chance to get out of the house. Sport was everything to me, it was the meaning of life itself.

I could do a bit with both bat and ball at cricket but, inevitably, football became my priority. It was inevitable once I discovered that goal-scoring was my speciality. I never wanted to be a wing-half – they call them midfield players today – because that job basically meant you were a provider, rather than the one who applied the glorious finish. I did fancy myself at the back, defending: the easiest position, since most of the time you are facing the ball. But my forte was scoring goals, the most difficult task in the game. Then, as now, the one who could put the ball in the net, time after time, was in greatest demand.

I learned how to play by covering every single blade of grass in Middlesbrough. At least, looking back, that's the way it seemed. I learned my skills on Clairville Common, in Albert Park, and on a cinder pitch just down the road. Often we played in the road itself.

I learned most, I suppose, around the ages of fifteen and sixteen, when groups of older lads would sometimes let me join in. On other occasions they would say 'Get out of it' and I did exactly that, I scarpered. If you hung around they gave you a clip. It happened to me, countless times, but it did me no harm to learn when I was or wasn't wanted. When they let me play, my God, was I in my element! They used to whack me all over the place, leaving me on my bum more than I was on my feet. It was a form of bullying, I suppose, but I never looked upon it like that because the pain faded once you scored a goal – and I scored plenty against the bigger guys.

My introduction to competitive team football was playing with my brothers and a brother-in-law for Great Broughton.

We played on Saturday or Sunday afternoons – once we had managed to shift the sheep- and cow-shit off the pitch. The side was run by a very kind lady, Mrs Nancy Goldsbrough, who ran the Post Office. Great Broughton was a fair way from home, fifteen miles or so, and we rode there on the back of a potato lorry. Small wonder I appreciated the luxury of a coach ride to Wembley, years later! Get there by truck, move the sheep and clear the muck, pull on the No. 9 shirt and play – sheer bliss. And always the No. 9.

Somehow, playing for Great Broughton was more important to me than just a match, although it was my first taste of organised competition. It was a trip out. I was not allowed to go to many places. Our Joe and Des and Bill, the senior members, had much greater freedom. I dreaded hearing these words from Mam or Dad: 'You can't go.' I was always bursting to get out.

Mrs Goldsbrough organised the matches, arranged referees and linesmen, and helped clear the sheep from the field. She didn't attempt to coach us or tell me how to put the ball in the net. No need. There were no showers and no bath. We arrived dirty, went home a lot dirtier, and enjoyed every single second.

Goals came easy from the very beginning. I know that sounds rather boastful and I do find it difficult talking about the subject of goal-scoring because, which ever way you look at it, I was good at it! I was never frightened and always kept my eye on the ball. It was the only thing I had in mind and, years later, it was to be my undoing, the element of my game which brought a premature end to my playing career. Once around the penalty area there could be somebody pushing, somebody trying to hack me down, somebody clinging to my shirt. None of that bothered me. I was never, ever, physically afraid. My terms of reference were basic and simple: put the ball in the net. That was my job, that's the way I saw it, and I allowed nothing and nobody to distract me from that purpose.

Eventually I played with other teams: South Bank, a well-known amateur club in the area, and another with the peculiar name of Billingham Sinthonia – sounds more like an orchestra, doesn't it? That was the only time I ever cheated the Inland Revenue. Billingham used to give me a quid for playing, which I didn't declare. I suppose I regarded it as expenses and spent it on dubbin for my big old-fashioned boots. But my dear old Mam thought that I needed a proper job. When I left school at fifteen, she solemnly advised: 'Put in for a nice job as a fitter and turner at ICI.' So I did.

That massive ICI plant, the source of employment for so many people in the area, shocked me in some ways. I turned up for my first day at work feeling utterly bewildered. I was frightened. It was the first time I had been away from home on my own, and, for a few moments, before stepping through them, I just stood and looked at the big metal gates. They were the biggest I'd ever seen. I know it's a cliché and you've heard it many times before, but to a boy not yet sixteen, with his sandwiches and bottle of pop in his pocket, they really did represent the gates of hell. Maybe I would have felt differently if I'd known Barbara was to work at ICI, too, but at the time I hadn't even met her.

Once inside, I did nothing. I couldn't do anything. I was marched around for a while – can't remember why, probably to show me where I would be expected to do my bit – but after those glorious, innocent school-days and a childhood spent outdoors, it was like a sudden introduction to a military way of life. I simply sat around for most of that first day. Come to think of it, I did a lot of sitting around for the next few weeks: just sitting there and listening to all the talk and technicalities. I suppose they were trying to explain to me what was involved in becoming a fitter and turner. It meant nothing. I was never cut out for fitting or turning in the first place.

One day they trooped us off to an anhydrite mine. What a shaker! I hated the lift and wasn't too keen on the rest of the mine either. I still don't like being in the air or below ground, preferring both feet on the floor and on the surface. That place scared me out of my wits. I wasn't prepared for the things I saw. Nobody told me there were lorries down a mine! Mam and Dad had always taught me to keep off the roads. But there I was, told, like the others, to press myself against the wall. I was petrified just being down there in the first place, and then there's a lorry heading my way carrying a load of white stuff that I couldn't even spell! I couldn't wait to get the hell out of there. Whatever they wanted to teach me after that, fitting and turning, geography or brain surgery, they hadn't a chance. They had scared me off.

Walking round that plant until fatigue set in, listening to the equivalent of schoolmasters telling us things I couldn't understand, equipped me for nothing. I didn't know what they were talking about and didn't particularly care, because I quickly lost any sense of ambition. What a frame of mind in which to take your first exam!

Excuse me if the detail seems obscure, but it struck me as bloody odd at the time. They stuck a tray in front of me, piled high with keys, locks, bolts, all kinds of metal objects. I hadn't the remotest idea what I was supposed to do with them – and still haven't today. I failed the apprenticeship miserably. They told me they thought I was sufficiently talented to become a 'junior clerk'. They couldn't kid me – I knew they meant 'messenger', but were trying to dress it up and make it sound more grand. It wasn't grand at all. I was sixteen and running about with notes from department to department. Finally I was recruited to what they called 'work study', which sounds a bit like time-and-motion but wasn't. It entailed filling in overtime sheets. Grand indeed! One thing puzzled me about my routine. I was told my working day began at twelve minutes past seven. Not ten past or quarter-past but *twelve* minutes past – I ask you! Over the week we were allowed five minutes' grace, apparently for late arrival. I was cycling to work by then – Mam and Dad had bought me a bike. Not one with the thick tyres like Dad's, but the narrow ones and the dropped handlebars which, to me, meant it was the real racer I never thought I'd possess. Why the hell didn't I keep it? I'd give anything to have it today.

Apart from anything else, it would remind me of the way I used to manipulate the system that gave us the five minutes' grace. I was always on time in the mornings, so I stored my five minutes until the end of the week. Then I'd be off home, on my racer, five minutes before the rest, having arranged for one of the other lads to clock out for me at the normal time. I suppose that was the first time Brian Clough stood by a principle. Who says time waits for no man? This young man didn't have to wait much longer for his escape from that military way of life. I'd known for a long time that I really wanted to be a footballer. I'd watched Middlesbrough players coming and going from Ayresome Park, only a quarter of a mile or so from home. I'd seen them living the dream that was shared by every boy who could kick a ball. The difference for me was that I knew I could be good enough to turn such dreams into reality.

Thank heavens for Ray Grant, a teacher at Hugh Bell School who had seen me banging in the goals for Great Broughton. He was the one who recommended me to Middlesbrough, then in the Second Division. After a spell playing for their junior side, which Mr Grant helped run, I was invited to sign as a professional. I didn't need asking twice. I didn't need to talk terms, either. They didn't give me the chance – £1 per week retainer and £7 if I was actually selected to play in any of the teams. Needless to say, the money went straight into a Post Office savings account. A few years later I had enough in there to persuade Barbara I was worth marrying!

But before I ever met Barbara I was called up for National Service. Funny, but whenever the subject of National Service is mentioned, the first thing I remember about my days in the RAF is the uniform. I'd hated the thought of leaving home for two years, but that uniform generated a strange sense of pride the moment I was kitted out and put it on. I suppose that, in one sense or other, I've been wearing a type of uniform all my life.

I did my square-bashing – twelve weeks' hard slog that wouldn't do any harm to the youngsters of today – at Padgate, near Manchester. After the first day I wrote home to assure Mam that I was fine. She had previous experience of offspring coming to terms with life in the Forces. Doreen had been in the Wrens – serving in this country during the final stages of the War; Joe had done his time in the Royal Navy, being sea-sick for much of his early time, apparently; and Des had served with the Marines. Dad's military days were the dramatic ones, though, and occupied many an evening around the fire whenever his children – and mine, in later years – demanded a story.

Dad saw active service as a private in the King's Own Yorkshire Light Infantry during the First World War. In fact, he was returned from the front and discharged as a result of wounds that had left him with a slight but permanent limp. For some time after coming home – a single man in those days, of course – he suffered temporary deafness, caused by the explosive sounds of the heavy guns. The story, or the version, we all loved to hear most, was the way Mam related the circumstances in which Dad was wounded in the ankle and was also left with a constant reminder of where a bullet nicked away a tiny part of his nose. 'Your Dad was running away from the Germans when he was shot in the ankle,' she would say, 'and he wouldn't have been shot in the nose if he hadn't turned round to see if they were chasing him!' It wasn't true but it made us laugh and, over the years, it became a traditional family joke.

After my initial training at Padgate, I seemed to spend the rest of my time in the RAF marching, occasionally standing to attention, swimming, running and playing football. Or sneaking off, given the slightest opportunity, to listen to the Test Match radio commentary. I was brought up listening to cricket – radio allows us to imagine far better pictures than television now provides. It was the era of the great spin duo, Jim Laker and Tony Lock.

I never reached a higher rank than Leading Aircraftsman and wasn't bothered. The friendship, the strength of the camaraderie among a group of young men reluctantly brought together, somehow produced a status far more meaningful than mere rank. In fact, only recently I heard from one of the members of the squad, Jimmy Holroyd. Another, a lad called Jackie Wilkinson who slept next but one to me, said one morning, 'You could do with your hair seeing to.' And he saw to it. He gave me the crew cut, the close-cropped hairstyle I kept through my playing days, although 'style' might not be the word Vidal Sassoon would use. It's nice that Jimmy got in touch.

The RAF allowed me to play a lot of football but, like England later, they failed to recognise real talent when it was under their noses. I played for the station side but was never picked for the national RAF team. I was a bit miffed about that, but grateful for other things my two years in the Forces taught me: how to use a shower, for a start. I'd never seen one before being called up. It had always been a bath. I wasn't embarrassed by communal showers in the RAF, they didn't bother me – it was the cold. Showers are *cold*. No wonder that even now I hate them, far preferring to wallow in a beautifully warm bath.

Travelling home on leave from the base at Watchet in the West Country was a long, long way by train. But it became extremely well-paid leave when I managed to get a game at £7 a time with the Middlesbrough third team or reserves. Bear in mind that I was being paid 37/6d (£1.87p) a week anyway, so those long trips across country were well worth it. Happy days.

Suddenly I was made aware of the opposite sex. There will be those to whom this particular item will be the most startling part of my book. Could anybody imagine, in this so-called enlightened and liberated age, that a fit and vibrant youngster nearing his twenties hadn't 'dabbled' with the girls in some way or another? But I was never one for the girls at that time – never bothered, honest. I hadn't even noticed, to tell you the truth. I was always too wrapped up with my cricket; until one night of discovery, after a football match we played at a base in Wales. The customary social get-together had been arranged, the local girls had been allowed in and everybody was dancing. Except me.

All the lads were sitting together and the rest of them had claimed a partner. I was the last one, sitting alone at the table with nobody to talk to. I didn't know what to do. You don't learn to dance on Clairville Common or in Albert Park or under the lamp-post with a ball at your feet or a cricket bat in your hand. I didn't know a single step. I was isolated, I was out of the game.

And then a girl, a dark-haired, pretty girl who couldn't have appreciated the extent of her own courage, took pity on me. She walked across to the table, promptly grabbed my hand and asked me to dance. It seemed more like a command than a request, and I didn't have the heart to tell her I couldn't dance at all. On reflection I probably didn't want to appear more of a prat than I already looked. So I wandered onto the dance floor with that pleasant young lady from the Rhondda Valley. There I was, decked out in RAF uniform, doing my level best to move my feet in time with the beat of the music. I remember being surprised at the slippery surface. My first physical contact with a girl, albeit sweet and innocent and in public, was hampered by not being able to dance and a bloody treacherous dance floor! But I persevered and shuffled on through a few dances – and then she bombed me out. Not nastily but there was no nipping outside, no taking her home. When time was up, when the social evening was over, she disappeared into the night.

She made a real impression on me, and on a couple of occasions I took the trouble to go by train to the Rhondda to see her. I bought a box of chocolates. She was the only girl I knew, the first one I met while doing National Service, and she had paid me a supreme compliment. When I was the last one sitting at the table and nobody wanted to look at me – probably because of my white face and the big ears that used to hold up the cap my Mam always made sure I wore when I was little – she had the courage and the kindness to ask me onto the floor. I had been brought up in a man's world, still am, and although I only saw the girl two or three times and nothing developed, I'll always remember that first dance. I am ashamed to admit I cannot remember her name!

I do remember Mary. Her mother used to cook me lovely meals. She was my first serious girlfriend, the first I 'courted', as we used to say in those days. I was out of the RAF and playing for Middlesbrough's second team by the time we met. I was full of myself, but my success didn't mean a thing to her. She once said to me: 'Who do you think you are? You're just a reserve-team centre-forward!' Can you imagine that? She flattened me! But we did get quite close. The courtship must have lasted beyond a year, and I actually asked her to marry me. She refused, unless I agreed to a wedding in a Catholic church. She missed out, poor girl. She was an absolute stunner, but the last I heard she was still single. She was such a good looker, an absolutely beautiful brunette. According to one of my sisters, she later worked in the Middlesbrough branch of Boots the chemists.

Then there was Wendy – oh, Wendy! Wendy and I played a lot of tennis in Albert Park. I'd become quite a good tennis player, in fact I was good at anything that involved a moving ball. Not good enough, though, for her father, who was soon to make that abundantly clear. Wendy's family lived in one of the posher parts of town – Devonshire Road, I think – and my first sight of her home was spectacular. It was a big house with a very big front-room. I didn't feel comfortable – you need to have lived in big rooms to feel at home in them. I was more familiar with a little back-kitchen, a sink, and a front-room where we were allowed to congregate only on Sundays. Still, I'd done the hard part – I'd made it through the front door. I thought I'd cracked it. Enter Wendy's father.

I'm not sure what her old man did for a living – insurance, possibly, or something similar – but he had 'got on' as we used to say. His delivery was sudden, frank and to the point. In fact, it was downright rude. He came straight out with it: 'I don't think you are the right one for my daughter.' I just sat there. I couldn't take it in. I honestly didn't know what the man was talking about. I had never spoken to Wendy about marriage or anything like that. Maybe he thought that I was not good enough, despite appearing to be a reasonable young man, because I came from a council house in Valley Road. I wonder whether he'd noticed the stuffing poking out of his settee – Mam wouldn't have tolerated anything like that at our house. Perhaps he thought his daughter would go on to better things, and I don't suppose there's a lot wrong with that from a father's point of view. We all want the best for our daughters. If yours brought home a bum for a boyfriend you'd tell her. I wasn't a bum at all, not by any stretch of the imagination, I was clean cut, absolutely

immaculate, and going on to a promising career. Not only that
but everybody who saw me in tennis shorts was of the same
opinion – I had 'lovely legs'!

When I had got on a bit and started banging in the goals for
Middlesbrough to the tune of 40 a season, would you believe that
Wendy's father had the audacity to write to me and say: 'You are
very welcome to come to my house and see Wendy'? I wouldn't
have gone round there to see her or him for anything. In any
case, somebody far more influential and important had entered
my life. Peter Taylor had been transferred from Coventry to
Middlesbrough.

At the time I was Middlesbrough's fifth-choice centre-forward.
Taylor's first words to me made a big impression: 'I don't know
what's going on at this club. You are better than anybody here.'

That was Peter. That was him throughout the rest of his life
– instant judgement, taking little or no time, as long as it was
based on what he considered to be solid evidence. And never
the use of six words where two would do. I was a wide-eyed
innocent by comparison and remember asking him in that first
conversation after training: 'How do you know I'm better than
that lot?' He said: 'You put 'em in the net better than anybody
else. I'm a goalkeeper, so I know.' As Eric Morecambe used to
say, there's no answer to that, and I was not going to argue.

Taylor's words were the first recognition I'd ever had as a
footballer. I'd gone through my early days with Great Broughton,
South Bank, Billingham Sinthonia, and nobody had ever said
much at all. I thought I was good, no, I knew I was good, but
everybody needs somebody to confirm their own belief in themselves. To me, scoring goals was just like other boys might
regard delivering papers. I just did it – every day. Though I
favoured my right foot and knew my left was a comparative
dummy, I scored with both. Any ball that came from the right –
unless I had time to manœuvre it to my stronger foot – I'd hit

with my left. And most of them flew into the net, especialiy as the weaker foot grew stronger.

I became close friends with Taylor, partly because neither of us had a car, so we travelled around together. Being married, he had a nice club house opposite Price's clothes factory. I used to go round to his house for lunch after training. His wife Lillian made smashing chips – she must have cooked me more chips than the local fish shop. Peter and I would walk home for lunch through Albert Park, talking football the whole of the way, until we were interrupted by the factory girls coming out of Price's for their break. Peter could never understand why I wasn't more interested, being single and not having much to do. It used to puzzle him. He'd say, 'They're looking at you, you know', but I wasn't a bit interested.

Taylor's interest in me meant far more. He boosted me. Over my years in management I have tried to do the same thing for the benefit of many players, even those in the million-pounds-or-more bracket, like Trevor Francis. Irrespective of their ability, you'd be absolutely staggered at how much they need a reassuring little lift at various stages of their careers.

Everybody needs a boost. Mam and Dad needed one – and got one from the wallflowers I brought home and planted in the garden for as many years as I can remember. The council lads put them out in the beds in Albert Park over a period of three or four days and when I enquired, walking to Ayresome on my way to training, they'd shout: 'Not yet, Bri,' or 'We're still eeking them out,' until I was given the go-ahead: 'We'll have 'em for you tomorrow.' That was the day I took Dad's barrow and filled the flower-beds at No. 11. And they didn't cost a penny.

3

GOALS, GOALS, GOALS

Barbara often asks me, 'What are you thinking?'
and I'll say 'Nowt' and she doesn't believe me, but
it's true. When I saw those goals in front of me, I
thought of nothing but putting the ball in that space,
everything else seemed to freeze for me.

PETER TAYLOR'S CONFIDENCE IN MY TALENT INTENSIFIED THE FEELING
of frustration that smouldered and burned inside me. I should have
been in the first team, but found myself confined to the reserves.
It led to a brief falling-out with manager Bob Dennison, a kindly,

old-school type of manager who was slow to spot my potential. I went to see him and asked for a rise. Very strict and very formal at that time, you weren't invited to sit down and you had to stand straight as a guardsman.

The system in football was crazy, then. Not only a maximum wage ceiling and bonuses of £2 for a win and £1 for a draw, but less money in the summer than during the season itself. Dennison was reluctant to pay me more but had to concede the point when I told him: 'I'm just as good a player as the great Len Shackleton – in the summer.' I don't think that smart-alec but true remark swung the matter, but I went from £9 to £11 a week. And soon, thank goodness, to the first team.

But I had to protest, first. I could acknowledge that Alan Peacock warranted a place in the side because he was good enough to become an international although, again, I was as good as him in the summer. That bristling arrogance of mine wouldn't allow me to accept what I considered to be injustice. Mam and Dad didn't allow us to be cheeky as kids, but if something irritated me I couldn't resist saying so. There were times when, as Taylor and I travelled from the ground by bus, the conductress would shout 'We're full' and ring the bell with people standing on the pavement. I'd shout: 'Oh no, we're bloody not – there are plenty of seats up here.' Like all youngsters we preferred the top deck. Taylor would hiss at me: 'You can't get away with this.' And I'd say to him: 'Oh, but I can. For a start, she's not bothered to check upstairs and, secondly, they're our buses!'

To my mind, my own position was just the same – the first-team bus would not stop for me. I sensed injustice. I was confined to the reserves, while Doug Cooper had the No. 9 shirt in the first team. I knew I was streets ahead of him, that he was too big, too fat, couldn't move, and that I could have stuck the ball through his legs five times before he blinked. It annoyed and frustrated me that he was in the League side rather than me. And it didn't help when I went home and thought of what Mary had said: 'You're just a reserve-team centre-forward.'

My début was against Barnsley at Oakwell. I can't remember the score but do recall that I didn't! What stuck with me most of all was the important lesson that I would eventually take with me into management. I was eager to get out there and justify my belief in myself, but nervous. One who was to become notorious for his apparent self-confidence was again in need of that vital, well-timed little boost.

At the very moment I walked towards the dressing-room door, on my way out with the rest of the team, Dennison called to me: 'It's up to you now.' That was wrong. He should have cuffed me on the back of the head or shoulder and said, 'Good luck, son. I know you'll do well.' He sent me out on a downer. He put fear in my heart when he should have put me at ease. It was a mistake I never made in twenty-eight years as a manager. When footballers go out on the field they have to be relaxed, not frightened. Sometimes that frame of mind is difficult to achieve, but they simply *have* to relax. I don't know anyone who can do anything to the best of his ability if he is taut with apprehension. You can't work, play, sing or enjoy sex to the best effect unless you have peace of mind. There was no point in my spending all week training and motivating players and then sending them into a match as tight as guitar strings.

Taylor always seemed to be relaxed at Middlesbrough, even though he was in and out of the first team. He was a Midlander, born and bred in Nottingham, and Dennison was a Coventry man. They were of similar ilk and inevitably soon became friendly. It was difficult not to become friends with Peter Taylor.

I can see him now, street-wise Pete, on the occasions Middlesbrough played at Plymouth. We'd go by train to Darlington and then by overnight sleeper to Devon. The first thing I was interested in on Darlington platform was finding my compartment on the train and getting settled for the journey. Taylor had other ideas. Invariably there were spare tickets and Peter would be up and down the platform, selling them. I'm sure he used to split the money with Bob Dennison. It was my first insight into the Peter Taylor business acumen!

I was always a good watcher, I suppose, and I didn't miss much. I certainly didn't miss the vision in the café where some of us called after training – Rea's Café, belonging to the family of Chris Rea, the talented singer-songwriter of today. I'd spotted a girl in there with a smile as wide as Stockton High Street. Little did I know then that my future wife had been brought up so close to where I lived – just on the other side of Albert Park. It was some time before I plucked up the courage to introduce myself. The prolific goal-scorer, the so-called star of Teesside, bought himself a strawberry milkshake, wandered over and said: 'Hello, my name is Brian.' Such silver-tongued charm! Not much in that introduction for a James Bond film, is there? I did follow it up and buy her a coffee.

Who cares? That was the start of an extraordinary relationship that has endured thirty-five years. I often wonder how, but I know that without Barbara's love, loyalty, understanding and remarkable tolerance, Brian Clough would not have succeeded or survived.

Barbara Glasgow lived in Gifford Street with her Mam, Winifred, who made gorgeous coconut cakes, and her Dad, Harry. I'd ride round there on my bike several nights a week. I still wore the flat cap and I think Barbara's Dad approved of that. Everybody living in Middlesbrough had a hat because it was darned cold. As a nipper, the last words I heard from my Mam as I left the house were 'Get your cap on', and on it went, 'cos those were the days when children did as they were told.

When I started taking Barbara out I was still expected to be home at night by nine-thirty. I sometimes missed the curfew as my obsession increased, but on the occasions I arrived home around tennish Mam would say: 'You're not going out tomorrow.' And I couldn't. I had to stay in, simple as that. It didn't matter that I was in my early twenties and a forty-goal-a-season Middlesbrough centre-forward, I had to be in on time, no ifs or buts. Next morning there were 2 lbs of sprouts to be picked from the garden and in Middlesbrough in January, the frost nips your fingers when you don't have gloves. The rules began to ease in time and the relationship, thank God, flourished.

We got on well from the start. I was totally infatuated by an extremely attractive girl who became, as she is now, an extremely attractive woman. It just developed. We used to go to the pictures, basically because there was little else to do.

Sunday afternoons were different. We used to go walking in Albert Park – but not together. Barbara walked with her friends, while I walked with my own pals. Blissful days, when you could walk along the pathway from the cannon to the fountain or down the avenue of chestnut trees, picking up conkers along the way if it was autumn. I wonder how many of today's footballers gather conkers on a Sunday afternoon!

Invariably, on those Sunday afternoons in the park, I wore a ribbed sweater that somebody had knitted a couple of sizes too big, plus a scarf – or a muffler as we called it – tied in a knot. And my cap – always wore a cap. When Barbara saw me coming, she'd turn off rather than pass close by. 'I don't want to be seen with you in that sweater and a muffler,' she'd complain to me later.

Eventually you would reach the lake where the ducks and the rowing-boats were. If you had a 'tanner' (two and a half pence in modern money) for a boat, then you felt as if you were in paradise. If you were lucky enough to have a watch as well you made sure of being at the furthest point from base when the boatman yelled: 'Come in, Number 6, time's up.' There were two or three little islands in the lake and we would moor our boat on the far side and sit, out of sight. The boatman would call three times – after that he had to leave his tickets behind and get on his bike to try to find you. When you were spotted you had to go in.

I eventually acquired a bit of taste in clothes. I used to pop into Marks & Spencer and buy Barbara twin-sets, matching jumpers and cardigans, for her birthdays. I always chose the mauve ones because it was my favourite colour. I'm not sure whether Barbara liked mauve – I never asked her. She wore them because beggars couldn't be choosers, and in those days our drawers were not overflowing with clothes. Despite this she was very particular about her appearance, still is to this day. She won't go round the corner without lipstick.

Barbara taught me to dance. She was puzzled that I wasn't a dancer, knowing my interest in music and knowing that I had been brought up around Mam's piano. I can hear her saying it now: 'Get it into your mind – one, two, three, hitch: one, two, three, hitch. You don't have to do anything else for a start.'

It had an uncanny effect. From not being able to dance at all, suddenly I was doing a Fred Astaire. After about a month I thought I *was* Fred Astaire. I probably danced more like Fred Flintstone – but it was a great eye-opener to me. What young men nowadays don't realise is that ballroom dancing can be such a source of enjoyment. In my day, to hold a girl close to you on the dance floor was a thrill in itself, because it was usually a case of hand-in-hand only on the way home. Even that was assuming you had the courage to take her hand. I've lost count of the occasions we would stand chatting, both leaning backs against a garden wall, before Barbara would say she had to go in.

It was odd that we had lived so close together – no more than three-quarters of a mile apart – but never knew of one another's existence before we met in Rea's Café. Well, I didn't know Barbara existed, anyway. When she left Kirby Grammar School I think her parents would have liked her to go into teaching, but she'd had enough of schools for a while and became a shorthand-typist at ICI, working at the same plant as me. Again our paths crossed without our knowing it.

Lindy Delapenha, a West Indian who played on the wing and who now, incidentally, works for radio in Jamaica, was the only Middlesbrough player who had a car. Not a luxurious vehicle by any means but a car none the less, and he kindly offered to drive Barbara and me to Stockton-on-Tees to buy the engagement ring.

Though I was utterly besotted, the proposal, such as it was, had not been conducted under particularly intimate circumstances. There had been no hanky-panky or anything like that in the relationship. When I said, 'Are you going to marry me?', she simply replied: 'Yes.'

So Lindy took us to Stockton. He was known for giving players lifts from the ground but, as a junior by comparison, I was well down the pecking order. 'You can get in,' he'd call to the lads lined up. 'And you, and you.' Then he'd glare at me and say: 'You – out.' That was young Clough taken care of and put in his place – forty goals in a season, but not entitled to a ride in the maroon Ford Anglia!

So I was honoured when Lindy volunteered to take us to Stockton. As I was getting out of the car, the door fell off. I was still trying to put it back while Barbara went into H. Samuel's and chose the ring. It cost about £30. She still has it, of course, and you can't put a price on those kind of memories.

My career was really taking off. I couldn't fail, really, considering the number of goals I was scoring. The start had not been spectacular, exactly (three goals in nine League games during the 1955–56 season), but my response was. It was not long before I told Mr Dennison I wanted out – I wanted a transfer. I think we were into my second season – a season I would finish with forty goals from forty-four matches – when my patience snapped. Middlesbrough were letting them in quicker than I could score them. I told the manager I was sick and tired of banging goals in at one end, only to turn round and see the team conceding even more at the other. No, it was not the kind of response I would have either encouraged or tolerated from a player once I had joined the managerial ranks, years later. But times were different, then. And, in any case, if I'd had a forty-goals-a-season centre-forward I would have made darned sure I had a defence that was worthy of him, not one that let in goals at the slightest threat.

How did the Press find out about my little disagreement? I can't recall the exact details. Maybe they were just good journalists in the North-East at that time. Or maybe I let them know. I think it was the second reason. I quickly learned how to use the media. I didn't get my transfer, but Dennison did give me the captaincy!

Some of the other players didn't like that, and my appoint-ment as skipper led to a bit of a bust-up. In fact, there were two 'camps' in the squad – and the division was never more obvious than when we all wandered into Rea's Café after training. There would be the Clough clan on one side and the others grouped some distance away. Talk about team spirit!

I have a distinct recollection that it was a lad called Brian Phillips who began the revolt – if that's what you'd call it. He was a centre-half of limited ability, and I remember him saying to the other players, after I was made captain: 'I can get as much for us as he can get.' Heaven knows what he intended 'getting', because it was four quid for a win and two for a draw in those days, with no perks. He resented my getting the captaincy, and he persuaded some of the others to sign a round-robin protest. It made no difference.

Phillips finished up in the nick. He was one of the players suspended for life and jailed for their part in the 'soccer bribes' scandal of the early 1960s.

The early playing days taught me other things. So did the long train journeys and the overnight stays, particularly, for some reason, the trips to Plymouth. It was probably on the first of them that I sat, young and inexperienced, quiet and straight-faced, at a table in the hotel dining-room. I froze when a man in a black jacket, white shirt and dicky bow arrived at my elbow and asked: 'What would you like as a starter?' A what? I'm telling you, I'd never had a starter in my life. As luck would have it I was sitting alongside Lindy Delapenha. When he said: 'I'd like a prawn cocktail,' I immediately jumped in: 'And I'll have the same.' I wouldn't have had a clue what to choose. I have been enjoying prawn cocktails ever since.

When I think of the training sessions at Middlesbrough my immediate recollection is of Harold Shepherdson sitting on a radiator, chatting with Jimmy Gordon. Harold was already working in the England set-up under manager Walter Winterbottom, and was to become part of dear old Alf Ramsey's regime that won the World Cup in '66. The sight of Harold leaping around celebrating that historic moment at Wembley tickled me. A nice man, a good man, but his long career in football rarely demanded great responsibility. He was spared the heavy burden of management in his own right – the trainer, No. 2, coach, call him what you will. But we shouldn't begrudge him occasions in the limelight for not everyone is cut out to be *the* boss.

Jimmy Gordon was to become a colleague in later years, as my trainer at Derby, Leeds and Nottingham. He was one of those wise old characters of the game, who contributed greatly and valuably to my managerial career. He also worked with a ball a darned sight more often when he worked for me!

That familiar cry at Middlesbrough still springs to mind, even today: 'What are we doing this morning?' The trainers would ease themselves off the radiator and one of them would announce the dreaded schedule: 'Laps – six doubles, six singles . . .' I was among the more fortunate, being a good runner. I still failed to fathom, though, why training was run, run, run, and why we hardly saw the very thing we were expected to use on match days – the ball. Whenever they broke the routine monotony it was a sheer delight. Oh, what a pleasure it was when Jimmy told somebody to go in goal and said to me: 'You . . . just strike it!' They would knock the ball to me from all angles and I would put it in the net.

We didn't have many team-talks, as such, but I was aware of a certain amount of resentment towards me from some of the other players, partly because I always said what I thought, but mainly because I was bloody good at what I did and made no excuses for believing I was the best. Dennison informed me on one occasion: 'There has been a complaint from one of the lads that you yell "give it to me" every time he gets the ball, even when he has the chance of a shot at goal himself. Why?' The answer seemed obvious to me, so I told him: 'Because I'm better at it than he is.' My record at Middlesbrough surely proved my point.

	League		FA Cup		FL Cup		All	
	Games	Goals	Games	Goals	Games	Goals	Games	Goals
1955-56	9	3	0	0	–	–	9	3
1956-57	41	38	3	2	–	–	44	40
1957-58	40	40	2	2	–	–	42	42
1958-59	42	43	1	0	–	–	43	43
1959-60	41	39	1	1	–	–	42	40
1960-61	40	34	1	0	1	2	42	36
Totals	213	197	8	5	1	2	222	204

Have you taken a good look at it? Go on, have another look, because I know it takes some believing. What would a striker with a record like that be worth today? In the Fifties and early Sixties he wasn't worth an England shirt – well, hardly.

Things looked quite good to start with, when I was selected for an Under-23 tour behind the Iron Curtain in 1957. It wasn't to be a particularly happy trip for me, despite getting a goal on my début – against the Bulgarians, I think, but the clearest memory is the fact that we lost. What I couldn't understand – and still can't – was why I was bombed out for the next game and replaced by Derek Kevan of West Brom. He was to be a pain in the arse as far as I was concerned, because he was one of those who were preferred to me by Walter Winterbottom at senior international level. Derek Kevan was a big, willing centre-forward, not blessed with quickness or outstanding ability to put the ball in the net. It was not simply a disappointment that Kevan was selected ahead of Clough. It was a crime!

The tour was educational. In Moscow they showed us Red Square, the Kremlin and Lenin's Tomb. We were honoured, I suppose, although you don't appreciate it at the time. Local people seemed to be queuing for everything, particularly to see Lenin that day. We were guided straight to the front of the queue, but the experience left no lasting impression apart from the chilling spectacle of the guards outside. There is still something awful to me about soldiers marching the goose-step. As for Lenin himself, I remember remarking to one of the other lads: 'He doesn't look too good.' I didn't feel too good either. I wasn't particularly interested in cultural tours when I was out of the team and feeling homesick. No thoughts of socialist ideology crossed my mind – all I knew was it seemed an awful long way from Moscow to Middlesbrough.

Bobby Charlton was a comfort. He had warned me before

35

we left England that I wouldn't like the food. That was hard for me to comprehend, having been brought up to eat anything, but Bobby insisted that I took plenty of chocolate. It wasn't long before I appreciated his advice. The very first meal began with a clear soup – I believe the technical term is consommé. I could cope with that but not with a raw egg looking at me, like a single eye, from the bottom. I did my best because I was hungry, but I was grateful for the Charlton chocolate diet. I think chocolate was about all I had packed, apart from a couple of pairs of socks and pants. We ate it every minute of the day – or that's the way it seemed.

Bobby Charlton was a good room-mate, and I believe I taught him something as well. At the hotel, prior to leaving on international tour, it was easy to become bored – something I tried my utmost to avoid as a manager. There is only one thing worse than a bored footballer – a footballer who can't play. I suggested to Bobby that we go bird-nesting in the hotel grounds. He had no idea. I had to show him how to find the nests: blackbirds', hedge-sparrows', all sorts. Back to childhood adventures, if you like, but it was a lovely time.

Under-23 football was hardly kind to me, while I didn't exactly set that scene on fire. It is so irritating to look back to important matches in which I failed to do justice to my talent. A match against Scotland, north of the border, was such an occasion – a draw in which I missed three scoring opportunities, the kind I would normally have knocked in with my whatsit. Young Clough was full of his own importance and ability, but he was also a severe self-critic when things didn't go his way. Those missed chances absolutely deflated me.

No reminder was necessary, but I received one during the rail journey home to Middlesbrough. It involved changing at Darlington where the train driver got off too, strolled along the platform and said to my face: 'Hey, you should have done a lot better against the Scots, lad.' I could have chucked him under the wheels.

As for my England prospects, they were to remain in the tunnel for some time. I was not even included in the squad for the World Cup of 1958. Kevan was regarded as the better bet, although I considered I'd had a reasonable season with Middlesbrough once again: forty-two League and Cup appearances, forty-two goals. But not good enough to warrant a place in the squad for the World Cup. It would be some time before Winterbottom came to his senses and picked the best centre-forward in the country for the full England team. Why couldn't that man recognise a golden nugget when it was shimmering there, right under his nose?

Brian Clough, in the meantime, was to make the best move of his life. No, not to Sunderland. Not yet. Far more important than that. I married Barbara.

4

SUNDERLAND

Hey! I played for England, you know!
Don't forget that!

APRIL THE FOURTH 1959 WAS THE MOST IMPORTANT DAY OF MY LIFE
– apart from the day I was born. Barbara and I were married at
Middlesbrough's St Barnabas Church, choosing the month of April
in order to qualify for a tax rebate. I remain convinced to this day
that she married me mainly because of the tidy sum I'd managed
to put away in the Post Office!

Today's players may be surprised to learn that my wedding

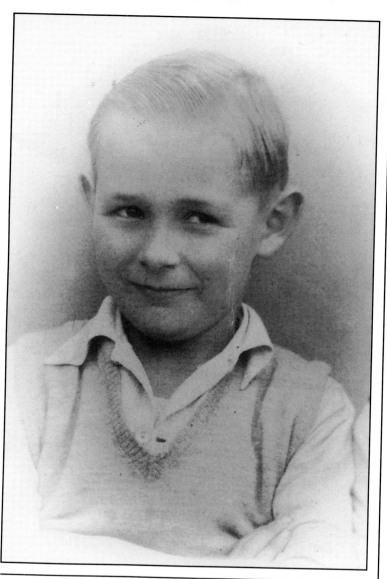

A cheeky sev[...]
year old.

triding out in front of the family, Blackpool, August 1947.

Posing on the romenade with (left to right) eanna, Doreen, Mam, Barry and Gerald. I am behind Barry.

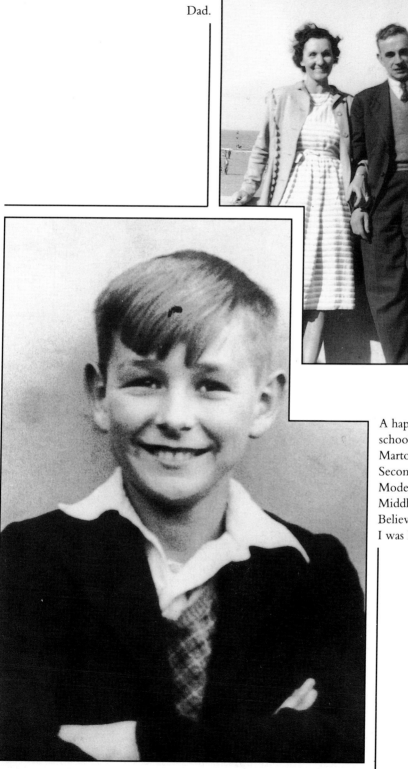

Mam and Dad.

A happy schoolboy at Marton Grove Secondary Modern, Middlesbrough. Believe it or no I was head boy!

Mam had her hands full with eight of us. I am the cherub on the far left with my brothers and sisters: (back row, left to right) Des, Joe and Bill, (front row, left to right) Gerald, Deanna, Barry and Doreen.

On the left again, with my brothers, about twenty-five years later.

Doing my
National Ser\
at RAF Watc
Somerset. I a:
standing, thir
from left.

With my new fiancée, Barbara Glasgow, Jersey 1958.

The most important day of my life: our wedding, 4 April 1959. I'm not sure the police officer on the far right saw the joke! *Northern Echo, Darlington*

Off on a
Mediterranean
cruise, 1961.

Barbara and me
with baby Nigel,
19 March 1966.
Sunderland Echo

day was a match day, like any other, and that I was expected to play. Could you imagine that, these days? They'd demand a special clause in their contract, the agent would be trying to negotiate a few thousand quid in added bonus and the Players' Union would be ringing the manager to protest. Well, we got married on the Saturday morning, and the reception was held at the Linthorpe Hotel. I handed brother Des £25 and said: 'Get everybody a drink.' He replied, 'Let them buy their own.' Once a Yorkshireman, always a Yorkshireman.

The speeches, such as they were, had to be short, because I needed to be at Ayresome Park before two o'clock to play against Leyton Orient. It was touch and go, especially as the car due to take me to the ground was late. I tried to recruit the help of a policeman who was on duty outside the hotel. I had noticed a police vehicle parked close by and saw no reason why he couldn't have given me a lift to Ayresome. 'Sorry, Brian, it's not possible. I'm not the driver of that car.' If the arranged lift hadn't arrived soon afterwards I might have been arrested!

We beat Leyton Orient comfortably and I notched up a goal. Yes, before you mention it, I heard the obvious wisecracks about scoring on my wedding day – even before the honeymoon. That was spent in London, at the Russell Hotel in Russell Square. We had a lovely few days. Like all good footballers I seem to remember spending most of the time in bed – no, not with my new wife all the time, either. She was out, taking in the sights of London. In the back of my mind was the thought that I had to get to Anfield in time to play against Liverpool on the Wednesday.

It was one of the few occasions Barbara ever sat in a directors' box. She had been kindly invited by the Middlesbrough chairman, which struck me as a not unreasonable thing to do seeing that we had travelled, direct from honeymoon, so that I could take part. Liverpool were beating us and looked all-over winners until I popped up with goals in the 89th and 90th minutes to snatch victory. Bill Shankly couldn't bear it. Dear Bill – how I still miss that wonderful man – walked on to the edge of the pitch and snarled at Harold Shepherdson. I happened to be wandering past and heard Bill's angry response to my match-winners. 'He's not had a f**king kick.' Harold's response was brilliant, worthy of Shanks himself: 'Well he's had at least two, to my knowledge.' Next morning, Thursday, I was back in training as normal. The honeymoon was over.

The honeymoon period with the full England side was to be just as short – only two caps in the autumn of the 1959-60 season, during which I collected another forty goals in forty-two matches for Middlesbrough. England memories, for me, are somewhat desolate – all frustration rather than fulfilment – in fact, the most pleasant memory of all reaches back to my meeting with the great Tom Finney. That adjective has been vastly over-used, too easily allocated to too many people, in all sports and other forms of entertainment down the years. In Finney's case it was utterly appropriate. Tom, among the nicest men you could wish to meet – then and now – was, quite simply, one of the finest footballers I have ever seen. And I am not forgetting the likes of George Best, Johan Cruyff, Pele. Finney could play almost anywhere. I don't know of many players who spent several impressive years on the wing – and ended up performing just as effectively at centre-forward.

I was in awe of the man as we assembled, prior to what was to be my first appearance for the senior side, against Wales in Cardiff. At the team hotel I felt nervous and vulnerable, twenty-four years old but a young twenty-four and hardly a man of the world. The first meal the players had together did nothing for my image or confidence, either. No sooner had I begun tucking into a breakfast of bacon and beans than I spilled them into my lap! No problem for the England player of today but to me, the naïve lad from Middlesbrough, it provided the real meaning of the word 'crisis'. That pair of flannels was the only pair in my possession. Finney noticed my problem. I suppose somebody sitting at a table, staring down at a lap-full of bacon and beans, does tend to attract attention. 'Not to worry, lad,' Finney said to me. 'Up to the room and get out of them. Leave the rest to me.'

He took the trousers and arranged for them to be cleaned and returned to me within hours. Kindness such as that, though it may sound simple now, is something you remember for the rest of your days. I remember it more than I remember the details of that début, but I'm sure I didn't do too well. As for my second and final game for my country, against Sweden at Wembley, I still argue that I was unlucky. A lot of players claim bad luck at Wembley, usually the ones who were never good enough to play there in the first place. We lost, 3-2 I seem to remember, and I could have saved the game.

One of the Swedish defenders attempted a back-pass. I was always ready for that kind of thing, I saw mistakes before they happened! But this time everything happened very quickly. I was on to it and hit an instant shot. I can still see that ball hitting the bar. If it had gone in, perhaps history would have told a different story. Perhaps they would have given me a third England cap. Perhaps I would have played at Wembley one more time.

But it hit the bar, and when I moved in to try and finish it off on the rebound I finished on the deck instead, rolling on the line with the ball trapped against my midriff. I couldn't get a foot or a head to it, even though it just needed knocking over the line. Some would call it fate. I called it a bloody nuisance. There were to be no further chances for me. I was cast aside at the age of twenty-four by a manager who, in my opinion, didn't know his job.

Winterbottom, later Sir Walter, was a pleasant, charming man. A soft man. Not like me – I have been a harsh man

41

on many occasions. I'm not sure if he had the first idea about management, though. He captivated people with his eloquence but it did nothing to change my mind. I regarded him as a man who did not possess the moral courage to stand up for what he thought should be done. It rankled with me that, as I continued scoring goals for my club, they didn't select me again for England. Winterbottom had used Bobby Charlton, Jimmy Greaves and me in the middle of the attack together. It didn't work, it couldn't work, but it was his job to find a way of producing a combination that made the best use of us. He failed.

My international career amounted to a miserly two full caps, an England 'B' cap, and appearances with the Under-23s. I also played for the Football League representative side against the Irish in 1959. The match coincided with Barbara's birthday and, like many others, I was not the best at remembering to buy cards and presents in time. I have tried to improve over the past thirty-odd years, but I didn't spend much time thinking about such things then. Before leaving for Ireland I promised her I would get a goal for her birthday. I did better than that. We won 5-0 – and I scored all five.

We couldn't have been as conscious of our image as the international players of today seem to be. Certainly I wasn't. I thought nothing of regularly collecting coal from the beach. I would ride my bike to Seaburn harbour, or get a lift with Ambrose Fogarty, the impish Irish player who was with Sunderland at the time, in his little van. Sea-coal is brought in by the tide – the loose stuff from the mines up and down the North-East coast – and left scattered across the sands. I would take a rake and a sack and I'd sling the full sack over the crossbar of my bike or, on easier days, into the rear of Fogarty's van before dropping it off at Valley Road: still called 'home' despite the club house Barbara and I shared. It was darned hard work but it was valuable fuel for Mam and Dad. Once dried out and put on the fire, sea-coal would burn all night. It somehow had a warmer glow – probably because it had cost nothing apart from hard work. On those occasions the work had been a labour of love.

At the end of the following season, 1960-61 (thirty-six goals in forty-two matches, in case you didn't read the chart), I decided Barbara and me needed a treat and opted for a cruise. I wasn't that keen, to be honest, because I'm not the best sailor in the world. I suppose I just wanted to spoil her. The weather was gorgeous and there was something romantic about life on board a liner, calling in at places like Cannes and Lisbon. Cannes was the place that turned me on. You could walk for miles along a dramatic sea front, beneath cloudless skies. It was a little different from Middlesbrough or Blackpool beach. The only thing that spoiled it, ever so slightly, was the insistence of the French on charging for the use of a deck-chair. We arrived back at Southampton to a surprise. Unknown to us, Alan Brown, the manager of Sunderland, was waiting on the other side of the barriers as we disembarked. He called us over and although I didn't know him personally, I recognised his face. There was a slight embarrassment initially when he forked out half-a-crown to the porter who had carried our luggage. I hadn't learned about tipping at that stage. For a start, I had no money in my pocket – and secondly, I had no idea.

Mr Brown lifted our cases onto a trolley, turned to me, and asked: 'Will you sign for Sunderland?' I presumed he had approached Middlesbrough first, so I didn't think to ask. With Barbara standing behind me I said 'Yes', just like that. Brown said: 'Fine. I'll see you at Roker Park in a week's time.' He told me I would be among the top earners at Sunderland – I can't remember exactly how much that was – and his word was good enough for me. He had broken a holiday in Cornwall to meet us, so I told him to get back to his holidays and I would sort out any other details that might crop up. I was supposed to be an awkward bugger, a cussed, headstrong so-and-so, but mine must have been one of the quickest and smoothest transfers of all time. Brownie could not believe his luck. From my point of view, well aware of my new gaffer's strict, straight and honest reputation, there was immediate respect. That was probably the reason why I didn't argue. That's exactly the way it should be. Sunderland paid a fee of £42,000 for me in 1961, but I can only wonder what a player with a scoring record like mine would cost today.

It was Alan Brown who taught me about discipline: the value of decent behaviour which, years later, was to become a hallmark of Clough teams and the reason why we were the favourites among referees. We made their job so much easier. The Sunderland manager's approach was a shock to my system. He stood as straight as a Buckingham Palace guardsman and when he delivered a bollocking – my God, did you know you had been bollocked! There were occasions when I was downright scared of the man. He detested shabby clothing and insisted his players always had a regular trim. There was never a sign of long hair at Roker Park. He made an immense impression on me. I hope – indeed, I know – that I carried his influence and sprinkled it through the game for a long time after he and his dear, late wife Connie retired to Devon. I sent her flowers for years. I still write to him.

He ran Sunderland from top to bottom, I recognised that from the start. What he said mattered and people responded. He was *the boss* in every sense of the word and I said to myself, even then: 'If ever I become a manager – this is the way the job should be done.' You can have your chairmen, chief-executives, secretaries and the blokes who run the 'development funds'. They are nothing, nobodies, and have no chance of succeeding unless *the* most important figure at the football club gets things right in the first place. The manager in charge of the team is the key. I smile when I hear people insisting that 'football is all about players'. I know what they mean. But who brings those players to a club in the first place – assembling a team to win a championship or a cup? Unless the manager has sound judgement, all the other football club employees might as well stay at home. And although the game has changed down the years I remain convinced that the manager has to be the boss.

I don't care how comfortable and swanky those glass-fronted executive boxes can be, the businessmen, second-hand-car sales-men and corporate entertainers won't spend thousands renting them unless the team on the other side of the glass is worth the money. Watching failure can be bloody uncomfortable, even when you're doing it in luxurious surroundings.

Alan Brown was not simply my manager, he was my mentor. He wasn't to know it at the time, of course, but he was teaching me the right way to go about a task that was to present itself far quicker than anyone imagined.

5

UNLUCKY BREAK

All washed up and only twenty-nine!

IT WAS ONE OF THOSE GREY, BITING, FORBIDDING DAYS THAT ONLY the North-East can produce. An afternoon with sleet driven into your face on the wind, ice under foot, and penetrating cold. Not an ideal day for watching or playing football, but it took more than Siberian conditions to cause a postponement in 1962. The match against Bury went on, the usual 30,000 or so braving the elements at Roker Park.

There was not only sleet in the air, there were already

thoughts of promotion from the Second Division. Wear-side folk were in festive mood, all right, that particular Boxing Day. Funny, but whenever I hear people asking one another, 'What did you get for Christmas?' my mind flashes back to '62 and I think: 'I remember what I got for Christmas, that year – I got done.'

No score – and just another loose ball, or so it seemed. I have read that full-back Len Ashurst has talked about my resenting him for the stray pass that brought about my downfall. If I was hard on Lennie, then I'm sorry – particularly as, according to my memory of the incident, it was Jimmy McNab who played the ball.

The rest is crystal clear, as if it happened yesterday. I sprinted across the heavy, muddy surface towards the ball, my eye on it the whole time. I was never to be distracted in circumstances like that. I sensed an opportunity to score another goal, to add to almost thirty I'd already scored that season. Suddenly it was as if someone had just turned out the light. The Bury goalkeeper, Chris Harker, had gone down for the ball, and his shoulder crunched into my right knee. I was slightly off-balance, with my head down. If I'd seen him coming I might have been inclined to kick his head off, but I didn't see him. My head hit the ground, and for a second or two I didn't know a thing. Only blackness.

It must have been a fleeting moment, though, because I spotted that the ball had run loose again, and my instinct told me to get after it. I tried to lever myself off the ground, but couldn't. I started crawling. Something kept urging me: 'Get up, get up.' Bob Stokoe, the Bury centre-half, said to the referee: 'Come on, he's only codding.' 'Not this lad,' the ref replied, 'he doesn't cod.' Johnny Watters, the physio, arrived and did his best. Blood was running down my face, but it was the knee that was hurting. The cruciate ligament was torn – similar to the injury Paul Gascoigne sustained through his own stupidity at Wembley, but it was much more serious then. In my case, repair proved to be out of the question.

They took me to the dressing-room, where I was lifted onto a kind of plinth covered in a white sheet. Within seconds there seemed to be blood all over it. Johnny Watters turned to Alan Brown and said that I should go to hospital. When he made a move to take off my boots, Brownie barked that he should leave them alone. I'm sure his first reaction was that I might be all right to resume the match, but it was a forlorn hope. The hospital operated on the medial as well as the cruciate ligament, and my leg was set in plaster from my ankle to my groin, with the knee in a bent position. That's the way it had to be for three months.

Alan Brown virtually isolated me in that hospital. He stopped friends coming to see me – although I didn't have that many, I did have a few! Something began to puzzle me. Though family were allowed in, I hadn't seen Barbara. Whenever I asked about her, they changed the subject without telling me anything. Eventually she arrived, after four, maybe five days, and she was paler than the white sheet draped over me. 'Hey, what's going on?' I asked. She said: 'I've been in bed . . .' and then floored me with something I'd never expected to hear: 'I'm afraid I've had a miscarriage.' I hadn't even been aware she was pregnant! Well, you didn't ask at that time.

I had stitches in my face, my knee was giving me hell inside a plaster encasing my entire right leg, the surgeon couldn't tell me whether I would play again, and my wife arrives to announce she has lost the baby I didn't know we were having. It was not exactly the best moment of my life.

The so-called rehabilitation period was hard. I became difficult to live with, although Barbara would no doubt tell you I've been even more difficult in later years! We had a red settee, G-Plan they called it, and I would rest my damaged leg on the cushions.

Whenever Barbara came in she told me to take my foot off – I could have thrown the settee at her. The knee was shattered, the career under threat, and the nerves were definitely frayed. Neither Alan Brown nor Johnny Watters said anything, but both must have realised that there was no earthly chance of my ever being the same player again.

The physio had cut two holes in the plaster enabling him to work on the muscles with electric treatment, so the leg itself didn't look too bad when I came out of plaster. Determination took over from depression. There was work to be done, and no-one had more determination than me when it came to fighting the odds. I ran up and down the Spion Kop at Roker Park, up and down, up and down, often with Brownie running alongside me for moral support. I spent hours, alone, doing the same, up and down the 'Cat Walk' by the beach at Seaburn. I must have spent the best part of a year going up and down those steps, happy to be in the open air, content with my own company and never doubting, for a moment, that I would make a full recovery. Eventually I was told I could have another shot at playing again.

The surgeon, I remember, wasn't keen on my attempting a come-back at all, believing that any further damage to the knee might leave me crippled for the rest of my life. But the pursuit of a threatened career does not recognise caution of any kind. I thought that I could be as good as new. I was dreaming, in much the same way as I'm sure young Gascoigne dreamed, but he, mercifully, had the benefit of far more sophisticated medical and surgical techniques.

The first time I played again was at home to Leeds in September '64, the very day that Barbara's Mum died while staying at our house. Sunderland had been promoted by then to the First Division – what has since become the grandly named Premier Division. The match went well – I stuck the ball through Jack

Charlton's legs and scored – but Brian Clough, Sunderland and would-be England footballer, was to play only two more matches in the First or any other division. The finest goal-scorer in the country and one of the best the game has ever seen, was no more. I left with the quickest 250 League goals ever scored – a career record of 251 in 274 matches. Eat your hearts out, Jimmy Greaves, Ian Rush, Gary Lineker, Alan Shearer. It's a record that I don't believe will ever be beaten.

Barbara still reminds me how badly I reacted to the news that I could never play again. I was worried about what the future might hold, what I was going to do. I wasn't qualified for anything beyond the insular world of football. I hadn't made it as a fitter and turner. I had been earning only £45 a week, but at times I had felt like a millionaire.

During my rehabilitation attempts I hadn't a clue that I was insured for £40,000: peanuts now, but a princely sum then. Alan Brown left to become manager at Sheffield Wednesday, and, looking back, I'm convinced that Sunderland were more interested in getting their hands on the insurance money than seeing me back in the game.

I had been happy at Sunderland. My sons, Simon and Nigel, were born there, and we had made many good friends. One was the West Indian bowler Lance Gibbs, who was playing league cricket in the area at that time. The night Simon was born I celebrated, comprehensively, with Lance, who bought me champagne at Wetherall's Club before I went to the hospital to see this new child, my first. When I arrived Barbara was obviously shattered, so I got hold of the matron and said, 'I want to see my son.' 'Have you been drinking?' she asked. I admitted that I had. She stuck a mask on my face and pointed to a group of about a dozen babies, every single one of which looked the same to me. 'That's yours,' the matron snapped. 'And don't you be hanging around here too long.' Some welcome to fatherhood.

Sunderland banked their insurance money, settling with me for little more than £1,000 as I recall, but the new manager, George Hardwick, offered me something that was to be far more significant than cash. He gave me the chance to work with the youth players. I found, instantly, that I could teach. I'd only been doing the job a matter of months when Hardwick made me youth-team manager. It was George who suggested I attend an FA course in Durham, where I could qualify for my coaching badge. That's where I first came across Charlie Hughes. Though he was supposed to be running the course, Hughes' primitive tactics were obvious from the start. To think that this man became Director of Coaching at Lancaster Gate, and even reached the same short list as me, years later, when I was interviewed for the job of England manager! That says everything about the way football is run in this country.

Hughes preached a theory that the quicker you could shift the ball from A to B, the more likely you would be to score a goal. It was a theory that encouraged a primitive, so-called 'long-ball' game, based on percentages – one that I regard as absolute bloody garbage. I'll say one thing for Hughes, he has somehow managed to hang around. I don't know what he does at FA headquarters, whether he just sits at a desk and writes letters, but he has made a good living out of my industry. I've worked with a few coaches and managers in my time, but never with anyone who had less idea about football than Charlie Hughes.

The course included all types – schoolteachers, accountants, post-office workers, the lot. Among them was Bob Hardisty, famous in the region as a Bishop Auckland player during their domination of the old FA Amateur Cup. Bob must have sensed my irritation with Hughes, because he said to me: 'You'll just have to bite your lip, Brian, and put up with him.'

There was no chance of my putting up with a man who had no idea. He set up 'little exercises', as he called them, where one of us had to run down the wing, cross the ball, and another had to head it into the net. Eventually, one of the teachers or accountants (none of whom looked as if they had ever kicked a ball properly in their lives) managed to get his foot round the ball and lift it into the middle. I was the one expected to place a deliberate header on goal and I did – with the side of my head. I was a cocky, blasé sod, and I did it my way.

Hughes stopped the session there and then and told me: 'You can't do that.' I said: 'I've just done it,' and he hit me with the question, 'Which is the hardest part of your head?' It was too daft for words, and I couldn't resist a cheeky reply. 'The forehead – the part I have used to score a lot of my goals. Have a look at my record.' Hughes was adamant: 'Well you've got to head it with your forehead.' I said: 'Bullshit, when you score a goal you can put it in with anything that's legal.'

It was a two-week course, but after only a couple of days Bob Hardisty took me to one side and said, 'Listen, you're pushing it a bit too far.' But I pushed even harder. I volunteered for every exercise presented to us, and if there was a chance to prove Hughes wrong, or to demonstrate to the others in the group that there was a simple and effective alternative, I did it. If I had been expected to lecture them on the Battle of Waterloo I would have been on thin ice. But this was football, my subject, and I was full of myself. They couldn't play and I could. I'm sure they finished up learning more from me than from Hughes. They certainly listened. When you are coaching, trying to get your point across, you have to make people listen. I don't know how many of the schoolteachers and accountants qualified from that course, but I was one of the youngest in the game to earn my full badge.

The Sunderland youth side had responded to me immediately, because I scrubbed those dreadful, monotonous laps from the training routine. I put a ball down and we played football –

five-a-side, six-a-side, anything that enabled them to practise the way they were expected to play as a team.

I adored that part of my life, despite the shattering blow that had ended my playing career. I had discovered a new challenge, and my liking for management – such as it was at that modest level – was immediate. The response of those young footballers at Roker told me I could do the job. I was going to be bloody good at it, and anyone who got in my way would have to watch out.

The chance to spread my wings came out of the blue. When George Hardwick lost his job as Sunderland manager in 1965, I went to see his successor, Ian McColl, to confirm that I could continue working with the youngsters. He refused, saying: 'I don't think the directors will be too pleased if you stay here.' It was an excuse. He wanted his own men around him.

My popularity on Wear-side was proved in spectacular fashion when my testimonial match was staged at Roker Park. More than 31,000 fans packed the ground. I played – scoring, of course – and ended the night around £10,000 better off. I ended it with a new job, too, because in the boardroom afterwards I was approached by Hartlepools' chairman, Ernie Ord, who offered me the chance to become their manager. I accepted on the spot, because I was out of work. At only thirty years old, I had become the youngest manager in the League.

I wasn't to know it until sometime later but I'd just agreed to work for one of the most evil men I have ever met.

6

ON THE BENCH

In this business, you've got to be a dictator or you
haven't got a chance.

MY VERY FIRST MOVE AS A FOOTBALL LEAGUE CLUB MANAGER COST
me £200, paid, in cash, to Peter Taylor. The formation of the
most successful double-act in the history of football inevitably had
its price. Taylor, bless his soul, demanded a 'bung'.

By the summer of '65 we'd gone our separate ways. While
I had been cutting my teeth with the youngsters at Sunderland,
Peter had entered management with Burton Albion in the

Southern League. I telephoned the night I was offered the job at Hartlepools and told him: 'I've taken up management – do you fancy joining me?' Of course he did. He was longing for a job in the League, but couldn't get in under his own steam. Here was his chance to get in through the back door. We met at the Chase Hotel in York. Taylor said he would have to take a large cut in salary to join me. He wanted a few quid, which wasn't unusual for Peter, so I handed him £200 out of my own pocket. I suppose we can say it was partly to cover travelling expenses and partly a kind of signing-on fee! There was no chance of my reclaiming it from Hartlepools, since they didn't have a penny.

That dreadful man, Ord, was unaware of my plans until I had done the deal. I didn't ask him, I just told him that Peter was coming to Hartlepools. But there was no prospect of a hard-up, broken-down club appointing two men for one job. Even the major clubs in the country didn't have managerial partnerships, so Peter agreed to come along with no grander title than that of 'trainer', the bucket-and-sponge man. At least we were together and on our way. It was time to begin putting theory into practice.

Two other men inspired my approach to the job: Alan Brown, who ran Sunderland like the dictator I was accused of becoming later in my career, and a craggy wise old owl of a man, Harry Storer. Taylor and I had Storer in common – he had been Peter's boss at Coventry City for several years and Peter first introduced me to Storer when I was a player at Middlesbrough. Storer went on to manage Birmingham City and was in charge of Derby County prior to Tim Ward, from whom I was to take over after quitting Hartlepools.

When I first met Storer I was a young man. I remember his square jaw, that looked as if it had been sculpted from a block of granite. He had a reputation for toughness, and I was in awe of him. He wasn't large physically but he was the rugged, tenacious type – the classic wing-half of his day. As a player, he had been known to kick people, and I could well imagine that. Maybe it was his reputation, maybe it was the surroundings in which we first met – a British Rail hotel which was quite posh by my standards – whatever the reason, I was wary. I didn't say a great deal, but I listened and learned. I was plonked in one of the biggest chairs I had ever seen and he took the trouble to talk to me as if I was a grown-up. I took to him because of that.

The first subject he discussed was football club directors – and, oh, what a breed of men they are! Dear old Harry startled me with his first words: 'Don't ever forget – directors never say thank you.' I didn't quite know what he meant, but subsequent years proved him right. To my credit – and I don't wish to sound boastful – I have seen off a few of them during my time. I only wish I could have seen off a few more. Whatever you do for them, whatever you win, however many times you take them to Wembley, they never say thank you.

As for management in general, he told me I would have to accept responsibility for *everything* at the club. 'Once you accept the job,' he said, 'it is all down to you. The supporter who bangs his head in the stand, the player who gets spat upon, the seat that doesn't work, the letter that arrives on a Monday saying "Your team is rubbish" – all of it eventually finds its way back to the manager's office.' He warned me that it would be difficult not to resent the criticism I could expect between one Saturday evening and the next time my players took the field. And I have sometimes resented it – although, to be fair, my teams haven't warranted too much criticism.

Harry Storer's pet subject was courage – the need for moral as well as physical courage in football. He told me how he once literally dragged one of his players out to the touch-line, and demanded: 'I want you to take me out there and show me the hole.' The player was nonplussed: 'Which hole, boss?' 'The f**king hole you were hiding in, every single minute, on Saturday.' Funny, but so true. I have worked with players who have hid down a hole, and with others who have shown outstanding moral courage – as Alan Hinton did, on the left-wing, at Derby.

'If and when you become a manager,' Storer advised, 'always bear this in mind. When you are leaving for an away game, look around the team coach and count the number of hearts. If you're lucky, there will be five. If there aren't, turn the coach round and go back!' Sound words from a good judge and a dear man. He had a lovely wife and after Harry died, we spent a lot of time with her and became great friends.

How valuable was Storer's advice all that time ago? Just look at the calibre of players we bought and captains appointed over the years: Dave Mackay, Roy McFarland, John McGovern, Stuart Pearce. Different types, different players, but all courageous men who led by example. The teachings of Storer, witnessed and absorbed by Taylor first-hand at Coventry and related to me over several get-togethers, were to form the basis of our approach to management.

One of the first things I had to do on my arrival at the dilapidated and dripping Victoria Ground was to place buckets in the boardroom, to catch the rain as it dribbled through the holes in the roof. On reflection, I should have left the buckets in there permanently – they were brighter than the directors and certainly more trustworthy than Ernie Ord.

My office, if that's the right word, was smaller than the downstairs toilet at my current home. The club secretary was an accountant, so if we needed him he had to be contacted at his office. A girl came in a couple of mornings a week to sort out the mail, but Barbara did any typing I needed. The stands were in poor shape, the pitch always seemed to be saturated, and we had to train at a place that must have been one of the coldest spots in Britain, Seaton Carew. On the beach! And the players who came in early were the ones who grabbed the few items of clean kit. Those who arrived later had to make do with a sock here, a shirt or top there, anything they could find from a table scattered with soiled and grubby items not necessarily meant to be worn together.

Having joined Hartlepools in the October, we had to act quickly, because at that early stage the club looked destined for oblivion. With only seven points, the team was bottom of the Fourth Division, their annual request for re-election to the League already on the cards. The first thing I learned was that those in the dressing-room had so little talent. Poor lads – I couldn't give them a hard time because they had a big enough problem with their inability to play. At the start Taylor and I just tried to encourage them. We had a goalkeeper called Simpson who was tubby, unmarried, staying in digs and living the life of a rake. He was on about six quid a week, Hartlepools were bottom of the League, and then I walked in. Just as he was thinking nothing could get worse.

I think my arrival was a boost for him for a while. I soon found out, or Taylor did, where he spent his evenings – in a pub drinking Cameron's beer: a strong, clear, beautiful beer, the best in the North-East. I told him: 'If I catch you in that pub one more time I'll kill you.' He switched pubs. He didn't survive long, though, because we signed the former Forest keeper, Peter Grummitt.

One of our first signings was a full-back from Forest, Brian Grant. That deal taught me a lesson, when I encountered the first manager who was ever rude to me. John Carey, the former Manchester United and Northern Ireland international defender, broke off our negotiations and said: 'I'm going for lunch.' There was I, trying to knock £100 or so off a £2,000 fee, and the manager of Nottingham Forest tells me I'll have to wait while he goes for lunch! I was sitting in my car when he emerged from the main door, smoking the pipe for which he was well known. I tried again. 'Any chance of completing our business, Mr Carey?' That blasted man walked straight past my car without a word, simply raising one finger like a schoolteacher telling a child to wait. It was unnecessary and unforgivable behaviour towards a beginner who had been in management only a matter of weeks: something I have always taken care to avoid. Any young manager who wanted to see me I met and spared as much time as possible.

I eventually completed the signing of Grant, and a few others followed: a goalkeeper here, an outside-left there. I signed John McGovern while he was still at grammar school. His headmaster told me, pleasantly enough: 'You really do have no right to be here, Mr Clough.' When you walked into a headmaster's office in those days, it felt very austere. Young McGovern beside me wasn't the only one standing to attention. I was wanting to take John as a full-time professional footballer and put him in my first team at the age of only sixteen. But the headmaster, peering at me over his spectacles, said: 'Mr Clough, it is my opinion that young McGovern should go on to study A levels and then to university.' I chipped in: 'Life doesn't very often give you choices. I think we should let him decide.' Despite the headmaster's reservations I knew John wanted to sign with me, and I'd already spoken to his mum. As soon as the headmaster gave his permission I was out of there, knowing that I'd made one of the most significant signings of that era. McGovern, who followed me first to Derby County and then to Nottingham Forest, went on to lift more trophies than any A levels he might have gained had he stayed at school. How many team captains have lifted that mighty European Cup above their head in successive seasons?

Pete and I would be at the ground six days a week, and did a lot of talking in the dressing-room. He was forever telling me that his wife, Lillian, did not approve of one of the forwards, Ernie Phythian. It was our first difference of opinion, I suppose, as I told him: 'I don't give a toss what Lil likes, Ernie's the best we've got.' He was, he scored a lot of goals, and he helped raise us from the foot of the table to eighteenth place by the end of that first season.

How Taylor survived I'll never know. I wanted him with me because he was a friend who had always supported me, and he had a great knowledge of football. But you should have seen him with a bucket and sponge! We sat in a little wooden shed that was supposed to be the dug-out. It was hardly big enough for two rabbits, let alone me and a bloke Pete's size. But in he went with his bucket of water and his sponge. He had to, it was a case of keeping up appearances. The chairman was wary of us, particularly Taylor, and although we were working as managerial partners Taylor had to be seen to be the trainer. I'm telling you, my retriever 'Del' knows more about injuries than Taylor did! When one of our players needed treatment Peter would simply wring out the sponge over him and say, 'Get up.' He could have been dealing with a broken ankle, a twisted knee or a dislocated shoulder – the diagnosis and cure was always the same. A squeezed out sponge and 'get up'.

I've always advised anyone entering management, or moving managerial positions, to make the difficult decisions as quickly as possible. You never know how long you will survive, so the first three months are vital. Problems don't come from the players – it's easy dealing with them – but from the chairman and directors. You need to set the ground rules. You are going to spend part of your life working there, so you must establish your territory. Sure, I was new to it, Taylor and I were cutting our teeth, and we were finding out as much about ourselves as our club. It was important to have a sanctuary. Barbara found us a warm, pleasant and secure home on the Fens estate, West

Hartlepool, a new semi-detached that was the first house of our own, bought for £2,300. Not a lot of furniture, but enough. No lawn either, because I never made the time to lay one, although I was forever saying to our Nigel, below school age but already obsessed with a ball, 'I'll get you some grass soon, son,' but, of course, I never did.

It wasn't long before I was found in another familiar position – at loggerheads with the chairman. Ernie Ord annoyed me. His size annoyed me, he was a tiny man who drove a Rolls-Royce and when it passed in the street it looked like a car without a driver. He had been what was called a 'credit draper', and he owned the club from top to bottom. Once he had sold out his business, the club had become his life. He would come in every day, demanding to know what I was up to and not happy at being told it was none of his business. I took exception to his interference in my job. It reached such a pitch that I eventually said to him: 'You get out of this little space I'm working in or I'll put you out.'

He didn't seem to be able to appreciate what Taylor and I were doing for Hartlepools. I knew how the media worked and never missed a chance to get them there with their cameras and their notebooks. I helped give the ground a fresh lick of paint, I helped the lorry driver unload steel plates for the rebuilding of the stand roof, and I made sure the Press were there to see it all. Hartlepools had never known so many column-inches. Ord – dreadful little squirt – should have been grateful. Instead he tried to sack Peter Taylor. He never could understand the need for two of us, despite Pete's regular appearances with sponge and overflowing bucket, and eventually decided he wanted Peter out. It coincided with Ord taking me to one side and announcing: 'From now on my son is going to handle all publicity at this club.' I said, 'Piss off', and carried on with whatever I was writing at the time.

He confirmed at a board meeting that Taylor and I had been dismissed, but we refused to go. I think he had tried to get at me through Taylor, who was touchy about criticism from directors at any time. We felt that Ord was trying to divide and rule, trying to undermine the confidence of a new young management team, perhaps for no other reason apart from his desire to run his club and take all the credit – and the realisation that I was preventing him from doing both. I even learned to drive the team coach. It wasn't done simply to seek publicity – it's a long way from Hartlepool to Southend. We must have had the oldest coach driver in the country, and I thought I might be needed. Thankfully I never was.

The team was doing well. Instead of fighting battles at the wrong end of the table, we finished our second season in eighth position and were improving all the time.

The nicest thing that happened while I was at Hartlepools was the birth of our daughter, Elizabeth. We could not welcome her straight away, unfortunately, because of some problem, some bug-scare at the hospital, which restricted Simon, Nigel and me to a view of Barbara and our eagerly awaited newcomer through a distant window. But the family picture was complete, although the plan to lay that little bit of grass at home was shelved for good. The Clough clan was about to move on, to a bigger club and bigger headlines and to create a kingdom that should have become the biggest in the game.

7

BUILDING A TEAM

*I have to smile at all the players who think they can
take off their boots one day and put on their suits the
next. They couldn't be more wrong.*

DERBY COUNTY SHOULD HAVE BEEN ONE OF THE BIGGEST AND MOST
successful football clubs, not only in Britain but in Europe. They
should have achieved the levels of triumph that Liverpool enjoyed
for more than a quarter of a century.

Oh yes, Derby should have been as big as Liverpool –
possibly even bigger. And there is only one man to blame for

the fact that they didn't reach such status: Brian Clough. To be strictly accurate, there are two culprits: me and Peter Taylor. When we walked out of the Baseball Ground in October 1973 it was the worst move of our lives. We were stupid, we were headstrong, we were stubborn and full of our own importance, but we were terribly, terribly wrong.

The day we resigned together was the day we turned our backs on the chance, if not the absolute guarantee, of turning a small-town club into a major power in European football. I honestly still believe that had Taylor and I not quit, we would have led Derby to the kind of unprecedented glory that set apart Liverpool from the rest from the 1960s onwards.

We didn't simply build a great team and the makings of a great club at Derby. It developed into something more than that – I suppose modern terminology would call it a 'dynasty'. Looking back now, I can isolate two little incidents, perhaps insignificant in themselves, which signalled the beginning and the end of the empire on which Taylor and I had set our hearts and our ambitions.

First was the moment when Dave Mackay, the truly great Dave Mackay, put his foot on the ball under the most intense pressure in his own six-yard area and then calmly and deliberately played us out of trouble with a pass that immediately switched defence to attack. I'm not sure of the venue – I think it may have been Leeds Road, Huddersfield – but I clearly remember Taylor's reaction. When Mackay stopped the ball somebody else in the dug-out was yelling: 'Kick it, shift it, get rid.' Taylor whipped round and shouted: 'That's what we bought him for. That's what we want him to do – put his foot on it. They'll all be doing it from now on. We're on our way.' And we were. Confidence swept from one player to another and the successful Derby era was born . . .

To be ended the day director Jack Kirkland caught Taylor's

eye across a crowded room at Old Trafford after we'd beaten Manchester United. Kirkland crooked his finger at Taylor, beckoned him over, and said: 'I want to see you on Monday morning to ascertain your exact duties at the club.' That was the humiliating demand which eventually triggered our resignations. It had begun with a foot on the ball, it ended with a 'come hither' finger in a boardroom; but, my God, so much happened in between.

Taylor had become restless at Hartlepools before I had. We had beaten the despicable Ernie Ord who had wanted to sack Peter and also tried to fire me, and a new chairman had been installed. But Pete insisted we were worthy and capable of bigger things. He was constantly in touch with Len Shackleton, the former Sunderland and England player, who had moved into journalism in the North-East. Taylor knew 'Shack' had contacts, and that if anybody could help get us a better job it would be him. Sure enough, Shackleton set up a meeting for me at an hotel at Scotch Corner. I was to see the chairman of Derby County, Sam Longson, a blunt, plain-speaking millionaire who had made his fortune in the road haulage business. Longson had the kind of voice that could shake stone from quarry walls. He also had a football club that had done nothing since coming out of the Third Division ten years earlier. After yet another season of nothingness Longson had sacked their manager, Tim Ward. It took Shackleton and me hardly any time at all to convince the impressionable Longson that I was his man. The job was mine before we left Scotch Corner.

Days later I had to attend a meeting of the directors at the Baseball Ground "cos it all has to be ratified and confirmed by the full board', as Longson put it in his inimitable style. So we all travelled down to the Midlands in the blue Rover, and I left Barbara and the three bairns in a public park while I went to meet the directors. She was there for hours, Simon and Nigel on the swings and Elizabeth in the pushchair. The meeting took some time, because it was there that I announced to Longson and Co. that they would not be hiring me alone. I told them I would be bringing Peter Taylor as well! We were never to be in greater need of his ability to spot talent, because Derby were in an awful mess.

On a hastily arranged pre-season tour of Germany our eyes were opened wide. I discovered, to my surprise – and I'm still staggered by the thought of it even now – that half the players couldn't swim. Having arranged to 'see you in the pool at half-past ten', I arrived in swimming trunks with my hotel towel over my shoulder to be greeted by the sight of eight or nine professional footballers huddled in a corner of the shallow end, clinging to the handrail. But not being able to swim wasn't the worst of it. More worrying was the fact that half of them couldn't play, either!

Decisions came easily. Taylor and I were always at our best and fired with the greatest enthusiasm when we were dismantling teams and rebuilding them, rather than maintaining standards already set. Players simply had to go. Ian Buxton played county cricket for Derbyshire as well as being our centre-forward. Because cricket overlapped the start of the football season, this meant we had only a part-time centre-forward. Buxton had a clause in his contract allowing him a holiday at the end of the cricket season, which was understandable from his point of view. But I said to Taylor: 'This is bloody ridiculous – we could be relegated by October.' Derby was being run like an amateur club.

Taylor was adamant that I went back to the North-East to make our first signing. We payed £21,000 for John O'Hare, a young Scottish centre-forward who I'd worked with in the youth side at Sunderland. O'Hare was the obvious and natural choice to replace Buxton. I have to confess that he was one of my favourites who, like John McGovern, I was to take with me to Leeds and to Nottingham Forest. O'Hare was the gentlest of men but also, on the field, one of the bravest, because he always received the ball with his back to the defender. People used to say that he had weaknesses in his game. Absolute balls! O'Hare could receive and control a ball on his thigh, his chest, his head, his ankles or his knees. And he had a heart as big as a bucket.

Taylor remembered his old goalkeeper at Burton Albion, Les Green. He was not the tallest, but he had long arms and incredibly big hands. We had to sign a keeper quickly because the one who began the season, the former England international Reg Matthews, was well into his thirties and had clearly 'shot it', as we used to say. Perhaps all the fags he smoked had finally caught up with him.

Our centre-half, Bobby Saxton, wasn't any good by then, either. So, soon after O'Hare arrived at Derby, so did Roy McFarland, who in my humble opinion was to become the best England centre-half in post-war years. He was that good. McFarland was such a complete footballer that he would not have looked out of place in any outfield position. Taylor had watched him on a number of occasions and was baffled that McFarland had remained so long at Tranmere – beneath the noses of the Merseyside giants, Liverpool and Everton. We needed to move quickly. I suppose that the capture of McFarland was the first of the classic Clough–Taylor signings that were to become the hallmark of our managerial style.

Taylor and I arrived on the McFarland doorstep late at night. It might have been after midnight, but nevertheless we asked his father to get the lad out of bed. McFarland wasn't keen on signing. He wanted to sleep on the idea but I think, in his heart of hearts, he wanted to sign for Liverpool and was a wee bit disappointed when Derby knocked on the door. I said to him: 'I don't care how long you take or how many questions you want to ask. We are going to create one of the best teams in England and I'm not going anywhere until you decide whether you want to be a part of it.'

Even McFarland's father was a bit taken aback. I recall him saying something like: 'Blimey, son, if they want you that much . . .' Whatever swung it, we put the transfer form on the table and, baffled and bemused, he signed. The lad, who was to go on to manage Derby eventually, has since told me that when he woke the morning after signing, he regretted what he'd done. It was not long, of course, before he came to realise that he'd made the best decision of his life.

The team started to develop. It was a conscious decision to go straight down the middle of the side – goalkeeper, centre-half, centre-forward. The spine of the team had to be right. All clubs eventually followed that practice, but we set the pattern and it took time for the others to twig it. Good players, like the full-back Ronnie Webster, striker Kevin Hector and the Welsh midfielder Alan Durban, were already at the club, so the framework was nicely established.

Another key arrival was John McGovern, who was to play as significant a role in the development of Derby County as he was later to play for Nottingham Forest. He couldn't run and often looked ungainly on the field. But he would always stand up straight, he would always strive to get and to pass the ball, and he would do that whether the team was losing 3-0 on a filthy night at Walsall or winning 4-0 on a sunny Saturday afternoon at Wembley. He was the absolute, genuine article – one who made the utmost and more of the talent at his disposal, rather like O'Hare. My kind of footballer.

We developed a perfect mix, not least with the eventual arrival of Alan Hinton, an outside-left from Nottingham Forest, whose dislike for blatant physical confrontation had earned him the unfortunate nickname of 'Gladys' and the regular taunt from the terraces: 'Where's your handbag?' Hinton, one of the nicest of men, had pace, and used his excellent left foot to hit shots and crosses with equal accuracy. If he had scored some of his free-kick goals not for Derby County but for Brazil in the recent World Cup finals, the television companies would be replaying them for the next four years to illustrate how 'we don't have English players who can do this.'

The first season was not that clever – transitional, I suppose you could call it. When I first breezed into the Baseball Ground I had declared, publicly, that we would finish in a higher position than Derby had done in the previous season under Tim Ward. First clanger! We finished eighteenth – one place lower than poor Tim Ward had managed. And he had been sacked!

The foundations had been laid, though. We had virtually a new side. It was improved further by the arrival of Willie Carlin from Sheffield United. Taylor and I believed in balance as well as talent – and Carlin, a belligerent, aggressive little Scouser, gave us just what we needed in midfield. The picture was almost complete.

Later on there was an impression, a wrong impression, that everything had gone swimmingly from the start, that all was sweetness and light. In truth, we had begun to make progress despite a hostile atmosphere backstage, starting the job to the accompaniment of hate letters from supporters of Tim Ward. Tim was a dear, kindly man, who I'm sure did not have a bad thing to say about anyone. I was to get on well with him in later years, and I had the sad experience of attending his funeral in Derby little more than a year ago. But there were friends of Tim on the board, members of the same Lodge, the same Round Table, or the same Rotary Club. One such, Fred Walters, was anti-Clough before I stepped in the door. Men like that aren't clever enough to hide anything, and their resentment shows at every opportunity. He even seemed pleased at our initial lack of success. At a quarter to five on Saturdays, during a spell when we couldn't win a home game, Walters would bellow down the corridor from the boardroom: 'We've dropped another place – fifth from bottom now.' He sounded like the old comedian Al Read – only vicious with it.

Our vice-chairman, Ken Turner, was a cricket man, a committee man at Derbyshire, with a typically amateurish approach despite a charming personality. He once suggested we tie a weighted belt around Roy McFarland's waist and make him train in it during the week. On Saturdays, having taken it off, he would then be able to jump higher. Now that was a serious suggestion from board level! Although I didn't swear much in those days I seem to recall one or two unfamiliar little words slipping out.

Turner did contribute the occasional good idea. Having announced that I would be away for the club's annual meeting, he suggested that I record a message on tape, to be played to the shareholders. Apparently it brought the house down. Perhaps I should have adopted the 'recorded message' procedure for all board meetings and club annual meetings throughout my managerial career.

If there was a single moment of inspiration that transformed Derby from a humdrum, dilapidated, down-in-the-dumps club, it was when Taylor took me on one side, scanned the young names in the team like McFarland, John Robson, O'Hare and Hector, and said, in an extremely serious tone of voice: 'We must get some experience into this side. Go and try to sign Mackay.'

To me, like most people throughout the country, Dave Mackay was the famous Tottenham Hotspur wing-half, a very big name, someone we used to read about in the newspapers. 'Get Mackay?' I said to Taylor. 'You must be bloody joking.'

But he remained adamant – Taylor at his far-seeing, selective, inspirational best. 'Go and try,' he repeated. 'You've pulled off bigger things than this.' Even though he didn't offer an example, I jumped in my car and drove to London.

I was nervous as hell. Arriving at White Hart Lane from the Baseball Ground was like turning up at Buckingham Palace having just left a Wimpy Bar. I took a deep breath and just bowled in. I can't remember how it happened – whether he just wandered into the entrance or somebody marked his card – but Bill Nicholson suddenly appeared before me. Nicholson: one of the great managers, whose team had not only won major trophies but had done it with a style and flair and honesty that I hoped my teams might emulate. I felt like a bit of an imposter – a beginner in his field, about to try and take away one of his most influential and famous players.

I was in awe of Bill Nick at that moment, but I kept hearing the words of Taylor, repeated over and over in my head: 'Go on, go on – you've pulled off bigger things than this.' Like hell I had! But I was brash and cocky in those days. I dismissed my uncertainty long enough to blurt out: 'I've come to talk to Dave Mackay.'

I'm sure dear old Bill smiled a little in a fatherly kind of way while he resisted telling me to turn round and get back in my car. Instead he told me: 'Well, as far as I know, he's off to Scotland tomorrow to become assistant manager of Hearts.' I persisted. 'But can I have a word with him?' I never got an answer, because at that moment Nicholson's phone rang and he disappeared, saying only that Mackay was out training. I went and sat on a chair in a passageway and waited for what seemed like an entire day.

Eventually Dave Mackay, he of the barrel-chest, the League and Cup double and twenty-odd Scottish caps, came striding in, as only he could. Still in his training gear, he marched straight towards me, hand outstretched. I was only three or four years younger than him, but I remember thinking: 'Christ, he looks

71

ten years older than me.' No shuffling of feet or uneasy, embarrassing loss of words – I came straight out with it: 'I've come to have a word about you joining Derby.'

'There's no chance,' he said. 'I'm going back to Hearts tomorrow, to be assistant manager. That's it.'

'Tell you what,' I said. 'Go and get in a nice bath and then we'll have a chat. You never know your luck.'

He had his bath and then took me into the players' area. I still remember the impression that it made on me. Everything was immaculate. Women running all over the place making cups of tea and sandwiches. I'd never been in a players' lounge in my life. We didn't have one at Middlesbrough (although there was a snooker table) or at Sunderland. At Hartlepools we only had buckets to catch rainwater. The surroundings were plush, but the response was still the same, as Mackay insisted: 'I wouldn't come to you for ten thousand quid.' I told him, 'I'll give you ten thousand,' but he repeated: 'No chance – I'm definitely going back to Hearts.'

We talked for a while about various aspects of the game, footballing generalities, until I became impatient and asked: 'What would you come for, then?' and he said: 'I'd consider fifteen thousand.' Maybe these were the negotiations in which I learned my trade. Don't let the player have the last say if you can avoid it. Or maybe it was just the old Yorkshire trait of giving away as little as possible, because if a few thousand quid had been the difference between landing Mackay or losing him, I wouldn't have resisted for too long. 'I can't get fifteen thousand,' I said.

'Well, if you can't get it you might as well get off and thanks very much,' he said, making as if to get up. 'But I can get fourteen thousand,' I returned, and he said: 'Done!', just like that.

I'd spent around two hours at the Spurs ground and I'm not

sure whether I've ever matched the feeling of total elation that swept me along the return car journey north. I kept telling myself I'd nailed it, I'd nailed it – the feeling of triumph was quite brilliant. I hadn't just signed a player, I'd recruited a kind of institution, a legendary footballer who, despite recent setbacks of two leg fractures, was the perfect addition, the crowning glory for the young side we were assembling at Derby. I never made a more effective signing in my entire managerial career.

When I look back across all the many and varied signings during my time in management – Roy McFarland, Peter Shilton, Trevor Francis, Kenny Burns, John O'Hare, Colin Todd, John McGovern and many, many more – Dave Mackay has to be the best. Not only did he have everything as a player, but he was the ideal skipper: a supreme example to everybody else at the football club. He even taught us how to play cards!

I drove straight to the Baseball Ground where Taylor was waiting. 'Any luck?' he asked.

'Yes, I've got him. He's coming up here to finalise everything and to put pen to paper tomorrow.'

'I don't believe it,' said Taylor, the one who suggested I go for Mackay in the first place. 'Never thought you had a prayer. Brilliant! Shows I was right to suggest you had a crack at him.'

Typical Taylor. Waiting for me to return from Tottenham was probably the longest single spell Pete spent at the ground. It was very rarely later than one-thirty in the afternoon when he produced his immortal parting phrase: 'I'll be shooting off, then.'

Mackay's £14,000 was a signing-on fee, to be spread over a three-year contract in addition to his wages. When he arrived to complete the deal the next day, Taylor told me: 'You'd better get him in here so that you can talk to him.'

I said: 'No, *you* can talk to him,' but Taylor insisted I

was in there as well.

This was the meeting in which the Clough–Taylor negotiating routine was born. We used it for years, whether signing a player, bombing one out, dealing with transfer requests, or sorting out some cheeky sod who wanted his wages increased. The Mackay situation was delicate, though. He was not only facing a change of club but a change of job. 'Dave,' Taylor said to him, 'the gaffer's got a wee bit of a shock for you. He wants you to play a different role.'

'What role?' Mackay asked, clearly now wondering what he'd let himself in for, but surely not expecting the next announcement: 'We're going to play you as a sweeper!'

The great Dave Mackay then went through the kind of to-and-fro technique that baffled and softened many a difficult customer who found himself as the tennis ball in a kind of centre-court session, with Taylor and me on opposite sides of the net. 'But I can't play sweeper,' he protested, 'I just can't do it.'

That's when I had to butt in and say: 'We have the best centre-half in the League in Roy McFarland. He is so quick that your pace won't be needed. I just want you to drop off and control the lot, because you'll be in a position to see absolutely everything.'

He still protested. 'But I'm used to combing every blade of grass on the pitch.' And that's how the conversation continued – Taylor positioned at one side of the room, me at the opposite side and the target of our attention strategically placed in the middle. No, my office was not a nice place to be if you were a player under discussion. After twenty minutes of verbal tennis the player would be dizzy, baffled, almost pleading for mercy. I never heard Dave Mackay plead for anything in his career, but even he was eventually persuaded to give it a try.

Perhaps he was still a little uncertain about the anchor

role we had in mind until that moment when he put his foot on the ball, resisting the temptation to whack it any old how, so demonstrating to the rest of the team the value of a calm head and a determination to pass the ball whenever possible. That was the moment we knew Mackay was going to make better players out of those we had placed around him – not least McFarland, who developed into a magnificent defender of the highest class. I believe that was the moment when Mackay realised he could do the job we had in mind. He was about to add the glorious finishing touches to an already mighty playing career. From that moment on, we just went out and pissed on everybody.

We had so much confidence it was coming out of our ears. We felt unbeatable and it all stemmed from Dave. He brought a swagger to the team, to the whole club. He had turned thirty and yet, on the two or three days a week that he came in for training – still living in London but spending a few overnights at Derby's Midland Hotel – he was absolutely bubbling. Win, lose or draw – and we didn't lose that often – it made no difference to his mood. The younger players would look at him in open-mouthed admiration. During our favourite training routine of five-a-side he'd repeatedly shout: 'Erm . . . don't bother to move,' before plonking the ball perfectly at the feet of a team-mate.

They were happy, happy days. I've never known a collective spirit stronger than the one we built at Derby at that time. Don Revie talked about 'the family' he created at Leeds United, but no group of players in the country was more closely knit or fiercely committed than ours. If we'd been together in 1939, Adolf Hitler would have been finished in a matter of months.

Although I was the gaffer I was still fit enough and sharp enough and good enough to be part of the camaraderie in the dressing-room and on the training-ground. I still carried the best shot in the club, and did I enjoy demonstrating it at every opportunity! It wasn't long before they had the reference books out, checking my scoring record at Middlesbrough and Sunderland. John O'Hare was a Clough fanatic – I think he knew the place, date and time of every goal I scored.

In the meantime, Mackay helped teach Nigel some of the skills that eventually persuaded Liverpool to pay more than two million pounds for him. Maybe my elder son, Simon, would have made it too, had it not been for a serious knee injury at a tender age. Before training, or sometimes afterwards, Mackay would say to the pair of them: 'Come on, you two, let's get in that box.' He spent hours on end practising with the two bairns, kicking ball after ball into a wooden 'shooting-box' beneath the old main stand at the Baseball Ground.

Mackay gave the team that moral courage I've talked about, an air of confidence that produced a sense of adventure. Soon we were producing a calibre of football that excited spectators, which drew attention to a football club that had spent too long in no-man's land. Derby were being noticed nationwide. The young, loud-mouthed upstart Clough was showing the game that he had a lot more to offer than mere opinions that made headlines and often upset the people in power.

We won the Second Division Championship in 1968–69 – the same season that the rejuvenated Dave Mackay was voted the Football Writers' Footballer of the Year. He shared the award with Tony Book, whose Manchester City side had won the League title a year earlier and who won the FA Cup in '69. Book must have had some season at Maine Road but I still find it hard to believe he'd had one as good or as influential as Dave Mackay's.

We always got on very well. I don't recall having had any differences or arguments with Mackay. What I do know is I could have behaved better towards him when Derby County appointed him to succeed me as manager after Taylor and I walked out. But that's another story.

8

DERBY WINNER

Coaching is for kids. If a player can't trap a ball
and pass it by the time he's in the team, he shouldn't
be there in the first place. I told Roy McFarland to go
and get his bloody hair cut – that's coaching
at this level.

THE DEVELOPMENT OF THE DERBY COUNTY TEAM WAS SWIFT AND SURE.
I knew that, as the best young manager around, it was inevitable
that I would finish up with the best team – the League Champions.

That's the way I was, the way I thought, the way I worked. What point is there in sweating blood day in and day out, battling with directors and constantly putting your judgement on the line, if you're only thinking about finishing second?

It's funny now, but I still regard the football we played in that first season in the First Division as some of the best we ever produced. We were to finish only fourth, but we had beaten the big boys, Liverpool and Manchester United. The foundations for the future were laid.

Peter Taylor was at his brilliant best at this time, making subtle changes – only 'imports' of the highest quality could sustain and improve the standards of an exceptional side. I can think of no better example of the Taylor–Clough method than the signing of Archie Gemmill, the little Scot who was to work with me until the day I retired. Correction – there was a short gap in our working relationship when I sold him from Forest too early. It was a major mistake on my part. I thought his legs had gone, but he proved that I should have kept him on for at least another year.

Taylor was in an uncompromising mood. Drawing hard on a cigarette, he told me: 'We've got to get over to Preston. We've got to sign a little bugger called Gemmill. It's not a case of "if" or "maybe" – this is the one who will make our team. This is a must.'

I suppose the rest is regarded as 'vintage Clough'. Certainly, when I wanted a player and set my stall out, nothing would deter me. If I had been easily put off I'd have accepted Bill Nicholson's discouraging greeting at White Hart Lane and Dave Mackay would never have become a Derby County player. I refused to take 'no' for an answer in those days. In fact, the manager who allows a player to 'think about it over the weekend' is a fool. When you want a player, you stick with him and let nobody else get as much as a sniff until you know for sure, one way or another, whether you've pulled it off.

The sniff I got over the Gemmill deal was the wonderful aroma of bacon and eggs cooking in a pan. Arriving at his home I asked him right out to sign for Derby, but he wouldn't. Not immediately, anyway. It was the first evidence – much more was to follow in subsequent years – that Archie Gemmill could be an awkward little shit.

Gemmill's lovely wife, Betty, was heavily pregnant at the time, carrying Scot. Little did I know then that the unborn bairn would actually be playing for me at Nottingham Forest by the time I closed the Clough managerial chapter. How time flies and makes you feel old!

I had the feeling that somebody else was in the market for Gemmill, maybe Everton, and I wasn't prepared to let go. If he wanted to sleep on it, then so did I. 'I'll sleep in the spare room or anywhere you care to put me,' I told the Gemmills. I'm not sure I was invited to stay, but I was never one to wait for an invitation when there was business to be done. Betty was not too impressed with me at the outset. She'd probably seen me on television and formed her own impression, but I think she warmed to me a little bit after I walked into the kitchen and got stuck into the washing-up.

The next morning she cooked me a beautiful breakfast. Gemmill signed – another of the best transfers I ever made. I was later to sign him for Nottingham Forest, and then took him on my coaching staff. As a player he was superb. As a man, I'm not sure who disliked him more – those who worked with him or those who played against him. Once you stop playing, then you have to carry some warmth off the pitch. Whether it be with a journalist, a friend, a gaffer, or the wife of a player you want to sign – you have to know how to be warm. And when you go for a new job for which you are well qualified you need to stroll in for the interview with a little bit of panache. Archie, I'm sure, would walk in grim-faced and intense as ever – just the way he was when he played for a living.

As the Mackay era drew to its close another key component slipped into place. I went back to Sunderland and signed Colin Todd, a young defender I'd worked with during my short spell in charge of the youth side at Roker Park. Taylor had left this one to me, saying: 'No need for me to look at the lad. You know him better than anybody, so if you think he's the one – go and get him.' I was absolutely full of my own importance and ability by then. Our judgement of players was beyond doubt or reproach. We had nothing to prove in that department, and I didn't feel the need even to consult the chairman or directors before doing our business. The way I saw it was simple: I was the manager, the man in charge, who would sink or swim on the success or failure of the players hired. The chairman wouldn't pay with his job if I failed in mine and it wasn't his personal money we were spending, anyway.

Sam Longson was on holiday when I did the Todd deal for what was then regarded as a massive fee of £175,000. I told him nothing about it until I sent him a telegram. I can't recall the exact wording, but it went something like this: 'Just bought you another great player, Colin Todd. We're almost bankrupt. Love Brian.' Rude? Out of order? It may look that way, all these years later, but then I could do no wrong, and, after all, I'd just landed the best young defender in England, who was about to turn Derby into the best team in the country. The following year we won the Football League Championship. I had beaten Bill Shankly and Liverpool, Don Revie and Leeds, despite a far smaller squad of players than those at Anfield and Elland Road.

I still seethe at the things that were said back in May 1972 when we took the title. Fools in newspapers and on television tried to make out a case that we had won it by default. We had a fine team who had achieved the best results over a season of forty-two matches. To say it was won by default remains an insult. A full league season never has produced false or unworthy champions and never will. We'd hardly lost a match since the turn of the year, and we'd beaten Liverpool by the only goal of our final game of the season – a game in which, incidentally, we played Stevie Powell at right-back at the tender age of sixteen. How many managers, how many clubs would have been prepared to do that? Clough and Taylor at their incomparable best. Again!

Leeds, who had won the FA Cup that year, needed only a point at Wolverhampton on the Monday night to win the Double and deny Derby the Championship. We had dispersed and gone separate ways. Taylor had taken most of the players – those who hadn't to report for international duty – to Cala Millor, the resort in Majorca that became legendary to players and staff at Derby and, later, at Forest. Nobody ever wanted to miss out on a trip there – whether in the close-season, or in mid-season when we just fancied a break from the old routine. We've enjoyed some of the finest times of our lives in Cala Millor. In fact, I still follow the practice of keeping a few peseta notes in my bedside drawer. I take a look at them from time to time to remind myself that it won't be long before I'm out there again.

While the team flew out in '72 I headed for the Scilly Isles with Barbara, our three children, and Mam and Dad. Why not? No point hanging around at home waiting for Leeds to complete their fixtures. Nowt we could do about that, and in any case time with my family was always top of my list of priorities. I often took holidays at school half-terms during the season – much to the surprise and annoyance and, I suspect, envy of the directors. Stuff 'em!

Taylor had apparently told the players in Cala Millor that they had nothing to worry about – 'no sweat' was his favourite saying.

He convinced them the title was ours, but I can't honestly say I shared his confidence as I trickled sand through my fingers and built castles for the kids in the Scillies. I expected Leeds to get their result against Wolves because Revie was the most thorough of men who, wherever possible, left nothing to chance.

The Leeds match at Molineux was eventually surrounded by controversy. There were allegations of attempted bribery by Leeds, supposed offers of cash for a penalty. Some of the claims were legally disproved later and Revie threatened writs, although I never did hear whether he served them. What I do know is that Leeds lost. The news filtered through to the island of Tresco and the island of Majorca, and the celebrations began. I can still taste the champagne we drank that evening, and the surviving hotel guests all joined in. Those few days after learning we had won the most precious prize in football, the most searching examination of managerial talent, were some of the happiest I can remember. Typically, the *Sun* was first on the scene. I didn't too much mind having my family holiday disrupted, because the photographs they took remain among my favourites. It was nice that Mam and Dad were there to share the moment.

I wish I could have persuaded Mam and Dad to move ten years earlier into the bungalow I bought for them. But she would continue to protest: 'It's too late, son. Too late for us to move now.' It was never too late. The council house in Valley Road was a nice place, a beautiful place. It was what she had made it, but I knew it was time my Mam sat down for a little while. Eventually she and Dad agreed, and I bought them a little bungalow close to where my sister Doreen lived.

We put a fridge in it, but when Barbara and I paid a visit we found the fridge empty and switched off. 'Mother,' I called to her, 'there's nowt in this fridge.'

'That's right, son,' she said. 'Your Dad and I don't eat a lot and, anyway, it's winter, so it's a waste of electricity.'

Mam was apparently christened after one of the first famous women foreign correspondents, Lady Sarah Wilson. Many a pressman will smile at the irony of that – my Mam named after a journalist! I was by now a household name, featuring on panels of so-called experts, including the likes of Malcolm Allison and the former Wolves and Ireland centre-forward, Derek Dougan. I'll never forget the sight of David Coleman, seconds before we went on air, gathering himself like a coiled spring before that red light flashed on top of the camera. Like everybody else, I had regarded Coleman as a friendly, relaxed face in a corner of the living-room, looking perfectly comfortable and at home without nerves or tension. To observe him first-hand and at close quarters in his own working environment was a shock to the system. He was winding himself up for a theatrical performance. He was like the player in the Cup Final or the vital league game knowing that so many people were dependent upon him doing his job. I can think of no greater testimony, no greater tribute to the man, than the fact that he is still performing to the highest standards, even now.

Brian Moore, of the opposite channel, has been a good friend of the family for many years – from the time I took my first steps into the television field. It is with no disrespect to others that I say Brian has remained the best football commentator for a considerable time. Don't let any manager tell you that his job carries most pressure. To see television performers working at the sharp end is to appreciate that others have to contend with extraordinary tension as well. They don't make them like Moore and Coleman any more.

They don't make them like Frank Sinatra any more, either. I have spent thousands of pounds on tickets to see Sinatra. I've never missed him when he's come to England, and in more recent years I've often taken so many friends and colleagues with me that we used the team coach. I was never too happy about staying overnight – I always prefer to get there and back and to sleep in my own bed. On one memorable occasion, the lady who dealt with my tickets for Sinatra wrote and suggested that since I'd been to so many of his shows it was about time I met him. And I did. Briefly.

I said to the public-relations woman at the pre-concert reception: 'Surely, he'll be absolutely jiggered after the show – he won't want to meet me.'

'Oh,' she said, 'he sees nobody *after* the show. He doesn't even return to the dressing-room afterwards. He walks straight out, gets into the car, and is gone before people have started to leave the theatre. You can only see him before the show.'

It was quite a swanky do. Lots of photographers. Roger Moore was there with his wife. I gave him a kiss and when he looked a bit surprised, I said: 'I've been wanting to do that for years.' In the background, Sinatra had moved quietly into the room and was having photographs taken with American Veterans of the Vietnam War. I was not about to delay the great man for very long. A lady introduced us.

'Are you all right?' They are historic words. They are the words, the *only* words Frank Sinatra uttered to me on that memorable occasion in London.

'Yes,' I said as we shook hands, 'nice to see you, thanks for coming over.' And that was that. Obviously, when he is asked to meet people he's never heard of, he still does it his way.

In the early days of our marriage Barbara dragged me along to the Globe Theatre to see Paul Robeson. Later, at my suggestion, we saw Nat King Cole in London – but we missed out on a notable hat-trick when we spent a few days in Brussels, for the World Fair, and could have seen Edith Piaf on stage. For some stupid reason, I think I said I wasn't bothered and we missed a legend performing live. Robeson, Cole and Piaf . . . what a threesome to tell friends about, especially coming from two Sinatra fanatics like Barbara and me.

It's not always turned out as intended. We once travelled down to see Liza Minnelli at the London Palladium. Trouble was, by the time we arrived in London, Barbara had fallen out with me and refused to go. I can't remember what I'd done to upset her but it couldn't have been anything too trivial! I was left with a spare ticket to watch Liza Minnelli three rows from the front. I thought: 'Sod it, I'm going on my own and I'll give the other ticket away.'

I gave it to the manager, who I knew. Who should turn up and sit next to me but Jack Jones, the American singer? I thought he'd had a few drinks because he was complaining, in a loud voice, to two women alongside him, about his car not having turned up, making him late. The show had started but Liza wasn't on, yet. Jones got up my nose. I was niggled, anyway, that Barbara hadn't come with me – I suppose, when you think about it, I was on my 'Jack Jones' twice over. The American was going on and on and on until I couldn't resist.

'Listen,' I told him, 'if I hadn't returned a bloody ticket you wouldn't be sitting in that seat now.'

'You mind your own business,' Jones said. And I just started to laugh.

'Watch it,' I said. 'You're sitting in my seat so you'd better be careful.'

I would like to go and see Elton John, but Barbara and the bairns tell me it's not my scene. I don't think they're too keen on being seen with me because there is usually a bit of a fuss when I turn up. Not my scene, indeed!

Although the League was always *the* trophy I most wanted to win, each and every season, they don't make too many European Cups, either. My heart was still in the First Division, but my eyes

ying to make
:ome-back at
Sunderland.

Stretchered o[ff]
Roker Park,
December 19[ ]
A cruel injury
that spelt the [end]
of my playing
career. *Newca[stle]*
Evening Chro[nicle]

Putting a bra[ve]
face on it: on
crutches
afterwards.
Sunday
Pictorial/
Syndication
International

Showing the
r Sunderland
ow it's done.
Larkin Fotos

ngland XI to
play Sweden,
Wembley,
ctober 1959.
en won 3–2.
hough I was
twenty-four,
this was my
cond and last
game for the
national side.
by Charlton
Don Howe
at the back;
my Greaves
s with me at
the front.
Popperfoto

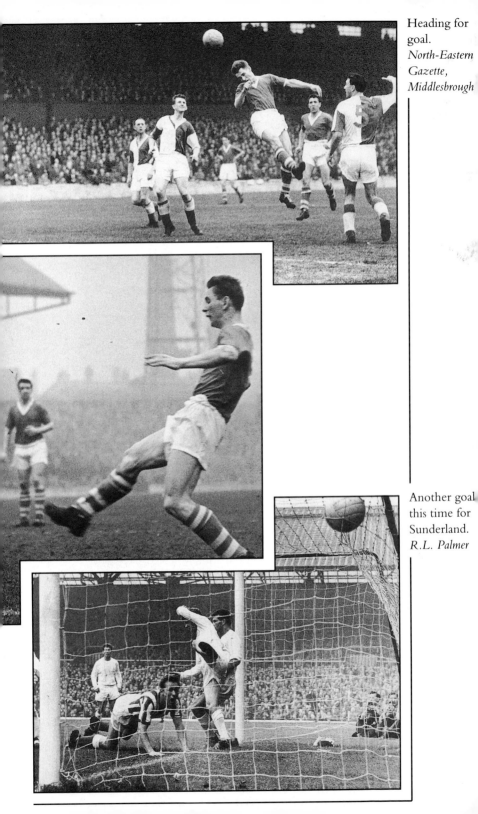

Heading for
goal.
*North-Eastern
Gazette,
Middlesbrough*

Another goal
this time for
Sunderland.
R.L. Palmer

hooting from
st outside the
penalty box.

*Northern Echo,
Darlington*

Celebrating
ther goal for
ddlesbrough.
this day no
has reached
League goals
quickly. Eat
ur heart out,
Alan Shearer!
*North-Eastern
Gazette,
Middlesbrough*

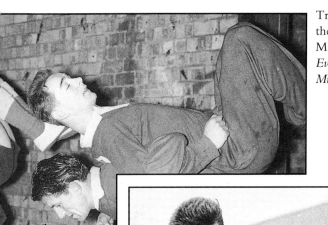

Training with
the other lads at
Middlesbrough.
*Evening Gazette,
Middlesbrough*

Middlesbrough
FC centre-
forward.

Marton Grove Secondary Modern team, me sitting in the middle.

t Broughton, eland League Champions, 952-53. I am nding, fourth om the right. *W. and C.D. hardson & son*

Success for R.
Watchet durir
my National
Service.

were set firmly on the trophy they hand over to the champion of champions in Europe. With the arrival of full-back David Nish from Leicester, the squad might not have had much depth in numbers but we felt we had the ideal set-up – a bloody good side, me and Taylor, plus Jimmy Gordon, the coach I had known as a player at Middlesbrough. We felt we had enough talent and know-how to be virtually unbeatable.

We sailed through the early rounds of the European Cup. The Portuguese giants, Benfica – Eusebio and all – were not in the same league as that Derby side of ours. I went over to watch them and afterwards, when Taylor asked what I thought, I daren't tell him. They were that bad! In those days, remember, they were household names, but if I'd told Taylor I thought they were crap he might have blabbed it to the lads and they might have become complacent. So I just told him: 'Well they're not bad, they drew 0-0, but they could easily have won.'

They had no chance at our place, absolutely no chance – especially after I arranged for half the River Derwent to be piped onto the pitch the night before the game. On match night itself the old FIFA president, Sir Stanley Rous, was sitting next to me in the directors' box. 'Er, Brian,' he said, 'I didn't know there had been a downpour last night. I wasn't aware of one at my hotel.' So I put him right. 'Oh yes, Sir Stanley,' I said. 'It rained extremely heavily, here.' Early in the game he had another little dig at me, this time for bellowing instructions as I was inclined to do. By the time we were 3-0 up the old bugger leaned across and said: 'There you are, Brian, you see, there really is no need to shout, is there?' People like him, all charm and diplomacy, don't have a clue about the passion and heartbeat of sport.

We murdered Benfica. I've never known an atmosphere, before or since, to compare with the Baseball Ground, packed for a big-match night. The opposition couldn't live with it –

a howling crowd almost within touching distance of a small pitch. The press boys used to joke that they loved covering Derby matches because they could get quotes from the players while the game was in progress. If any journalist had wandered onto that sludge-heap that night his weekly expenses would have included the cost of new shoes!

We were quick to master the technique of playing away in Europe. That team was quick to learn everything. In Lisbon's famous 'Stadium of Light' we were in the dark for twenty minutes. They came at us from every conceivable angle. There was only one way to describe their superiority – they pissed on us. We couldn't get a kick, but we hung on and the match remained goalless.

March 1973 was one of the blackest months of my life – so black that the clouds lingered for years and, I'm sure, were part of the reason why I never became manager of England. It was the month when the Football Association convinced themselves I could never meet what they considered to be a crucial demand of the job. The role of diplomat.

The semi-final of the European Cup took us to Turin for a first leg against Juventus. It wasn't the result that incensed me – a 3-1 defeat that left us needing one of those miracle nights at the Baseball Ground a fortnight later – it was the nature of it. The lousy stench still fills my nostrils when I think of the attempts at corruption. UEFA later carried out some kind of inquiry, but the truth has remained somewhere swept beneath the carpets in the corridors of power.

We got wind that the referee for the second leg of the 'semi' had been offered some kind of bribe (although UEFA's investigation never found out who had tried unsuccessfully to nobble the ref). I couldn't believe my eyes at some of the things that happened in Turin. One of the Juventus substitutes – I think it was the German, Helmut Haller, was seen going into the referee's dressing-room before the match and again at half-time. I'll never know what was said, but one thing's for sure – he wasn't in there to brew a pot of tea. There was no proof of any irregularities between Haller and the fellow German ref, who might just have been friends, but I was livid. We had two key players booked well before half-time, Roy McFarland and Archie Gemmill. As far as I can remember their only crime was to stand somewhere adjacent to an opponent who flung himself on the floor. Now wasn't that a coincidence? McFarland and Gemmill – two players who just happened to have been booked in previous games – would now, automatically, be ruled out of the second leg. It stank to high heaven. I'd heard lurid tales of bribery, corruption, the bending of match officials in Italy, call it what you will, but I'd never before seen what struck me as clear evidence. I went barmy.

Our anger afterwards saw Taylor arrested – for something minor like a murder threat to the referee, apparently! Meanwhile I was ranting on to the Press about 'cheating, f**king Italian bastards', and I meant every single word of it. We had been done, but we left Italy still believing we could 'do' them at our place. The referee had been useless and had been duped by the cheating Italians into overreacting to trivial offences.

The scene was set, the Baseball Ground was heaving and swaying and generating the kind of atmosphere capable of unnerving the toughest opposition. And it was 21 March, the first day of spring – my birthday. Unfortunately it turned into a night of 'ifs' and 'maybes'. Juventus were under the cosh and showing signs of buckling when we were given a penalty – only for Alan Hinton to miss the bloody thing. When Roger Davies was sent off we were effectively finished. We were out of the European Cup. The feeling as Taylor and I left the ground that night was one of disappointment and frustration, still mixed with the anger that had overflowed from that decisive first leg in Turin.

Within hours, Derby County's elimination from Europe's prem- ier club tournament was rendered meaningless. It was eleven- thirty that same evening, and I was in bed with Barbara, when I heard the phone ringing downstairs. When I picked it up my brother Joe's voice was hushed and brave, but what he said hit me like a sledgehammer: 'We've lost our Mam.'

I had known that she was dying. She had cancer. I had only recently spent three days in the North-East, on hand to visit her at Eston Hospital, between Middlesbrough and Redcar. It isn't often you are made to feel utterly helpless, but that was precisely the way I felt then. 'Hello, it's our Bri . . .' were just about the last words she said to me. I sat and held her hand and said: 'Are you OK?' – futile things like that. She gestured that she needed a drink, but the best I could do for her was to rub her quivering lips with ice.

Nothing prepared me for the news that she had gone. I'm sure I didn't say a word for several seconds. I immediately saw her face. I thought about her in that little woolly hat. I thought about her cleaning all those pairs of shoes. I thought about her hanging out the washing and standing at the mangle and leading us like a row of little ducks to church on Sundays. I thought about her always being there when I returned home from school. And I cried a little. I went back to Barbara and told her: 'We've lost our Mam,' and I cried, because it hit me that I would never see her face again.

Suddenly, devastatingly, I was in the real world. Away from the smell of the liniment and the roar of the crowd. Within the warm comfort and reassurance of my family and my own home, but engulfed by a desperate feeling of overwhelming loneliness. What was it they called me in those days? A genius? I'd just been knocked out of the European Cup and had a player sent off. And now all that meant nothing because we had lost our Mam. Some genius. Some birthday.

Joe and the rest of the family still in the North-East handled the funeral arrangements. At the service itself I just sat and repeated to myself: 'I've lost my Mam.' You only have one Mother. Only one. Barbara keeps reminding me today that our grandchildren only have one Grandad and that I'm precious to them.

Mam was cremated, but I wish now there had been a burial instead. It is a purely personal and selfish thing – the selfishness of a man wanting what he can't have. The family still send flowers to the place of remembrance, but I wish there was a grave so that I could have the sensation of actually visiting her. I think I would go every week.

I don't believe in an afterlife. When Mam went, she went. I am an avid reader of newspapers but I've yet to see proof of anyone dying and coming back after the funeral. I have been introduced to many churchmen down the years and none of them has convinced me either. Nor am I a church-goer any more. When my elder son, Simon, was marrying Susan, the local vicar at Quarndon refused to arrange the service on a Sunday. 'I don't do marriages on Sundays,' he said. He was wrong. It is their job to preach, baptise and marry people in the church. And Sunday, surely, is one of their working days. We switched the service to nearby Allestree and I've never been back to his church since.

No, I'm sure there is no afterlife. The loss of Mam was final, as was Dad's death four years later, at the age of eighty-one – or that of Des, who died of cancer in 1987, while he was still in his fifties. Mam was seventy-three when we lost her, and I still see her face, most days. And Dad's and our Des's. So they are always there, but I can't bring myself to believe I will ever meet them again.

Our Mam . . . what a lady. What an example and source of inspiration to the entire family. Oh yes, she is up there with my greatest heroes. Just below Len Hutton.

9

SO LONG, SAM

We sit down together and discuss things carefully
and in detail. Sam has his say and I have mine.
And then we reach a decision and agree that
I am right.

MY SELF-CONFIDENCE AND, YES, MY EGO KNEW NO LIMITS. I KNEW THAT
we at Derby were on the way to becoming a major force, part of
the élite of English football. On a personal level I was well aware
of my notoriety and popularity as a national figure on television.
Even though I possibly annoyed and upset as many viewers as I

impressed, I'm certain very few reached for the 'off' button while I was on the screen. I loved all that!

I loved what we had created at that old, unfashionable club, too. All the confidence I had experienced as a goal-scorer of exceptional ability was flooding through my veins again. I realised I could be as a manager what I had been as a player – the best in the business. It was a feeling that I simply could do no wrong. The players we had signed – Dave Mackay, Roy McFarland, John O'Hare, Alan Hinton, Archie Gemmill, Colin Todd and the last of the arrivals, Henry Newton – were all of the highest class. Taylor had an unrivalled eye for talent, and no-one could match my recruiting skills. Our ability to blend them into a balanced, exciting and successful team was proven for all to see. The record books showed Derby as League Champions and semi-finalists in the European Cup. Nothing could halt the march.

That's the way it seemed and that's the way it should have been – but for a combination of my ego, Taylor's pride, and the stubbornness of an old man who wanted to be seen to be running his club and regaining control of his outspoken, outrageous manager.

When Sam Longson brought Taylor and me from Hartlepools he had a vision. He wanted Derby transformed from the ranks of the run-of-the-mill, the humdrum, into something special, a club that could challenge the powerful élite for the glittering prizes and back-page headlines. Let this be a lesson to all young, would-be managers. Beware the 'friendly grandfather'. Beware the ambitious chairman who will 'give anything' for success. Beware the knife behind the smile!

In the beginning, there was no relationship in football closer that the one between Longson and me. It went beyond the normal chairman–manager partnership. It was a genuine, close friendship, between an old man and a brash young upstart, in whom he saw an opportunity to fulfil his dreams. There was a theory, and I cannot deny it, that Longson – the father of three daughters – regarded me as the son he never had. He certainly treated me as if I were of his own flesh and blood. He'd often call at our house, dropping off a leg of lamb and the mint sauce to go with it. He took my Mam and Dad to his holiday home close by the beach on Anglesey. He drove me thousands of miles in his cars – the Rolls-Royce or the gorgeous, sporty, silvery Mercedes. He allowed me to treat his Merc as my own. I didn't even need to ask, because the keys were always available and the open invitation was constant: 'If you want it, take it.' He gave me money, he gave me booze, he would have given me anything I wanted.

The first thing he gave me was a room in the Midland Hotel soon after I first moved down to start the job. Initially, I was 'billeted' in the more modest York Hotel across the road. One morning I saw the Indian cricket team leaving the Midland, and their skipper, the Nawab of Pataudi, wandered across to have a few words. It was him who recognised me – honest! I told Longson: 'If the Indian touring team is staying at the Midland, how come your new manager is at the bloody York? I want to be where they are.'

I was moved straight away. It was there that I met Billy Wainwright, the hotel manager who became one of my closest friends, travelled throughout Europe with the team, and remains in regular touch today, although he has retired to his home town of Sheffield. The Midland Hotel became our second home. Mackay stayed there, McFarland lived there for a long spell, and the entire Derby side spent Friday nights there before home games. We even arranged for a barber to call in on a regular basis, to give a trim to those who needed one. I couldn't abide players turning out with untidy hair on a Saturday.

Longson once took Wainwright and me into Burberrys in

London and bought me a beautiful, three-quarter-length suede coat. I'd never had a suede coat in my life. I trusted Billy's judgement on such things – he was always spotless and immaculate – and when he told me that the coat was 'top quality', that was good enough for me. I wore it for many years.

Taylor, as usual, was first to spot possible problems. He began telling me that I was getting too close to the chairman. 'The old bugger will do you if you're not careful.' I didn't understand his reservations at first. Everything was going so well. The team was brilliant, we knew we could make further signings, and we thought that it could only get better. Sam was treating me like a son. For my part, I was opening doors for him. I was taking him to matches and because he was with me, people would ask: 'Is that Sam Longson, chairman of Derby County?' That kind of thing grew on him. He enjoyed the notoriety.

We were on tour in Germany once, and West Ham were also there. Sam and I were sitting in the stand when he nudged me and said: 'Will you do me a favour?'

'Of course,' I said, 'what is it?' thinking he wanted me to nip out for a cup of tea.

'Will you introduce me to Bobby Moore?' I took him to the West Ham dressing-room, spoke to their manager, Ron Greenwood, and set up the meeting. I asked Sam if he'd like to meet Martin Peters and Geoff Hurst as well – seeing that we were in the company of World Cup heroes – but he said he only wanted to meet Bobby Moore. I don't think he'd heard of the other two!

Gradually I became more and more of a television personality. At first I would notify the board in advance of any planned appearances on the box. I didn't see the need – what business was it of theirs? And, in any case, the exposure was good publicity for the club – but Sam assured me it would keep things on a nice even keel. Taylor, meanwhile, was egging me on to do all the television I could. He was the best 'egger-on' in the business, just so long as he wasn't involved. He would say: 'Go and do the telly and take the chairman with you.' At the same time, remember, he expressed fears that we were getting too close.

On one particular occasion, when Barbara and I were invited to the BBC's Sports Personality of the Year Awards, we took Sam along. Taylor, who normally wouldn't venture as far as the local pub, came with us, bringing Lillian too. The late Graham Hill, Damon's father, who had I think finished third in the voting, later offered Barbara a lift back to the hotel. When she explained that we were with friends, Sam broke in, saying: 'I'll go,' and jumped into Hill's car. That was the man. And that was the life I had enabled him to lead. It was a relationship that seemed unbreakable, but then how many football managers have said that through the years? And finished with the sack?

Not only did my success allow him to rub shoulders with the rich, the not so rich, and the famous, but I also built him a new stand – the Ley Stand, opposite the players' tunnel at the Baseball Ground. Not only did we pay for it, with money generated through the turnstiles – we wouldn't have had it at all if I had not bargained with the managing director of Ley's steel factory. The plans revealed, apparently, that we didn't quite have enough room for the new structure. To accommodate the stand we needed another eighteen inches, encroaching into Ley's property. Crisis! So I went round there, alone as usual, and told the big boss what we needed. 'It's looking a bit run-down out there,' I said. 'I'll take down your old corrugated fence, replace it with a new one, and move back your pylons. After a week, you'll never know it's been done.'

I'd never been in a factory since my early working days at ICI but, again, my self-confidence outweighed any uncertainty and the direct approach such a feeling inspired must have startled anybody who got in my way. 'I'll have to put it to the board,' he said. 'Will there be any compensation?'

'F**k compensation,' I said. 'The eighteen inches of ground is no use to you whatsoever. We'll name the stand after your factory and give you season tickets.' I think it was what they would now call a 'package deal'. In any case, it did the trick. I went back to Longson and told him he could get on with building the new stand.

Trouble was lurking just around the corner, though. I gave him those few inches, but eventually he took a yard. I don't think there was one specific thing that soured our relationship, but my 'spies' began to notice and report back little instances which told that the old man was going cool on me. He had become something of a local hero in his home town of Chapel-en-le-Frith, basking in my reflected glory. What we had achieved at a relatively small-town club in the space of three or four years was unheard of. Longson found himself surrounded by 'friends' he didn't know he had. But they all began to ask the same question: 'Who runs Derby County – you or that big-headed manager of yours?' That sowed the seeds of concern in Longson's mind. If truth be known, the old so-and-so had an ego as big as mine.

Somebody else, somebody closer to home, helped ruin the relationship as well. Taylor! He began telling the chairman: 'It's time you realised how well Brian runs this club.' He was right. I did run it. I swept the terraces, I signed the players, I took the training every day, did the mail and walked the pitch every Sunday morning, plotting what was to be done next. I virtually lived at the Baseball Ground, and when I wasn't there I'd be visiting local hospitals, speaking at Rotary Clubs, and suchlike. Or appearing on national television, bringing the club the kind of publicity and exposure it had never known in its history. But instead of heightening Longson's appreciation, Taylor's words had the reverse effect. Longson began to believe that we had

CLOUGH: THE AUTOBIOGRAPHY

too much power and, to a certain extent, he was right. I had let it go to my head.

Something else was going wrong. The relationship with the club secretary, Stuart Webb, was cooling too. Football managers should be careful about the people who fill three specific jobs within their club – the secretary, the coach driver, and the lady who does the laundry. All are in positions where they know things, hear things. You have to be sure they are people who are totally trustworthy, who will not 'blab'.

Webb, or 'Webby' as he was known, had been recommended by Jimmy Gordon. We didn't know where to go for a secretary, being new to the game, but Jimmy said there was 'a lad at Preston who's supposed to be good'. I interviewed him with the vice-chairman, Sidney Bradley, who later asked me what I thought. 'He's quite impressive as far as I'm concerned,' I said, 'and I think we should give him a run.' Webb also looked immaculate – always did. He was perfectly summed up, years afterwards, by the late Geoffrey Green, football correspondent of *The Times*. Glancing at Webb, adorned in green evening jacket at a presentation dinner, Geoffrey described him as 'that most perfect of polished penguins'.

Webby was never a major problem. It's just that he tended to play both ends against the middle. He used to put on a front as a friend, but he wasn't one. Taylor twigged him before I did. 'Don't trust him,' he would warn, when Webb had left the room. I grabbed Webb by the lapels one day and told him: 'I'll put you through that bloody wall if you ever cause me any trouble. You came here to join the secretarial staff – you were nowt. Now you're walking round with 20,000 pesetas in your back-pocket' – as he did, being in charge of the money when Derby went on tour.

The secretary's position is a difficult one. It's never easy for a manager to have the club secretary as a friend because he has to serve his board of directors. I saw the secretary as the one who should mark my card about everything and everybody – and no bloody secrets. I was as open as any book anybody has ever read – as open as the Book of Remembrance.

Webby was clever. I saw, first-hand, the lengths he was prepared to go to in order to keep directors happy. On one occasion we were on tour in Spain. I had taken our Simon and Nigel with us and we ended up at an hotel with no swimming facilities. I told Webb: 'Just you find a pool for my kids.' Typical Stuart – on the phone for a minute or two and he came up with the use of the most beautiful pool at a private club. My kids were first in. I lay on the side, chuntering about this and that, while Taylor sat there smoking his fag. We heard Webby say to Jack Kirkland, the director in charge: 'Do you swim, Mr Kirkland?'

'Yes, I swim,' the director replied, 'I'll race you.' Webby mumbled something about not being that good a swimmer himself, but the bet was struck for a fiver. I acted as starter. One, two, three – and in they went. Kirkland, who had only one eye, still had his bloody glasses on. If the pool was fifty yards long Webby had swum twenty-five by the time one-eyed Jack had done ten. Suddenly, politics jumped in as well. Webby was that shrewd he started to back-peddle, and Kirkland beat him on the touch. Taylor drew on his cigarette, nudged me and said: 'Webby could have done two f**king lengths there and still done him. We've got to keep an eye on the secretary.'

When Taylor called to Kirkland: 'I'd no idea you could swim like that,' I had to bury my face in a towel. Taylor was the best and the funniest at taking the piss with a one-liner without them knowing it. Within seconds Webby had dived back into the pool – to retrieve Kirkland's specs off the bottom.

Taylor always kept Webb at arm's length. One day when I buzzed Stuart in his office, he said he'd be along in ten minutes. Taylor grabbed the phone and told him: 'You get down here. Now! When the gaffer asks you to come, you get your arse down here or I'll come and drag you down.' He was with us in the space of seconds.

Webb's power gradually increased. He opened a travel agency. He organised travel for our club and several others. He began attending league meetings. It's a strange thing, but if you 'get on' a wee bit in football all the doors start to open. Two or three years beforehand, nobody knew he existed. Once we had started being successful, Webb became a personality in his own right. Many years later, of course, he recruited the help of Robert Maxwell to save Derby from bankruptcy. I haven't seen Webby for several years but Barbara received a warm, complimentary letter from his wife, Josie, when I retired. That was a nice touch.

It's odd how Kirkland, a cantankerous old sod who eventually triggered the parting of the ways, kept cropping up or poking his nose in. There was the day he summoned me to his office and said: 'I'm going to give you some good advice – and listen to it. No matter how good you are, or how powerful you think you are, Stuart Webb has the ear of the chairman.' I didn't understand. 'The chairman listens to his secretary, all chairmen listen to their secretaries. They get to know everything and they pass it all on.' Sound advice – which I learned to appreciate a lot further down the line when I worked with Ken Smales at Nottingham Forest: the most trustworthy secretary I ever knew.

Slowly but surely, Longson began chipping away. There was a bar in the boardroom that I used as my office. It was a perfect arrangement for entertaining the callers whose numbers increased in proportion to our success. I remember David Coleman sitting on the steps that led to a little office next door. He had an entire camera crew with him. It was a case of 'Have a coffee, fellas, or would you prefer a beer, a Scotch or a nice little brandy? Oh, this is the chairman, Mr Longson. Chairman –

have you met David Coleman?' It was always like that. If not David Coleman then some other celebrity – and old Sam lapped it up. Trouble was, nobody was that interested in what he had to say.

Local journalists, like George Edwards, Neil Hallam and Gerald Mortimer, were regulars to the 'inner sanctum'. I've known some journalists arrive before ten and not leave before four. But after that 'Hello, chairman' there was nothing else for Sam. He had nothing to contribute, and anyway they didn't want his bloody name in the paper. There was no copy in the old man. Finally, the bar had to go – or at least my use of it did. Sam turned round and said: 'I think this club is becoming a sanctuary for journalists. You are doing too much entertaining.' He had the security grille pulled down. And locked.

I had become too big for him. He wanted more of the limelight for himself. He even offered himself for a place on the League Management Committee. Now that was a joke if ever I heard one! But never let anyone underestimate the power of those in charge of football clubs. When I joined Derby one of the first things Longson told me was that directors had to stand down at the age of 65. The second he reached 65 – he changed the rule!

He became more and more envious of me. He was forever chuntering in the background: 'I was the one who signed him. I was the one who gave him his big break. I was the one who allowed him *carte blanche*.' There had been many a controversy since our arrival, not least the fiasco over the proposed signing of winger Ian Storey-Moore in 1972. He was on his way to Manchester United for £200,000 when we stepped in. We almost kidnapped him – Taylor and I were past masters of the cloak-and-dagger transfer – we tapped more people in our time than the Severn-Trent Water Authority!

United thought they had him nailed but we shipped him to Derby, and hid him away like Salman Rushdie before unveiling

him as 'our new signing' to a packed house at the Baseball
Ground. Even I hadn't bargained for the kind of shit that hit
the fan over that. You couldn't mess with Manchester United,
the great Matt Busby's club, in those days. We were left waving
goodbye to Storey-Moore as he departed for Old Trafford and our
tails were very definitely between our legs.

A fine of £5,000 over the transfer cock-up followed a fine of
£10,000 two years earlier for negligence in the books, which
also cost us a place in Europe. Longson's tolerance was being
stretched. He saw my flourishing television 'career' as a threat
to his own ambitions among football's hierarchy. He was being
badgered by fellow chairmen, and other idiotic hobnobs who cling
to the game: 'You'd better get a grip on that manager of yours.'
For years he had pushed me and encouraged me to go on TV, but
suddenly he announced: 'You're spending too much time on telly.
Your job is here.' He insisted that my television appearances be
reduced, and permitted them only when the board agreed. He
even wanted to inspect newspaper columns before they went
to print. He didn't have a hope in hell. In any case, they were
only excuses to force Taylor and me out of the club. And they
worked!

We beat Manchester United 1-0 that October. Unusually,
Barbara and Lillian were there, although I don't think my wife
had been to ten games in the previous ten years. In the Old
Trafford dressing-room later, Taylor said: 'Winning here doesn't
happen very often, so we ought to go upstairs.' I was reluctant.
I've never been one for mixing in boardrooms, home or away,
but this time I went along. There were plenty of others milling
around, and we were greeted by the then United chairman, Louis
Edwards, who said: 'This must be the first time you've been in
here,' immediately cracking open a bottle of champagne. The five
of us stood around exchanging pleasantries until, after finishing
one glass, Taylor began to shuffle. 'Time we went back down,'

he said. 'But we've only just bloody come up,' I said, 'and you're the one who insisted on it.' Pete took another look at his watch and then, by an absolute fluke, caught Kirkland's eye.

What happened next went unnoticed at the time, but it was certainly noticed later. When Kirkland crooked his beckoning finger at Taylor he was effectively squeezing the trigger. Pete wandered back into our company but didn't say a word. It was on the coach, on the trip home, that I learned what had happened. He came and sat next to me and asked: 'Do you know what that bastard said? He said he wants to know exactly what my job is. I've got to go and see him, Monday.'

Pete and I met at the ground prior to his meeting with Kirkland. His first words to me were: 'They're coming on strong, aren't they?'

'Yep, it was inevitable,' I replied. 'They think we've become a bit too big for our boots.' After his rendezvous with Kirkland, Taylor's chin was on his chest. 'I don't think there's any place for me here, now. As usual, like Ernie Ord did at Hartlepools, they're trying to get at you through me, but this time I'm getting it as well.'

Taylor had to sit through the humiliation of detailing his duties for the benefit of a stupid man who didn't have the first clue about football management. He was degrading a man whose record was unequalled. Peter Taylor had nothing to prove to anyone but a complete fool. How do you tell somebody exactly what you do for a living? I've lost count of the occasions when I've returned home in the evening, only for Barbara to ask: 'What have you done all day?' I couldn't tell her – not every moment of it, anyway. Phone calls, training, interviews, directors sticking their noses in, spending two hundred thousand quid. All I could tell her was that I'd never had a minute to spare.

Kirkland's questions were not only unnecessary – they were totally out of order. He was new on the board and there by invitation. Longson had given me the excuse that it was better to have the enemy inside the club rather than outside, stirring it. Until then he had been stirring it for the board as well. 'I'll get him in and that will shut him up,' Longson said. It did – he stopped criticising the directors once he became one of them. Then he turned his nasty attention to us.

During the same week Mike Keeling, a director who had become a friend, met me with the club's president, Sir Robertson King, at a pub on a back-road near Turner's laundry. He was a trustworthy man, one of the old school, one of the gentlemen of the game. Tweed suit, waistcoat, walking-stick – a monocle would not have been out of place. He was settled into retirement and would dawdle along to the match on a Saturday afternoon. An accomplished speaker, the ideal president. He had said to Keeling: 'Bring that dear boy to the local and we'll have a little chat with him, Michael.' Leather chairs, discreet alcoves, the local was reminiscent of a gentleman's club. He told me to think very seriously. 'There is no way you should resign,' he insisted.

In all honesty I wasn't ready to leave Derby. I knew things were going well, I believed we were building an empire to match anything in the English game. I was so full of myself that I believed I could handle Longson, given time. But Taylor's pride had been dented. That's what hit him harder than anything. You could do anything to Taylor – call him a thief, call him a woman-iser, call him what you wished, but if you ever questioned his ability to do his job or showed him up, he'd go berserk.

An example. I was playing cards with Dave Mackay and Alan Durban in Spain and the clock was pushing close to a pre-arranged press conference. I was in the middle of a hand when Taylor tapped me on the shoulder and said: 'Are you ready? You're not even bloody washed.' I said I had washed, but he jumped in with: 'Well, you haven't shaved.' Still looking at my cards, I said: 'Hey . . . piss off.' He lost all control, hauling me from the chair and screaming in my face: 'Never ever tell me to piss off.' His pride had been hurt. He couldn't bear to be shown up in front of anybody.

So when Jack Kirkland belittled him, Taylor's mind was made up. He was adamant – he was off. His pride was more intense than mine. When he caught me sweeping the terraces or watering the pitch on Sunday mornings he would say: 'You're crackers. Get in the bath – we can pull somebody in to do that job.' Those tasks didn't trouble my pride. On the contrary, if you've gathered sea-coal on a freezing beach on a wet Wednesday you can actually enjoy sweeping terraces on a sunny Sunday morning.

Taylor wasn't there when 'we' resigned at the weekly board meeting. As usual, he stayed at home and left it to me. The most momentous decision of his career, and he let me make it on his behalf. I quit for both of us! I walked into the boardroom and looked at those pathetic faces, chucked the keys onto the table, and said: 'Accept our resignations.' Sir Robertson King, to his eternal credit, spoke up: 'We'd like you to reconsider.' Guess what? In leapt Longson: 'He's resigned, and I propose we accept it.'

I never actually saw any voting take place because, by then, I was blinded by anger and maybe even hatred. I was thinking: 'I don't give a toss whether you vote or not – here are my keys, I'm out.' I was in there, oh, two or three minutes, but I do remember Stuart Webb shuffling. I had the feeling that he was thinking: 'Once they've gone, it's wide open for me.' It was – but perhaps I was being unfair.

I kept my car keys, because I had to get home somehow. From the Baseball Ground I went straight to Taylor's house where I told him I had quit. And that he had as well! Neither of us was compensated one penny. I'd recently signed a four-year contract and it had all been thrown through the window – a major mistake. If we had taken our time and I had tried to negotiate a pay-off I'm sure they'd have handed over a tidy sum to the pair of us, but Taylor always needed to do things now, this second, today. We were fools. We made the wrong decision. We should not have left Derby to the care of others and it was to be some time before we came to terms with what we had just done.

We had no fears about getting another job. I had the offer of a six-month contract from London Weekend Television – a lot more money than the £20,000-odd Derby had been paying me. But, with Taylor, first things first. 'What will you do?' I asked him over a cup of tea. 'I think I'll catch a plane to Majorca.' His first bloody thought was a holiday. Absolutely typical! In fact, he hung around at home for a week or two, before he set off for Cala Millor.

We should have known that the bust-up at Derby was far from over. From the ground, I had driven round the corner and filled up my Mercedes on the club account. Later I had some new tyres fitted. I kept the car for a few days until a policeman friend came to see me and said: 'Brian, I must mark your card. You do know you're not insured, don't you? Be careful – you could run into one of our lot who won't give a shit who you are.' Kirkland again. It was his idea to cancel my insurance. And it was the first sign that things were about to get extremely nasty.

10

REVOLT

*Of course I am prepared to bury the hatchet – right
in the back of Sam Longson's head.*

NOTHING LIKE IT HAS OCCURRED IN ENGLISH FOOTBALL BEFORE OR
since. The reaction of the Derby County players after Taylor and I
resigned became national news – front page as well as back – for a
period of weeks. The whole town was caught up in an atmosphere
of revolution.

And I have to confess, for the first time, that I was behind
much of it. I was involved in the meetings where the players

plotted and planned their moves that brought a state of siege to the Baseball Ground. It was ironic that Dave Mackay, my key signing, who launched the great revival of the old club, would be brought in to replace me as manager. He once said that his biggest problem in taking over was that I wouldn't let go. He was absolutely right.

Some of my fondest and dearest memories are from my time at Derby – despite even greater achievements at Nottingham Forest. My ambitions were there, too, but they were snatched away by the hands that were only too eager to grab my resignation. No wonder I tell anybody who seeks my advice: 'Never resign. If you think of it, sleep on it. And if you are of the same mind the next morning, go back to bed.'

I suppose I could have forced them to sack me. I could have pushed it to the limit and discovered whether they really wanted us out. I could have then collected about eighty grand from the contract I'd just signed. I've always had something of a reputation for liking money but if it had been my god, as some seem to think, I would have set my stall out for a handsome pay-off. It never really occurred to me. Emotions were running so high at the time that cash was never part of the question. Deep down, I thought our resignations would either be rejected immediately, or that the board would have a rethink and eventually call us back. It turned out to be wishful thinking. That old bugger, Longson, was as hard as the stone his lorries delivered. He was forever bragging to friends, even years later, that he had called Clough's bluff. I have to admit that he did just that. Clever sod!

How could we have given it all up – the achievements, the good times and brilliant memories, and the promise of untold further success that lay ahead? Imagine Kevin Keegan quitting at Newcastle, because Sir John Hall objected to his television appearances, or because a director had asked his assistant, Terry

McDermott, to define his duties! That's a reasonable comparison – although, on second thoughts, Keegan doesn't need the money as much as I did. He could walk away at any time, so Sir John had better tread carefully!

Even I underestimated the impact our resignations would have. Bedlam broke loose. I've never known a group of people so united as the players Taylor and I had assembled. Michael Keeling resigned from the board in protest, and has remained a close friend and business associate ever since. For a time he wondered whether he had made a mistake – whether he might have been more effective remaining as a director and carrying on the fight from within. We'll never know, but he fought with the rest of us from the outside.

The English game was as near as a toucher to an historic non-event – the postponement of a match due to one team's refusal to play. Leicester were due at the Baseball Ground on the Saturday, but our players were so incensed, in such a rebellious mood, that they talked of getting on a plane for Cala Millor instead. I had to step in. 'Hey, hang on a second, you can't do that. That's pushing it too bloody far.'

Had the players gone through with their threat, God only knows what would have happened. They would all have been in serious breach of their contracts. They might all have been suspended. They could have caused the shut-down of the entire club. But, given the slightest encouragement from me, they would have gone through with it. Their determination to have us reinstated became a crazy crusade that threatened to get out of hand.

I have admitted being part of it, but I didn't really orchestrate what went on. I still harboured thoughts of going back, of something happening to smooth the way for our return, and the players seemed to hold the key. Key? Rather than turn it in the lock they were more inclined to break down the bloody door! The street outside what passed for a main entrance to the Baseball Ground was reminiscent of Coronation Street. But if someone had written a mini soap opera based on the events of the next few weeks at Derby, the script would have been torn up and discarded as unbelievable. Even I sometimes have trouble believing it all really took place.

The immediate aftermath of our departures produced not only furious but comic scenes. To the delight of a handful of pressmen who had been admitted from the hundreds gathered in the street, Alan Hinton marched up and down with a large tea-urn thrust above his head. 'This, gentlemen, is the only bloody cup we'll ever win from now on.' The protest went on until the early hours of the morning. Some good sense prevailed when they agreed, or conceded, that the Leicester match just had to be played.

Taylor, meanwhile, wasn't directly involved in any of it. There was all hell let loose over a decision that was basically his idea – and yet he was sitting in his bloody house all day long or taking his beloved black Labrador, Bess, for a walk. I drove round to see him and he had the cheek to say: 'You've got to let it die down. It's getting out of hand. There's only one lot winning and that's the Press. They're dipping their bread to such an extent that if you're not careful we'll destroy everything we created.' Notice the convenient use of the words 'you' and 'we'. I wish I had a fiver for the number of times during our years together that Peter Taylor said to me: 'We've got trouble – you'd better sort it out.' Oh no, he didn't want to become embroiled in the bedlam that followed our walk-out, but he was on the phone every day, sometimes every hour, demanding to know what was going on.

I made up my mind to go to the Leicester game – not out of mischief, although I don't suppose many will believe that. We had built up a terrific rapport with the fans and I wanted to say 'cheerio' to them, nothing more. Well . . . yeah,

I suppose in the back of my mind there was a feeling that my appearance might spark enough of a reaction to bring about our eventual reinstatement. But my main aim that afternoon was to say goodbye to the supporters.

And what an afternoon! I drove myself to the ground in a Rolls-Royce, lent to me by a builder-friend, David Cox. He had been lunching with us at his hotel, the Kedleston Hotel, not far from my current home. It was a favourite meeting-place with the players and, in my early days at Derby, with a few local journalists on Sunday mornings. It remains a favourite eating place for me and my family.

I parked right outside the ground. When a policeman sidled up and asked: 'Brian, how long do you intend staying?' I replied, 'Five minutes, no longer.'

'So you're not going to watch the match?'

'No,' I replied, 'believe it or not, I'm just nipping in to say "so long".'

There were banners everywhere. There must have been more banners than we saw at the recent World Cup Finals in the United States. But they were in protest, not in celebration: 'Clough and Taylor in' and 'Longson out'. I can't remember a single one that said 'Well done, Sam.'

I hurried through the entrance the players used and went up into the front row of the stand, not too close but not too far from the directors' box. I'd never heard louder cheers, not even when we were beating the likes of Liverpool or Manchester United. It was wonderful, exhilarating, thrilling. I waved to all four sides of the ground – and as I looked to my left I saw Longson waving to the crowd as well. The silly sod thought the cheers were for him! Two or three minutes and I was away. Back to the Rolls and home. That night I went down to London and appeared on the Michael Parkinson show. See? I did say I had become quite famous!

The anarchy intensified after the Leicester match, which Derby won 2-1. The players said that my appearance had put them in the mood that made victory a certainty. A series of meetings followed at Archie Gemmill's house, at Colin Todd's – where, as the players and I trooped in, his wife Jenny would say, 'You go through, I'll get in the kitchen and make the buns' – yes, and occasionally at mine. It wasn't just a few of the players who turned up at those houses: it was all of them. We had developed as a team, won the Championship as a team, been cheated out of the European Cup as a team, separated as a team. We wanted the team to stay together.

So did the masses – and I do mean masses – who formed an official Protest Movement that marched through town, held public meetings all over the place, and enjoyed the support of the local Labour MP, Phillip Whitehead.

Unknown to us, we were meeting at a serious disadvantage. Longson and his cronies were one step ahead. They had already earmarked Mackay to take over, realising that a quick appointment was in their best interests. They didn't have much trouble either, seeing as Forest were quite happy to get rid of him. He'd hardly been an unqualified success since moving into his second managerial job. I suppose, to Longson, he was an obvious choice. Mackay had played a magnificent part in Derby's recent history. He was a strong man, who took no nonsense from anybody. If anyone could withstand and overcome the seething turmoil that had engulfed the club, Sam decided, Dave was that man. You didn't muck about with Mackay.

To be fair – and there was nothing in his managerial background at Swindon and Forest to suggest he was capable of such achievements – he did a terrific job. He made brilliant signings like Franny Lee (now the owner of Manchester City), Bruce Rioch, and Charlie George, who played possibly the greatest football of his career in his short time with the club. Derby went on to win the League title two seasons later, and Mackay deserves the utmost credit for the way he tackled and endured the task he inherited.

The players didn't want him. Once they got wind of his proposed appointment they converged on a Baseball Ground already under siege from the media and public alike. The street was jammed. There were cameras, lights, microphones, and more notebooks and pens than you'd find at W.H. Smith. The players were determined to see Longson and beg him, if necessary, to reinstate us. They stormed through the place banging on doors, shouting and yelling. At one stage – and this hit the national headlines both in the newspapers and on TV – they threatened a sit-in at the ground. The scheming Jack Kirkland and the secretary Stuart Webb locked themselves in the boardroom, after refusing the players' demands for 'consultation'. The two of them daren't even sneak out to the toilet. They were holed up for so long that they had to relieve themselves by piddling into an ice bucket. I've never checked it out, but I do hope they weren't drinking champagne!

Not content to see Taylor and me through the doors, Longson then launched into print, in the local paper, the *Derby Evening Telegraph*. He alleged that we had been on the fiddle – making false expenses claims for attending matches on scouting missions, meal bills, that kind of thing. The allegations were made more at me than at Taylor, so I called the press boys together and announced I was suing for libel – not just Longson, but the entire board.

Rumours swept Derby – it was that kind of town. I've never known a place where rumour, gossip, speculation and tittle-tattle spread so rapidly. There was talk that, during what we called the 'boom days', I had helped myself to a waste-paper bin full of money – between £7,000 and £10,000. I think the rumour still exists to some extent, so it's worth an explanation even this far down the line.

Fans would queue for tickets from eight o'clock in the morning. The Baseball Ground was besieged most days of the week, but the general office was understaffed and couldn't cope. It was no good trying to telephone the club, in those hectic, frantic, times. The phone would just ring all day!

I was leaving the ground at around five o'clock one evening and went through the general office to say 'so long'. Normal procedure. Not only was I polite – I was a nosy sod who wanted to know what was going on in every nook and cranny of the club. I spotted a large waste-paper bin, stuffed with money, propping open a door. I'd never seen so many bank notes and cheques in my life! I thought: 'I know this lot are under pressure in here, but this is bloody ridiculous.' We operated one of the most open, accessible grounds in football. Anybody could walk in and wander all over the place. Surely even an understaffed office couldn't leave a fortune just lying around?

So I took it. I just picked up the bin and carried it back to my office. I sat there, alone, for about a quarter of an hour waiting for them to discover its disappearance. They didn't. They eventually locked the office and scarpered, leaving me with the best part of ten grand in a bin and thinking: 'What the hell do I do with this now?' So I took the money home. The next day I returned it all to the secretary, telling him that this couldn't go on. Webby seemed relieved, I think because he had an idea a lot of cash had gone missing. He certainly thanked me profusely.

There was no fiddling as far as I was concerned. Taylor may have charged a bob or two for the occasional match he didn't attend, but then he probably did other things for which he didn't charge. Me? I wasn't fiddling threepence. But after we walked out I think the staff, including Webb of course, were asked to go through the paperwork. When they found one or two alterations here and there, Longson dived in head first.

I wonder if they included the changed bill from a pub just outside Lincoln, where we stopped for a half a beer and a pie on the way home from playing a testimonial at Peterborough? Sidney Bradley, the vice-chairman, was there, so he picked up the tab. He was a director, he would pay – simple as that. Until, as we were leaving, the barmaid called: 'I've forgotten to charge you for the pies.' About sixteen of 'em! Sidney told her to alter the bill and he paid the extra. When Longson made his libellous allegations, I told him and Webby they'd better check up on the vice-chairman's pie-bill – just in case they thought he'd gone bent as well.

The libel case dragged on. I didn't want to go to court, particularly, but the directors wanted to go even less. They knew they couldn't prove the allegations Longson had made. Respected businessmen – or businessmen who believe they are respected – don't much like the prospect of being humiliated in court. Stuart Webb came to me one day and said: 'They want to settle.' I said: 'Fine, let them settle. I don't want to let them go to court either, and I'm sick of going to London – I hate the bloody place. I'm sick of seeing lawyers who are making fortunes out of it.' We must have laid out between £12,000 and £15,000 by then. Taylor had weighed in with a little bit of it, but most of the money was mine. Eventually and inevitably they settled. They paid me £17,500 in all, but after the time it took I was basically only interested in retrieving my legal fees. In all, the action cost Derby around £41,000.

The Press, of course, loved it. We made sure the players' next move was leaked to them. As captain, Roy McFarland was asked to appeal to the man who had helped him become such a fine footballer. He phoned Mackay at Nottingham and said: 'Don't come to Derby, Dave. There is a lot of turmoil, we think we can get Cloughie and Taylor back, so don't take the job. We don't want you here.'

We should have known that the response would be a forthright refusal. You don't muck about with Dave Mackay. We were totally out of order, and in many ways it was shameful. But for months, as the official protesters did their bit, we intensified the pressure. If I had been in his position I would have gone totally berserk. But Mackay was Mackay, as solid as the player on whom I had pinned my faith, and he saw it through with a great deal of dignity.

He even withstood another threat from the players, whose wives had by then involved themselves in the protests. There were doubts about them turning up in time for a match against Leeds. He did precisely what I would have done, announcing that if they weren't there on time he'd play the reserve side. They turned up!

I warned McFarland and the players to be careful. They had to work under Dave, and you can't work for an out-and-out enemy. 'Sod it, we're all leaving anyway,' was the attitude, but of course they didn't leave. Things blow over – even turmoil on such a level as this. Eventually players realise they have enough on their plate keeping fit, getting in the side and trying to stay there, and looking after the few bob they make from doing so.

I've never experienced anything like the reaction to our resignations and never want to again. Taylor? It wasn't too bad for him – he spent most of the time at his villa in Majorca. He didn't live as long as he would have wished, dear Pete, but while he was alive I can't help thinking he got it right, most of the time.

I was always careful about my part in those secret meetings. The players were acting out of friendship and loyalty, at times out of character, and although I didn't instigate much of their action I was carried along by it. But enough was enough. Several of them had progressed to international status and I didn't want to be part of anything that would embarrass them or in any way jeopardise their careers. Nor did I want to squander the support I had throughout the town. It's a very thin dividing line. People can worship you one minute, but if they think for a second you are harming their club, they'll drop you like a stone.

But I didn't want to let go.

11

BRIGHTON

I found a bunch of third-division footballers who were the palest people I've ever come across at the seaside. I think I frightened them to death.

PEOPLE GO TO BRIGHTON FOR VARIOUS REASONS. FOR A HOLIDAY, FOR a day-trip, for a place to retire, for a Tory Party conference. Or for a dirty weekend. With all due respect to the club and its fans, you don't go there for the football.

Brighton is not a big-time club and is never likely to be.

But that is no reason for people to doubt my motives or my sincerity when I agreed to take over as manager at the Goldstone Ground, late in 1973. The fires were still burning in Derby, the protests surrounding our resignations raged on, but the flames were beginning to die down a little, and it was obvious to anyone but a complete idiot that there was no immediate way back for us. Longson had called our bluff if you like, and felt entitled to preen himself. Our departure was his personal triumph. For a while Derby prospered but, eventually, like all badly run clubs, they went through three or four managers who couldn't run a corner shop. They finished up in the Third Division and on the brink of closure, before they were rescued by a combination of Robert Maxwell's money and the managerial know-how of another firm pal of mine, Arthur Cox.

I ended up in the Third Division by choice. Brighton gave me the chance of a quick return to the only job I knew. It was a case of football management or drive a lorry – I didn't have the O levels needed for working in a bank. It was suggested at the time, and has been argued even in recent years, that I was 'playing at it' when I agreed to be Brighton's manager – that I regarded it as nothing more than a stop-gap, a temporary fill-in job, a convenient little earner until something bigger and better, something that appealed more to my ego, presented itself. Such accusations are as wide of the mark as those Italian penalty kicks by Baresi and Baggio in that bloody awful World Cup Final in the United States.

Does anybody seriously believe that Brian Clough, one of the worst travellers on God's earth, would have agreed to a job on the south coast of England unless he intended staying? The only form of travel I genuinely enjoy is walking – even that's a bit of an effort these days, because of my dodgy old knees. I detest flying and have always needed a few drinks before getting on board. Even then, I've been known to stop an aircraft after an aborted take-off attempt – and get out with my team and return home. I hate road travel as well. If I tot up all the tedious hours spent on coaches I've probably lived twenty of my fifty-nine years on the motorways!

So Brighton was hardly an invitation from next door. Not only was I stepping down two divisions, I was lumbering myself with long journeys and, in the first place, life in a hotel. Hardly the kind of existence that appealed to the bloke who was supposed to like things his own way.

Those who doubted my motives insulted my undertaking to Mike Bamber, a wealthy, night-club-owning, gem of a man, who turned out to be the nicest and best chairman I ever worked for. Nothing was too much trouble. He looked after me like a king. Boy, was I cosseted! He put me up at the Courtlands Hotel, where I was treated as I can only imagine royalty are treated. They would bring me oysters, smoked salmon, champagne – the best of everything. I felt guilty when the time came to leave Brighton, because I know it broke Mike Bamber's heart. If he were still alive today and I was tempted to come out of retirement, Mike's would be the offer I'd take.

Taylor was keen, too. Mind you, seeing that he was the one who prompted us to leave Derby, he was entitled to be enthusiastic about the opportunity to get back to work. Not that he had a great deal to do with the negotiations. We were given £14,000 for joining Brighton – two cheques of £7,000. It was me who had the task of attending the board meeting that rubber-stamped our appointments. Yet again, he didn't go – he just sent me with the simple instruction: 'Make sure you pick up the cheques!'

Barbara wasn't able to spend too much time down there with me, because the kids were at school in Derby. People who have stayed in an hotel for any long period, alone, will understand the feeling of isolation I experienced down there.

It didn't matter how much I was cosseted. Somehow, even the best doesn't taste as good as it should when you're eating alone. They gave me the table in the window. Set for one. That made me feel like somebody who was 'getting on' a bit. Not in stature, just in years.

The feeling of isolation intensified because Taylor didn't spend a lot of time in Brighton early on, although he did eventually set himself up with an apartment there – with a sea-view, of course. Bamber kept telling me: 'If you're on your own and feeling in need of some company, come down to the night-club whenever you wish.' That was when I discovered I'd entered a different world. It wasn't a football town – the football club didn't even have a training-ground, but practised on some park near Hove. It was a showbiz environment, in which you could walk along the prom and bump into people you had seen on television. Barbara would recognise all of them. Some of the 'promenaders' actually recognised me!

Mike Bamber was well known in the entertainment world and had many theatrical connections. One Friday night prior to an away game in the Sheffield area he took me to the local Fiesta Club, where Bruce Forsyth was top of the bill. I don't know whether he'd been tipped off by Mike, but suddenly Forsyth announced that I was in the place. As I stood up to acknowledge the applause – and a fair bit of good-natured barracking – Brucie took the mickey a wee bit. Nothing nasty, all nice and gentle, but it made me feel uneasy and embarrassed. He didn't have to do it and I wished he hadn't.

Not all the showbiz fraternity made us feel ill at ease. In fact that wonderful lady, Dora Bryan, offered us the use of her home in Brighton. It was when we were looking for a house. We were introduced to her at a twenty-first-birthday party for Mike Bamber's son. Within minutes of first meeting Barbara, she came straight out with one of the kindest gestures we have ever received. 'If you would like somewhere nice to live while you find a place of your own,' she said, 'you can have our house. We have an hotel, so we spend our time there. Our house is empty. It's yours if you wish. Just move in and make yourselves at home. You will find the key under the plant-pot by the back-door.'

As things turned out, we didn't need to move in. The Leeds offer arrived – so we moved out of town.

I learned something in Mike Bamber's night-club from the late Les Dawson. Oh, how we miss those funny men – Les Dawson, Tommy Cooper and dear old Eric Morecambe! I still cherish the cap Eric gave me one night in his days as a director at Luton. I was suffering at a night match, not knowing I had the early symptoms of pneumonia. Eric's cap still generates a lot of warmth in my life, whether I'm wearing it or not.

Anyway, Mike Bamber introduced me to Les Dawson – or, at least, told me to wander along and have a chat with him in his dressing-room. I can still see Les now. He was sitting on a chair in a kind of passageway. He had a half pint of beer on a table. He was composing himself, gathering his thoughts before going out there to do his act in front of all those people who had paid good money to be entertained.

'Les,' I said, 'good to see you. How are you?'

'I'm bloody working.'

Nothing more needed to be said. My timing was wrong. I should have waited until after he'd been on stage and done his work. The comedy routine is funny to those who watch it, but to those who do the performing, it's a job. Like the chairman who wanders into my dressing-room or the hanger-on who ventures into my working day at the wrong time or in the wrong place, I was being told to piss off. I knew exactly how Les Dawson felt. The only thing that surprised me was his choice of three words, when two others must have crossed his mind.

Although Taylor began to make more regular appearances and

we had recruited John Sheridan from the Derby coaching staff, I still felt lonely at Brighton – on my own in a strange and different world. Friends supported me a great deal: Colin Lawrence often drove down and David Gregory, a gardener-pal who later helped landscape the grounds of my so-called Quarndon 'mansion' came when he could. Good people, good friends.

Pity about the results! You see, there is one thing that keeps you going more than any other in football management. No matter how black things appear, no matter if you're having problems with players or the directors don't like you, one thing puts it all right and shuts everybody up – a victory. But we couldn't win a match at Brighton to save our lives.

Less than a year earlier I'd been involved in the European Cup Semi-Final against mighty Juventus. Cheating bastards! Now I was involved in a first-round FA Cup tie against mighty Walton and Hersham! A bunch of bloody amateurs, and they beat us 4-0. I've had some bad days in football but that must have been one of the worst.

He won't know it until he reads this, or until a pal reads it and tells him, but comedian Eric Sykes had never been in greater danger of a smack in the mouth than he was that day. I think he was president of the Walton club, or at least held some position there. Anyway, he was perfectly entitled to feel chuffed, having seen the little team of nobodies produce possibly the greatest result in their history and one of the big Cup upsets of the day.

As I walked through a passage after the match I could hear his raised voice as he stood with a phone in his hand, obviously giving me some right stick. I heard him gloating something about 'Cloughie . . . ha, ha, ha.' I had never met him in my life but I'd laughed my socks off whenever I saw him on TV – and still do when they play the old clips. But that afternoon I would have taken sheer delight in punching him. If only I had shown similar self-control, years later, on that infamous night when supporters invaded the pitch at Nottingham Forest!

Brighton couldn't win because they couldn't play. I went on record saying they were crap. What alternative did I have? Their credentials were revealed for all to see in a home game against Bristol Rovers. Lost again – 8-2!

I would stay in the hotel for days and nights on end. John Sheridan noticed my dull mood and said: 'We've got to get out of this place – we'll go to the pictures.'

'Pictures?' I said. 'I haven't been to the pictures since Hopalong Cassidy was beating the Indians.'

'Well, we're going. You haven't been out of here for two or three nights. Let's be having you.'

He took me to see *The Sting*, but when we reached the cinema it looked as though we might miss out because there was a massive queue. I said: 'Forget it, I haven't stood in a queue for twenty years.' Just as I was about to buzz off the commissionaire spotted me and said, 'Come on.' He beckoned us both straight in, and when I asked where we should pay, he replied: 'Pay? You're not paying for anything.' Oh yes, it does help to be known. I've milked that privilege ever since.

Among my pet hates is putting petrol in my car. I hate the smell of the stuff, hate my hands stinking of it – so I won't do it. When I arrive at my local garage the lady leaves her till and fills up the Merc for me. I go in the bread shop while she puts in the petrol.

The greengrocer we've been using for twenty years has now gone self-service. The first time I went in and saw the new lay-out I said: 'Hey, I'm not having this. I'm not serving me bloody self with spuds.'

'Oh,' said the assistant, 'you don't have to.' And she went round the shelves and got everything for me. I've been spoiled down the years, haven't I? The difference with me is, I acknowledge it. The trouble with you is – you're jealous.

I have no problem with having money in the bank, a large house and a Mercedes, and still being a socialist. Barbara and I share an interest in politics, both believing in socialist principles, although my support of the Labour Party has not been as active in practical terms as some people think. When you are a Football League manager there is little time for any other involvement. Politics has been an interest, yes, but I could never allow it to occupy too much time in my life.

I have canvassed on behalf of Labour candidates and did my bit to help Phillip Whitehead retain his Derby seat just as he helped me in the aftermath of my resignation from the Baseball Ground. My involvement on behalf of the coal miners has been well documented, marching with them in protest and joining them on picket lines. When you now consider how their industry and their jobs have been decimated it is tragic that more people didn't listen when they were claiming that their livelihoods and futures were in jeopardy.

I did have opportunities to go into politics full time. Harold Wilson's regime wanted me to contest a Conservative majority of almost 30,000 at Richmond, Surrey, saying they knew I could not overturn it but it would lead to 'other things'. I was not to be tempted.

I must say, though, that the second approach from the Labour Party made me think hard and long about the possibility of becoming a member of parliament. They offered me the chance to fight Moss Side, Manchester, where Sir Winston Churchill's grandson held a vulnerable-looking 4,000 majority for the Tories. Now the prospect of taking on Young Winston appealed to me no end – as did the prospect of ruffling a few feathers in the House of Commons. I was seriously tempted. I knew I could oust Churchill. When you are asked to stand for parliament, they 'flannel' you with supposed jobs they have in mind. Maybe they weren't flannelling, but I did think it was a bit of blarney to get me interested when I was told: 'We have visions of you becoming Minister for Sport.' At that time I could have taken my pick of any marginal seat in the country. I decided to stick to what I did best – picking football teams.

I regret being rude to Harold Wilson on one occasion. It was at a dinner in Leeds, organised by Yorkshire Television, where he was guest of honour and I was due to make a speech. During a break in the proceedings I went for a wee. I became embroiled with some bloke in conversation about Ted Heath and his love of sailing. I knew I should have returned to the table, but I was so full of myself in those days as manager of Derby, I was so conceited and arrogant, that I thought everybody would be prepared to wait for me. What an idiot I was!

I remember making some apology around the time, but only a few months ago I wrote to the Wilsons, sending flowers to Mary and telling them that my rudeness in Leeds all those years ago had been 'on my conscience for too long'. They wrote back, a kind letter as always, and I'm glad I got it off my mind.

Failure, or the threat of it, never sat easily in my lap. I grew uneasy at Brighton, and I was delighted when a break, an episode of light relief, came out of the blue: Muhammad Ali meets Brian Clough. Ego meets ego. To be fair, there have not been many times when I have met someone with more talent in his or her field than I had in mine, but Ali was certainly one of the few. I don't need to add that Frank Sinatra was another.

I think it was the idea of somebody at the *Daily Mail*. They wanted a piece out of it. Either the *Mail* developed cold feet or I asked for too much money, I'm not absolutely sure, but the arrangements became slightly obscure. Anyway, we finished up on a charter flight packed with associates of the old Victoria Sporting Club in London, most of them villains, no doubt. They certainly looked like villains.

Colin Lawrence was with me, as we flew out of Heathrow

destined for that amazing title fight between Ali and Joe Frazier at Madison Square Garden, New York. I've mentioned my fear of flying but the trip to the United States was a one-off – the most fascinating, and the funniest, journey of my life. One of the villains – which is perhaps marking him hard in retrospect, because he was kindness personified – was called Harry. He ran a pub in the East End, apparently. He took it upon himself to look after me, to make sure I was well catered for, and that the stewardesses with the drinks didn't miss me.

'Hey, Brian,' Harry piped up when the plane had levelled out at cruising altitude and the seat-belt light had gone out, 'we've got a lad on here who can do two hundred press-ups, one-handed.'

'Don't give me that,' I said in the typical, dismissive voice you've heard a thousand times.

'Well . . .' Harry said in the kind of tone that made a single word sound like a serious threat. 'If you like to have a bet?'

I wasn't a betting man, particularly, which made me a rarity among those particular passengers. But I was intrigued and said I'd like to see him do it. No sooner said than obliged. The 'lad', never more specifically identified, was duly summoned down the aisle. He rolled up his right sleeve, stretched his six-feet-plus along the aisle and at 30,000-odd feet above the Atlantic proceeded to pump out two hundred press-ups. On one hand.

There were a few cheers but it wasn't over-done. It wasn't so much a party piece, more a chilling statement of fact. It was nothing more to him and his fraternity than ten orthodox press-ups would be to you and me. All right, five press-ups.

'Hey, Brian,' Harry growled, again. 'You know where he gets his fitness from?' Like a fool I fell for it, hook, line and sinker.

'No, I've no idea.'

'He's been in prison for the last ten years.'

I've never been better looked after on a flight in my life. I will always remember one of the stewardesses coming down the aisle with the drinks trolley. The saner among the passengers were asking for gin and tonics with ice and lemon. When she stopped alongside Harry's seat he just reached out, swept up a dozen or so assorted miniatures and told her: 'Now move on and stop when you get to him' – pointing at me.

As she moved off he shouted: 'Help yourself to whatever you want, Brian – just take as many as you like, son.'

I met Ali at one of the press conferences the Americans arrange so well prior to and after major events over there. The great man didn't know who I was and I don't think he was too chuffed about the meeting. But he warmed up after we'd shaken hands, and asked me: 'What do you do for a job?'

I said: 'I'm a football manager, actually.'

To his eternal credit and exquisite judgement, Ali laughed: 'Football managers are grey men. You ain't old enough to be a manager – you should still be a player.'

Some player, he was. It wasn't the fight, so much, that left a lasting impression. Ali demonstrated a level of grace and beauty and athleticism, coupled with an impression of utter tranquillity, that seemed totally out of place in a boxing-ring. It struck me that I was watching no mere boxer, no mere sportsman. He was unique, an artist who rose above his profession. The strength and the brutality, the sweat and the danger and the bloodshed were to be expected – although the intensity of it all, witnessed close-up, was frightening. I never was a fan of boxing, particularly, but I'm fascinated by class performers of all kinds.

Another diversion relieved the worries and concerns that crowded in on me at Brighton. The Shah wanted me to become Iran's national team manager. Just imagine if I'd taken it, he'd have been saddled with another Ayatollah!

What a trip! I took Billy Wainwright with me, and Vince

Wilson, a journalist pal from our days together in the North-East, who wrote my column in the *Sunday Mirror*. The Iranians flew us out first class, put us up in the most sumptuous hotel, and served us the finest caviare until it was coming out of our ears. To be strictly correct, Billy served it. Being in the hotel and catering game he was the only one of us who knew what to do and how to manipulate the silverware that was produced for dishing out the caviare – a huge mound of it, for which you would need a second mortgage if you wanted to buy as much today.

Some people doubted the sincerity of my interest in the Iran job. They were wrong. I took the trouble to call at the British Embassy to check out the educational possibilities for my kids. It was a double-check, actually, because before I left England I'd already had a natter with the Foreign Secretary – well, you do, don't you!

George Brown – later Lord George-Brown – was good enough to meet me at a pub in Belper. 'I've had an offer of a job in Iran,' I explained to him, 'and I know there is trouble bubbling up out there. I'd like to know what you think.'

'Well,' he replied, 'if you've gone through the right channels they'll treat you like a god. They'll make you a bloody king. Your kids will go to the American School, you'll have cars at your disposal, and you'll be able to pick exactly where you want to live. And as for the salary, they'll virtually invite you to write your own cheque.'

George was right. I was offered a lot of money to take the job – more than twice the £200 a week they were paying me at Brighton, and I'm sure I could have persuaded them to pay even more. It was a tempting proposition.

My talks were with a gentleman who had the grand title of Master of the Horse. They told us he was one of three right-hand men to the Shah – presumably he took charge of most things to do with major appointments in sport over there. It was in his quarters, in the early hours, that he agreed to let me see some of the most famous horses on earth. We were seated in a beautiful, ornate room, and in front of us was the biggest bowl of fruit I've ever seen in my life. If they'd removed the fruit and pumped water into it, the four of us could have plunged in for a midnight dip. He took us past the armed guards to see those exquisite thoroughbreds and, like a little kid, I fed the Shah's horses with apples, oranges and pears I'd picked from the fruit bowl. The 'Master' didn't seem to mind.

I don't know how I had the heart to reject their job offer after such a privilege, but I did.

Meanwhile, back at the Brighton ranch, my disillusionment increased. I was spending too much time away from my family and I missed them. The players Taylor had recruited weren't making any impression, and after drawing a match against Rochdale I went into the boardroom to hear Taylor say: 'We've shot it, haven't we?'

Pete, never comfortable in public and particularly when facing the media, was a brilliantly humorous man, capable of boosting the morale of everybody around him. Throughout our years together I had to keep reminding myself that he needed an occasional boost as well. When Peter Taylor was down, he was way down low. He'd go and sit in his house for days on end.

What preyed on his mind at Brighton was not that he had lost his contacts or his knowledge of what was happening in football. But he had lost some of his enthusiasm, his willingness to go out there and find players for himself. We were signing them on the recommendations of scouts like Peter's old mucker from Derby, Maurice Edwards, and David Blakey, a former centre-half at Chesterfield.

Taylor said he couldn't put his finger on the reasons why things were going wrong, but one problem was that he was only rarely seeing the Brighton team play. I was having to relate things to him, trying to placate him when he asked how the newer recruits were performing. When I finally lost my temper, I told him: 'The players you're saddling me with down here can't f**king play at all!'

The invitation to take over at Leeds United was a surprise but no, in all honesty, I can't say it came as a blow or as a disappointment! I said to Taylor: 'The offer's arrived – let's go to Leeds.'

'No,' he said. 'We're all right here. Let's give it another season.' When I told Taylor I was definitely going, I asked him outright: 'Are you coming with me?'

'No,' he said, 'I think I'll stay put.'

Think? He knew he was staying put, all right. He'd been to Mike Bamber and organised himself some more money. He thought he could do alone at Brighton what he and I had done together at Derby. Not a chance – not a prayer. He was not cut out for management, he didn't like the finer detail of the job and what is more, deep down, he knew it. But it was his decision to split the partnership that had achieved so much success over the previous nine years.

12

LEEDS

I'm frightened of many things. The dark, flying,
being out of work. But the thing I fear
most is failure.

DON REVIE TOOK GREAT DELIGHT IN THE 'FAMILY' HE HAD CREATED
at Leeds United. Close-knit, he said. Us-against-the-rest, never say
die, all for one and one for all. The man was forever going on about
how united they all were at Elland Road. It used to fascinate me
and then to sicken me. Was Leeds really such a happy family?

Then I found out for myself, first-hand. Revie had left to

take over as England manager, after what I, and many others, considered to be the unwarranted sacking of Sir Alf Ramsey. When I stepped into his shoes in July 1974 I found out all about Revie's so-called family. And I can tell you this – it had more in keeping with the Mafia than Mothercare.

I had regarded the Leeds offer as one I couldn't refuse – but I should have done. Their chairman, Manny Cussins, had rung me at Brighton. He and a senior director, Bob Roberts, drove down to see me at the Courtlands Hotel. Before we got down to any fine detail there was one thing I needed to know. I had to get it straight in my mind and I had to get it direct from the chairman himself. 'Why me?' I asked Cussins.

He didn't hesitate. 'I saw what went on when you left Derby. I want the kind of manager whose players are prepared to go on strike for him.' As Eric Morecambe used to say, there's no answer to that. Those first words from Cussins were brilliant. They told me what I wanted to hear. He didn't sound a bit like a chairman who would be booting me through the door little more than a month later.

I went to Leeds for the wrong reasons. Our experiences at Derby, particularly the rotten way in which we were eliminated at the hands of Juventus, wouldn't allow me to forget the European Cup. I wanted another crack at it as soon as possible, and Leeds offered me that chance on a plate. The club had already qualified by winning the League Championship the previous season. It was too good an opportunity to miss.

Did I say the European Cup? I hardly lasted long enough to be given my own teacup at Leeds – forty-four days, some of the loneliest and most miserable days of my life. They detested me – and it showed.

Little did I realise the extent of the dislike and resentment – if not downright hatred – waiting for me at Elland Road. And I faced it alone, apart from having Jimmy Gordon alongside me as coach-cum-trainer. Peter Taylor was not to be moved. Cussins and Roberts were a bit taken aback when I told them Taylor was not coming. But there was never any hint of them developing cold feet or pulling out. Cussins insisted: 'You're our man – you are the one we want.'

I have often wondered what difference it would have made had Taylor gone to Leeds with me. Though I have thought about it long and often, I still can't make up my mind whether it would have made it any better. I'm inclined to doubt it. He would have calmed things down, occasionally. He would have taken only a matter of minutes to establish who were the real shit-stirrers in the dressing-room and the potential trouble-makers in the boardroom. Oh yes, Taylor was very good at that. Would he have bought us enough time to establish ourselves properly, though? Would his good judgement on matters where I was explosive and headstrong have convinced nervous directors that we could cope with any number of dissenting voices among the players? No point in posing the questions, really, because we will never know the answers.

I do know that Taylor would have nudged me aside from time to time, and avoided a damaging confrontation. He would have stepped in with a quieter voice, a more controlled manner – and a wisecrack, a pearler of a one-liner that would have had even the most resentful player in a state of collapse, laughing. Yes, we could have done with at least one laugh during those forty-four days!

I had badly misunderstood, and underestimated, the anti-Clough feeling that existed within the club. Leeds had been the dirtiest and most cynical team in the country in the late Sixties and early Seventies, and from my soap-box as manager of Derby and the best pundit on television I had said so on numerous occasions. I prided myself on producing teams who didn't argue with referees and linesmen, who didn't blatantly waste time, and who could anticipate a bollocking and a fine from me if they resorted to any form of dissent. Derby County and, later, Nottingham Forest were the best friends English referees ever had. So many of them told me my teams were the easiest and most pleasurable of all to control. I can say, without fear of contradiction, that no referee ever said that of Leeds in the Revie era.

I despised what they stood for – systematically putting referees under intolerable pressure with their violent behaviour, both physical and verbal, their overreactions, and the unsavoury spectacle of skipper Billy Bremner running alongside the harassed referee, constantly yelling in his ear. They angered and offended me to such an extent that I took every opportunity to condemn their cynicism which, for me, devalued so much of what they achieved and the marvellous football of which they were capable – a high level of skill and organised teamwork that I, like millions, admired. Leeds, in those days, cheated – and I was more than happy to draw people's attention to the fact.

On one occasion I was so incensed by their flouting of the rules that I went on record saying Don Revie should be fined and his team kicked out of the First Division and dumped in the Second. They didn't like that at Elland Road. They gave the impression that they were prepared to trample on anyone who attempted to criticise their flawed talents. They were ready to eat me alive.

It wasn't fear, exactly, that I felt on my first morning. But there was certainly a feeling of apprehension in the car, even though I took my two young sons along for the ride. We had just returned from holiday in Cala Millor, and I had resisted all suggestions that I ought to have come back earlier. After all, their pre-season 'family day', or whatever they called it – involving the players and staff, wives included – was something not to be missed. Well, I regarded holidays with my family as something not to be missed. I wasn't hurtling back for them or for anybody else. Let 'em wait.

They waited, all right. In fact, to be deadly accurate, they were lying in wait! I could sense the hostility in the air. I should have known what to expect from the moment I drove my car through the gates and into the ground. A man, heavily built, red faced and aggressive – just a supporter, I assume – came striding up to the car and said: 'You're bloody well late.'

'It's got nowt to do with you whether I'm late or not,' I told him. I could have told him that when you're the gaffer it doesn't matter too much whether you're late or not, but I resisted it. He had made his point and he sidled away. The anti-Clough feeling had revealed itself before I had set my first foot in the ground. 'You're bloody well late.' Leeds United's inimitable way of saying: 'Good-morning and welcome to Elland Road.'

Don Revie had departed to become manager of England, but it soon became obvious to me that he hadn't really left at all. He was all over the place – down every corridor, round every corner, behind every wall, and in every room and cupboard. Or his influence was. Dave Mackay, remember, had rightly accused me of refusing to let go of Derby. I was about to experience the same handicap, the same bitterness that he must have felt. I was soon to know loneliness, isolation and despair.

Maurice Lindley, who had been Revie's assistant manager for years, gave me little help during my short stay at the club. They used to say of Lindley that he was a master of the art of looking busy at all times. Certainly, whenever I set eyes on him he seemed to be on the move, clutching a piece of paper. Somebody once suggested he'd been clutching the same piece of paper for years!

Syd Owen, known as one of Revie's loyal right-hand men,

could have provided a great deal of help to me – if he'd wished. I quickly formed the impression that he was only too eager to join the 'Anti-Clough' brigade. He refused to co-operate with me in the way a manager's staff is expected to – in fact, he was truculent and obstructive. His feelings towards me could not have been clearer if he'd come right out and said: 'I don't think you are the right man for this job and I don't like you, either.'

If he said, 'Good-morning,' it was snarled rather than delivered with sincerity. On occasions when I talked to the team, Owen stood at the back of the room and I had the impression that he was mumbling criticisms or whispering wisecracks.

'I've had a phone call for you,' he'd say.

'What time?'

'Oh, I took it yesterday but I just missed you.'

Things like that. I needed help at Leeds – certainly from people who were in the best position to offer it. Owen had worked with those players for years. He was 'one of them', and his priority seemed to lie on their side – certainly not on mine. If I had survived for much longer at Leeds, Syd Owen wouldn't have!

It was as if nobody wanted to let me in on how things had been done and achieved in the past. It was as if they wanted to keep it secret. It made for a dreadful atmosphere backstage, as well as on the training-ground.

I'm convinced that Revie must have been in contact with the players from time to time. So must his old Leeds trainer, Les Cocker, an aggressive, nasty little bugger who followed Revie out of the club to go and work with England.

I didn't hold back when I met the players. I repeated some of the criticisms and reservations I had expressed previously. I told Peter Lorimer he tried to con referees, I told Norman Hunter and Johnny Giles they were such good players they didn't need to go around kicking people. And I told Scottish international winger Eddie Gray that, with his injury record, if he'd been a racehorse they'd have had him shot. I honestly thought that a bit of friendly stick might have melted the ice, but I couldn't have been more wrong. They couldn't take it.

I joined in the first five-a-side game on the training-pitch opposite the main entrance to the ground. I wanted to overcome the feeling, no, the certain knowledge, that I was being ignored by players. Very little was said in that first training session. We seemed to have played for hours when, suddenly, they decided to make me feel welcome at last. Whack! Somebody came at me from behind – I think it was the England striker Allan Clarke – and stuck me on my backside. I didn't realise it immediately, but I lost my watch as a result. There was no obvious laughter, nothing out loud. But I could sense that every single one of them was hiding a smile of satisfaction.

For the first few days at Leeds I didn't have a friend – apart from the one I had brought there with me, Jimmy Gordon. The players were apprehensive and wary, there was even a separate place for me to strip and get bathed, so I wasn't part of any banter in the dressing-room. And always, everywhere, there was Revie.

When I retired from Nottingham Forest I recalled those awful days at Leeds and vowed not to go near the place or to speak to any of the players for the whole of the following season. I knew that Frank Clark had enough on his plate taking over from me as manager without thinking I was still physically around the City Ground and in touch with the team, individually or collectively. I didn't want to hamper him in any way – certainly not the way Revie had hampered me. My record at Forest was enough for Frank to contend with, and he did it superbly by restoring Forest to the Premiership at the first attempt.

It was a week or so before the groundsman at Leeds, John Reynolds, came to me and said: 'Gaffer, here's your watch.' He was one of the nicest men at the club – which isn't saying much.

Another was the scout, Tony Collins, who gave me some advice that might have kept me at Leeds a lot longer than forty-four days if only I had listened and taken it to heart.

'Let me give you a tip,' he said to me in that quiet way of his. 'I know you want to make changes and that one or two players will be on their way – but don't rush it. Don't be in too much of a hurry. They don't take easily to change here, so be advised – take your time.'

But I didn't listen or, at least, I didn't take his advice. I couldn't wait to improve on what already existed at Leeds. I knew how I could make the League Champions into an even better side. I wanted to do something Revie had never done. I was determined to start, straight away, creating a team good enough to win that European Cup.

A manager hasn't a prayer of succeeding if he doesn't carry the players with him. You can't laugh, you can't train, you certainly can't win matches, and you would have trouble assembling everybody for a squad photograph. I didn't carry the Leeds players. I never gained their confidence or support. Instead of unity and common purpose there was animosity, unrest and suspicion. I have never experienced anything like it before and would never wish such dreadful circumstances on my worst enemy. It was like trying to swim against the tide, in hot tar.

I handled the whole thing badly. I was faced with a group of hardened and highly talented professionals who had been used to a father-figure – nay, a godfather-figure – a manager renowned for his attention to detail. In turn, they were faced with a new boss who had savaged them, on television and in print. It was perhaps not surprising that they failed to display the same commitment and dedication on the pitch. We lost the first league game 3-0, and in the weeks that followed things went from bad to worse. Just four points from six league games, and the relationship between me and the players was getting no better. Something had to give!

My way – aggressive, blunt and hell-bent on making changes – was never going to work. The fact that Revie had left half-a-dozen or more players' contracts still to be finalised when he resigned didn't help my cause, either. His attention to detail seemed to have slipped, for once.

Rightly or wrongly, I had the impression that Johnny Giles was behind much of the hostility and opposition shown towards me. The little bugger was one hell of a player, who dished out his own shrewd, expertly delivered form of instant 'justice' on the field. Like all Irishmen, he also had the gift of the gab, but he was more eloquent and intelligent than most – a fact borne out to this day by his newspaper column, that proves him to be one of the more readable and perceptive observers of the game. Hardly surprising that when Giles talked, the other Leeds players listened.

I wanted him out – not least because when Revie left to take the England job he recommended Giles as his successor at Elland Road. He urged the directors to appoint the man he felt was best equipped to continue the same old methods that had served the club so well. Giles would also have been a popular choice in the dressing-room.

So it suited me down to the ground when I discovered a chance to move him on to Tottenham where, apparently, Giles would have been made assistant manager and groomed to take over from Bill Nicholson. I set up the deal, believing that Giles was eager to go. For my part, I saw it as the ideal opportunity to eliminate one major dissenting voice from the dressing-room. When Giles turned round and said he didn't want to go, I thought: 'You little shit, that means I'm still lumbered with you.'

Giles did eventually go into management, of course. He did well in his first spell with West Bromwich Albion, but struggled in his second run at the job in the 1984-85 season. He couldn't take the flak. He didn't weather the storm. Just like Ian St John – another of those professional observers or pundits or whatever you call them who tried management and failed. I got sick of seeing him on television telling everybody how it should be done. I've always had a mischievous little wish that was never granted. I wanted Bob Wilson, the old Arsenal keeper who's made a good living and done a good job with BBC Television and now switched channels to ITV, to have a crack at management – just to see whether he could have practised what he has preached. Television is packed with brilliant managers who have never done the job! Unless or until the likes of Alan Hansen and Trevor Brooking have had a stab at management, they cannot fully appreciate what the job entails.

I think Hansen would have had a chance. I'm not sure about Brooking, because management demands that you upset people from time to time: a chairman, a director, a player who isn't picked, or the wife of a player who thinks you should have picked him. Trevor always gives me the impression that he'd rather not upset anybody. I think the public could use a bit more opinion, more colour and more controversy than they are getting at the moment. Perhaps it's time I made a comeback on the box!

The television pictures from Wembley, for the traditional curtain-raiser of the Charity Shield, should have been different. They showed dear old Bill Shankly leading out his magnificent Liverpool side and alongside him, followed by the Leeds team with the glummest faces ever seen at such an occasion, there was me. Much as I admired Shanks, and I loved the man, I didn't want to march from the tunnel at the head of the Leeds United side that day.

I asked Don Revie to lead them out, instead.

Yes, I was prepared and eager to relinquish the honour of that managerial march onto the Wembley turf which was, and still is, the dream and ambition of everyone who enters the profession. I had turned down my first chance after winning the League title with Derby two years earlier. I refused to take part in the Charity Shield. Prior to winning the Championship, we had already arranged a tour to Germany, the following pre-season, for dates that coincided with the big occasion. And, much to the astonishment and dismay of the chairman and his board, I decided to stick to that long-standing arrangement.

Sam Longson never forgave me to his dying day. I lost count of the number of times he complained to me: 'You stopped us going to Wembley.' In the eyes of a football club director that is as big a crime as scarpering with the season ticket money! A place at Wembley – or, more important, the chance to sit in the Royal Box – is one of the perks that attract people to football directorships. You don't often see directors eagerly volunteering to board the coach for a reserve game on a filthy night away at, say, Bury, but they all clamour for a day at Wembley, to be seen in the poshest seats.

The circumstances were different in '74. I had not won the title with Leeds – Revie had. I phoned Revie on the day of the match. 'This is your team,' I told him, 'you lead them out at Wembley.' Apart from anything else, I thought it was a decent thing to do, a nice gesture towards a man who had just won the League title – the toughest test of management anywhere in the world. But he was not to be tempted.

'Pardon?' he said, obviously taken aback by my offer. 'You've got the job now, Brian. I'm not coming down to lead them out. It is your privilege.'

There should be a feeling of pride and immense satisfaction when you make that walk from the tunnel to the touch-line at what is still the most famous old stadium in the world. There always was on the umpteen occasions I did it with my Nottingham Forest team. I wonder how many managers have taken their teams to Wembley as often as I did? Not many.

I was proud – and, to use Revie's word, privileged – to walk out alongside Shankly. In fact, I remember turning towards him and clapping him as we walked. But there was no sense of togetherness with those who walked behind me.

And there was no sense of privilege during the match, either. Certainly not at the sight of some of the disgraceful antics the captain got up to. Billy Bremner's behaviour was scandalous, producing one of the most notorious incidents in Wembley history. It was as if the players were offering grounds for all my criticism that they had resented so much.

Bremner seemed intent on making Kevin Keegan's afternoon an absolute misery. He kicked him just about everywhere – up the arse, in the balls – until it became only a matter of time before a confrontation exploded. There is only so much any man can take. Eventually, inevitably, Keegan snapped – and they were both sent off, Keegan whipping off his shirt and flinging it to the ground as he went. It was a stupid gesture, but I could understand the man's anger and frustration. It was the action of a player who felt he had been wronged, not only by an opponent but by a referee who had failed to stamp out intimidation before it reached the stage of retaliation. Keegan will have regretted his touch-line tantrum immediately. A Liverpool shirt was not something to be thrown away.

I have been critical of Keegan over the years. I don't like it when people choose to live outside our country and then come back to drink our water or, in Kevin's case, have horses eating our grass. And I'm being serious. If they want to live abroad, then let them go, and good luck to them. But I see so many – sports stars and film stars – choosing to leave these shores and returning to make fortunes, drink our water and say what a lovely place England is. It makes me want to vomit.

Keegan had his spell living in Spain, so he got it out of

his system and I got my annoyance out of mine. Now he's back in the best country of all and has done a remarkable job in re-establishing Newcastle United among the leading clubs in the land. Yes, for a man of no previous managerial experience who spent so long out of the game, he has done extremely well.

Keegan was a victim, not a culprit, that day at Wembley. The double dismissal was all down to Bremner. Keegan was an innocent party who had been pushed beyond the limit by an opponent who appeared determined to eliminate him from the match, one way or another. I told Bremner afterwards that he had been responsible for the confrontation. He should have been made to pay compensation for the lengthy period Keegan was suspended. And I would have made sure he'd have paid it from his own pocket and not from the club 'pool' set up by Revie for the payment of players' fines!

That was Bremner – a fiery Scotsman with wonderful footballing gifts and a will to win that compared with the best of his profession. I know Bill Shankly regarded Bremner as one of the finest footballers in Europe in those days, and we should be thankful he never managed to add little Billy to that formidable bunch of his at Anfield.

I needed help. I needed friendly faces, people I could trust and whose support I could count on. Without my mate, I was more vulnerable than ever before, but Taylor was adamant that he preferred to stay at Brighton and refused to budge.

So I went back to Derby and signed John McGovern and John O'Hare – and, shortly afterwards, I spent a quarter of a million on Duncan McKenzie, from Nottingham Forest. The reaction at Leeds was fascinating but, in the case of McGovern, extremely distressing. O'Hare's talent was obvious for all to see. His ability to control and keep the ball with his back to goal and defenders breathing down his neck had earned him Scottish international caps as well as the acknowledgement and respect of his fellow professionals. McKenzie was an extrovert who, apart from puffing forty fags a day and being one of the most popular of entertainers on the pitch, had mastered the rare art of jumping over Minis in the car-park. Now there's a player, if you like. No wonder he's gone on to make his name on the after-dinner-speaking circuit.

Poor young McGovern was never accepted by the Leeds players or supporters. They thought he couldn't play. They thought he was a gangling, sparrow-footed, ineffective plodder, not fit to wear the famous white shirt they all cherished. There were occasions when, if I had thought the worst of them, I would have suspected that some of Leeds' players were playing passes intentionally short or slightly too far ahead of him – clinically contrived to make a fool of McGovern.

They were wrong about him, as he showed at other clubs. Amazing to think that within six years, as skipper of Forest, he would twice hold aloft the European Cup that Leeds never won! Yet, at Leeds, he became the most unpopular footballer I ever signed. They gave him a terrible time. It reached a stage when he was booed every time he touched the ball. I felt desperately sorry for the lad, but he never sought sympathy and never shirked a tackle. His mother – biased and protective like all caring mums – came to me and said: 'You're using my son as a whipping-boy.' I hadn't heard the phrase in donkey's years, but I told her: 'You're so wrong, it's incredible. I have done more for your son than anybody will ever know.' I couldn't blame her, though, or dispute the cause of her concern. McGovern was never given a chance.

It upset me to think I had tossed him into such an unpleasant environment. It hurt me to see him targeted for such terrible abuse. There was some excuse for those in the stands and terraces, because many of them are ignorant of the finer requirements of the game, but there was no excuse for the

Leeds players. Surely they were not so thick that they could not recognise McGovern's talent when it was put right under their noses?

Peter Shilton brought me the sack at Leeds. At least my attempts to sign him brought everything to a head. They already had David Harvey, the Scottish international goalkeeper, and clearly did not think they needed another. Harvey asked: 'Are you trying to replace me?'

'Yes,' I said, 'I'm trying to sign Shilton.'

Harvey said no more to me and I don't know what he said to the rest of the players in the dressing-room, but I sensed a hardening of attitudes towards me. I also sensed that it wouldn't be too much longer before my time was up.

It was claimed that the players had held a meeting and passed a vote of 'no confidence' in me, but I'm not sure that was quite what happened. I was at a meeting involving the players, Manny Cussins, and the vice-chairman, Sam Bolton – or the Black Adder as he was known – and I don't know what was said after I had left early. In any case, I was soon on my way. Cussins came to my office and said: 'It's not working.' That was his phrase.

'What's not working?' I asked. 'I haven't been working here five minutes so how can anything be working yet?'

'Well . . . the players are unhappy with you and the fans are unhappy.'

I sensed my chance. 'So what do you want to do about it?' I cast the baited hook and Manny took it in one. 'Well . . . if it's not working, we've got to part company.'

I then had one of the biggest strokes of luck of my life. Anticipating bother, I had taken Colin Lawrence to the ground. Having settled on £25,000 with Cussins but signed nothing, I was told by Colin to hang on while he contacted a solicitor friend, Charles Dodsworth in York. Charles was brilliant. He persuaded Cussins to sign an agreement that committed Leeds to pay my income tax for the next three years. So instead of paying me £25,000, it was eventually going to cost Leeds £98,000. Manny wasn't to know it when he made his first offer of the job but when you hire Brian Clough, even for a mere forty-four days, he don't come cheap. And he don't resign!

The only sign of genuine friendship in the dressing-room had come from Allan Clarke. I had given him a kiss when he scored the goal of the only victory we managed while I was running Leeds, and on the day I was fired he came to me and said: 'I'm sorry you are going – you've had a rough deal.'

I went from the ground to the studios of Yorkshire Television where, unknown to me, Revie was waiting to take part in the same programme – a studio discussion that was at times heated but which took us nowhere. In any case, I was preoccupied by thoughts of only one place – the bank. I wanted to get the Leeds cheque into my account as quickly as possible. Colin, Vince Wilson and I broke our late-night journey to Derby at an M1 service station. Sausage, egg and chips tasted as good as the finest caviare. As I lounged in the back seat of the car for the final few miles home I put my feet up, stretched my arms behind my head and said: 'Gentlemen, we've just won the pools.'

I had been in touch with my own bank manager, who advised me that the quickest way of steering the Leeds cheque into my account in Derby was to present it at the issuing bank, next morning. So Colin drove back to Leeds and handed in the cheque, which was then expressed into my personal account. Thank you very much, Manny Cussins – wherever you are.

The Leeds money enabled me to pay off the mortgage on my house in Ferrers Way, Derby, and move to my so-called mansion in Quarndon. Anybody who has the money and doesn't pay his house off is crackers. Banks and building societies are stealing money with their interest charges. Once Leeds paid me off I knew I was secure. They gave me independence and financial freedom. A beautiful wife, three gorgeous children, money in the bank – and no mortgage. It's a funny thing, but money has never been a problem to me. People just seem to keep throwing it my way – and one thing I've always been able to do is catch. I can't understand why they keep doing it – apart from the fact that I have so much talent!

Leeds reached their European Cup Final but lost in Paris. They had chosen Jimmy Armfield to succeed me – the man the FA employed to 'head-hunt' Terry Venables as replacement for England manager Graham Taylor. A nice man, Jimmy, and a good full-back in his time. But as a manager of a major club at top level – he had no idea!

Neither had almost all the Leeds players of that era. Most of them tried their hand at management and failed: Bremner, Hunter, Clarke, Gray and, to a lesser extent, Yorath and Giles. Terry Yorath didn't do badly with the Welsh side and Giles had his moments at the Hawthorns. Oh yes, and Terry Cooper has done the rounds and survived. But the only one of the 'Revie brigade' who has made a lasting name for himself as a manager has been Jack Charlton. Even he made the mistake of leaving my old club Middlesbrough before he should, and he quit Newcastle at the first sign of a dissenting voice from the terraces. But he had always looked after his money, enabling him to feel more secure than most of his fellow managers. Jack was to land the perfect job. He and Ireland were made for one another.

I was about to discover that strength of independence which has enabled big Jack to tackle the job with the air of a man who hasn't a care in the world. I might have been at Leeds for twenty years if Manny Cussins and his directors hadn't hidden behind the excuse of player unrest, lost their nerve, and sacked me.

Nottingham Forest and I remain eternally grateful that they did.

13

FOREST OUT OF THE WOODS

Firing people isn't hard.

THEY WEREN'T TO KNOW IT AT THE TIME, BUT THE MOST SIGNIFICANT aspect of my arrival at the City Ground in January 1975 was the car that carried me there. I was driving a beautiful pale blue Merc – a 'present' from Leeds as part of my pay-off for the most profitable forty-four days' work I ever did.

That car symbolised the feeling of freedom and independence that meant I could dive headlong into management again – this time without giving a toss about anybody. Don't get me wrong,

I have always cared about players, about people with talent. It's the rest that get in the way – the meddling directors and the parasites who hang around them and influence them and encourage them to get involved in matters that are none of their business. From the moment I left Leeds, some club was going to benefit from Brian Clough's belief in his own ability – and the sure knowledge that I could do the job precisely the way I wanted, on my own terms. And God help anybody who got in my way! The sack at Leeds hurt me badly, but it also set me up so that I need never fear the sack again. Now that has to be the greatest gift any manager can be given.

Nottingham Forest will never know how lucky they were, that day they asked me to get on with the job of rebuilding their run-down club. They didn't just need a new manager – the bloody place was so dead it needed a kiss of life. The old chairman at the time, Jim Willmer, couldn't have had a clue what he had done, the day he started me in the job. He had signed the best manager in the business who brought with him an absolute guarantee of success. To be fair, not even I imagined quite how successful we would prove to be. Funny how Leeds United still don't have a European Cup in their trophy cabinet. I have two – but I'm not gloating, honest!

It was the late Stuart Dryden, vice-chairman at the time, who pushed my case with the rest of the board. Dear Stuart . . . we were to share many fabulous times together after he became chairman, and we became the best of friends. He was a good man, a loyal man, whose dignity and support never wavered. Nor did my regard for him when, after being found guilty of some fraud at his Post Office, he was sent to prison. Poor man! I did what I could, but how can you help in circumstances like that? I hope my loyalty to Stuart at a time of great distress to him and his family was as comforting as the faith and friendship he always extended to me. The success I was to achieve on behalf of Forest would not have been possible without Stuart Dryden's support.

At the time I took over I remember saying: 'Nottingham Forest have one thing going for them right now – me!' I wasn't joking, either, although I suppose it did sound arrogant and flippant – typical Clough. Good headline material, of course, and there's nowt wrong with that, especially at a sleepy club like the old Nottingham Forest.

The club was languishing near the foot of the Second Division after just nine wins, with the season almost two-thirds over. Home crowds averaged around 12,000. Fine players like Martin O'Neill and John Robertson were on the bloody transfer list. The club was rotting on and off the field – an inevitable victim of their own stupidity in selling many of their better players.

The start of my eighteen-year career at Nottingham could not have been better. My predecessor Allan Brown's final match in charge had been a third-round FA Cup tie against Tottenham. Although the Second Division that season included the likes of Manchester United, Sheffield Wednesday, Aston Villa and Newcastle, a result against Spurs was regarded as something special. Unfortunately for Brown, a 1-1 draw at home wasn't enough to save his job. But it did give me an ideal first game: Tottenham, away, with little expectation of a win and nothing to lose. Not that I did a lot in the way of preparation. I just sat in the directors' box and watched my new team pull off something of a 'giant-killing', with a Neil Martin header and a little bit of luck. As I sat there, beaming, the thought crossed my mind that this was the place where I made the best signing of my life, Dave Mackay. It was another great result for me at White Hart Lane. We stayed down in London, training at Bisham Abbey before playing a league game at Fulham on the Saturday and winning again, 1-0.

Fulham were to become a thorn in our side. As luck would

have it, we were pulled out of the hat with them for the fourth round of the Cup. We went back to Craven Cottage a fortnight later, and scraped a goalless draw. Back to our place for the replay: 1-1. Back to London for a second replay: 1-1 again. The third replay, the fourth Cup game between us, saw Fulham beat us 2-1 on the banks of the Trent. So Forest had played six FA Cup matches that season, enough to win the trophy, and gone out in the fourth round. Is there any wonder I never managed to win the damn thing!

We didn't win many more games in that first season, either: just two more, leaving us with fourteen points from sixteen matches. We could quite easily have gone down into the Third Division, but we survived in sixteenth place. I've always said league tables don't lie. It is nonsense to talk of teams being 'too good to go down', just as it was nonsense to argue that my Derby County side won the Championship 'by default'. Forest could have been relegated, the season I took charge, for one basic reason. We were crap.

Some of our players couldn't play, some couldn't kick the ball from A to B, and several couldn't head it to save their lives. After watching John Robertson a few times in what he regarded as 'action', I was not surprised he was up for sale. Rarely had there been a more unlikely looking professional athlete. Some managers would have taken one look, laughed – or cried – and thrown him out. A scruffy, unfit, uninterested waste of time. I kept him on, as well as O'Neill. I don't know what it was with the dumpy little bugger, but something told me he was worth persevering with, and that in time we might find a footballer of some merit inside that shuffling hulk.

So let's make a quick assessment of the player who was to become such an influential member of our championship-winning team: an habitual smoker, possibly ten pounds overweight, indisputably the slowest player in the entire Football League.

My God, he used to drive me absolutely barmy! For a start, he detested training. His version of warming-up was to stand on the same spot with his weight on one leg – then shift the weight on to the other. He was fat, often unshaven, dressed like a tramp, and smoked one fag after another.

Originally Robertson tried to play in midfield, but he wasn't mobile enough. He was a late-nighter and used to eat all the wrong things. In fact, he was a slob – an absolute slob. But if a manager looks hard enough he may find talent which others can't see. Robertson was in and out of the side until the end of that season. We messed about with him at outside-left, but we were a poor side and he looked no better than the rest of them.

On a pre-season tour of Germany I'd sent the players out to warm-up, but I found Robertson just standing there in the dressing-room with his hands down his shorts, literally scratching his balls. I sighed in despair. 'They're out on the pitch warming-up and just look at you. What a disgrace you are!' He couldn't swim, he couldn't run, he hated the sunshine and you couldn't get him out of bed anyway. Strange lad . . . but I just sensed he had immense talent. As Forest developed as a team, Robertson's ability began to emerge. We bought a left-back from Manchester City, Colin Barrett, whose career was later to be cut short by injury. He used to surge forward, supporting Robbo physically and morally.

I pulled Robertson in one morning and said: 'I don't ever want to see you at the ground unshaven again.' I tried to discourage him from smoking – he used to carry his fag like the convicts did, pointing into the palm of his hand so I couldn't see it. He used to hide from me – he'd see me coming and run. I told him to eat properly, to cut out the chips and all the other fried stuff that seemed to make up his entire diet. Whenever he saw me, he'd breathe in.

He didn't look like an athlete at all, but then neither did Van Gogh look like a painter. By the time he lost his ear he must have looked like an accident – but when he took to the canvas he was brilliant.

I made him get rid of his beloved 'suedes'. Now there's nothing wrong with suede shoes, providing they're clean, but he must have spilled a pan of chips on the ones he insisted on wearing. Within a period of six months, because of me, he became the target of good-humoured ribbing from everybody in the dressing-room. It had the desired effect. In his own mind he decided: 'I'm not standing for this', and it developed from there. Robertson finished up with more medals than a Chelsea pensioner. He realised his dream of playing for Scotland, and he deserved even more than the twenty-eight international caps that came his way. Looking the way he did when I first came across him, even if he'd tried hitch-hiking, he wouldn't have made it beyond Scotch Corner.

My good friend Brian Moore, the accomplished ITV commentator, was to say to me some while later: 'This John Robertson you keep harping on about – I can't see what he does.'

'Put him up against the corner flag with the ball at his feet,' I replied, 'and he'll take on the full-back, dummy him, stick it through his legs, hold it and then cross it. He'll do this all inside a yard, before spearing the ball onto the head of a team-mate running in. Not a lot of players can do that.'

I didn't give Robertson any of his extraordinary abilities to manoeuvre and deliver a ball. All I did was to offer him the chance to use them. I didn't want him trying to run around, I didn't want him farting around playing passes that meant nothing. I wanted him to calm down, to get out on the left touch-line and to hold the ball – like Alan Hinton had done for me at Derby. Hinton was another who could cross the ball to where it was needed, and he had a thunderous shot to go with it. For some reason – perhaps a schoolteacher had told him – Robertson always wanted to play the ball quickly, before he had weighed up the options. He had the ability to hold it, to have a look, and to dart into space if it opened up. We simply told him to use that ability, to take his time and not to rush into trouble. We made sure he was never short of support from others in the side, so that the pressure of being tightly marked would never bother him. John Robertson became one of the finest deliverers of a football I have ever seen – in Britain or anywhere else in the world – as fine as the Brazilians or the supremely gifted Italians who seem to be all the rage at the moment.

He didn't become a great player by spending hours on the training-ground running laps or practising free-kicks. He responded to encouragement to do the things that came naturally. It would have been so easy to have shown the door to such a slob. Before any manager dispenses with a player who stands on one leg in training, I suggest he takes one more look, on the off-chance that player might be quite useful when he stands on two.

As a manager, or even in my playing days, I've sometimes had players come to me and ask: 'When do I pass the ball?' I've always given the same answer: 'Nobody can tell you that.' You cannot tell a footballer when to play it, only he knows. He has to look around, he has to have control of the ball, he's got to have options – and he still needs to be able to deliver when there is somebody kicking at his backside, digging at his ribs or tugging at his shirt. Robertson was a master of that craft, a bit of a shuffler, reminiscent of Stanley Matthews at times: a player from whom so many others, like Tony Woodcock, Peter Withe, Garry Birtles and, of course, Trevor Francis were to benefit.

Funny, but he was never popular with the fans at Nottingham, even when we were at our peak and winning European Cups. I found that very difficult to understand. It reached such a pitch that on one occasion he had to be stopped from climbing over the perimeter wall during a game to get to a bloke who had been calling him 'a useless, fat sod' all afternoon.

Sadly, Robertson was the central figure in the row that brought an abrupt and bitter end to my friendship with Taylor. It all revolved round his transfer to Derby. He would have been better off remaining with me at Forest for another couple of seasons – and he did, in fact, return to the club on a free transfer in 1985. But he was never the same player, as he acknowledged when he said to me: 'Effectively that move finished my career, didn't it?' I'm afraid I had to tell him: 'Yes, it did.'

One player I just didn't fancy. I had given a free transfer to Tommy Jackson, who tried to play in midfield. Tommy Docherty was manager of Manchester United at the time, and he gave Jackson a contract. Now we are talking, here, about a player who finished up with thirty-five international caps for Northern Ireland. There was concern at Forest when I made the decision to release him without a fee. Stuart Dryden came to me and said: 'You have let Jackson go for nothing and he's been snapped up by Manchester United?'

He was obviously suggesting that anybody signed by United *must* be good or at least be worth a transfer fee.

'I don't give a f**k if he's signed for Real Madrid,' I said. 'He can't play.'

But there were those who could – Robertson and O'Neill, Viv Anderson, Tony Woodcock and Ian Bowyer – and what a part they were to play in spectacular, future events!

Soon there was to be John McGovern and John O'Hare as well. Oooh, did I take some delight in going back to Leeds and buying those players for far less than I'd paid for them! By agreeing to the deal that switched O'Hare and McGovern from Elland Road to the City Ground, Manny Cussins and his cronies had effectively doubled my compensation.

While I had enjoyed the good life after Leeds, driving the Merc, doing bits of telly, and generally lapping up my new-found freedom away from the tension and loneliness of management, somebody else had found himself a job outside football. Jimmy Gordon had lasted only forty-four days at Leeds as well, bombed out with the man who took him there, but I made sure he was looked after. Once I got to Forest I was able to offer him a job working with me again, but in the meantime he'd gone to work in the stores at Rolls-Royce. What a waste.

Jimmy, a senior-pro when I was a youngster at Middlesbrough, had a great knowledge of the game. He was thorough and wise and as straight as a die. And players liked him. He became a friend of the family until, years later, he offended us with some comments he made in a book written by Tony Francis – a journalist I can't stand. We will never know what possessed Jimmy to become involved in such a venture. It seemed totally out of character.

The character I needed at Forest was Jimmy Gordon, the football man. The fair-minded old pro whom I could trust with my life and my wallet if I'd carried one. Funny, that. People talk about my wealth, millionaire status and all that, but I've never been one to carry money around with me. Maybe that's the reason I've hung on to a few bob.

There was progress in my first full season with Forest. I weeded out those who couldn't do it, encouraged those who could, made sure the directors knew their place, and guaranteed we figured in the papers on a regular basis with more than our fair share of back-page leads. Six wins out of our final ten matches took us to eighth place, which wasn't bad – but not as high as Brighton had finished in the Third Division. And nowhere near as significant.

Peter Taylor had staked everything on getting promotion for Brighton that season. I think he had spent the club's last few quid on Joe Kinnear from Tottenham, the full-back who has done such an effective job as manager of Wimbledon in recent seasons. There was some dispute between Taylor and Kinnear – probably to do with money, if I know Taylor – so things were not as they should have been between the manager and his new signing. Taylor's gamble – and he was a gambler by nature – had failed. For him, it was promotion or bust, and when he missed out by a whisker he packed it in. He did what he'd done before at times of crisis – he buggered off to his villa by the sea, just around the coast from our favourite haunt, Cala Millor.

He'd gone there with a sense of failure, having missed promotion, with a heavy if not broken heart. We had not been in touch very often since parting company on the south coast, but he could see that progress was being made at Forest – his home-town club, the one Pete always wanted to manage. He was Forest daft!

I think it was Michael Keeling who first put the idea in my big head. 'What's Peter doing?' he asked one morning. I said he was doing nowt as far as I knew, apart from lying in the sunshine with Lillian, and when Mike followed up with, 'Do you ever fancy working with him again?' my first reaction, as ever, was: 'Well, he could give me a ring.' But after giving it some thought overnight, I just got on an aeroplane, flew to Majorca, and said to Peter: 'How do you fancy coming to Forest?'

I could see the enthusiasm light up his suntanned face. I saw an immediate twinkle in his eye. He couldn't ever hide his enthusiasm from me, no matter how hard he tried – and he tried again on that occasion. I knew what was coming. I knew he would shift uneasily in his chair, waggle his tongue in his cheek, pause for about half a minute as if pondering the most profound of questions . . . and then he hit me with the question: 'What's in it for me?'

'I've got a contract, you will be given a contract, and I'll get you a few bob in expenses,' I told him. He still managed to stall for a while, although I knew he was longing to snatch my hand off and say, 'Done.' His agreement to join me at Forest was a certainty from the moment I gave him the chance – as inevitable as night following day. Some said he was the best signing I ever made at the City Ground and although I could dispute it, I know exactly what they mean.

Peter Taylor made me laugh, and I worked better with a smile on my face. His arrival at Forest immediately lifted not only me but the whole place. Show me a club that has laughter in its dressing-room and corridors as well as talent in its team and I'll show you a club that will win things. We were to laugh our way to Wembley so many times that our coach could eventually find its way there without a driver.

He would have me on the floor, laughing and begging him to stop the banter. His one-liners killed you. You could have a deathly hush in the dressing-room after training. There might have been a bust-up, a difference of opinion, I might well have been laying down the law. Players would move about, in and out of the shower or bath, just getting on with the business of cleaning up and getting dressed. In virtual silence.

'I do hope you've all washed your balls.' Taylor's voice broke the ice. Silence over, the banter was back, the atmosphere was healthy, and the place was alive.

Then he'd grab one unsuspecting and innocent player and drag him over to me. 'We've got problems,' he'd say. 'This one's been out for the last three nights, shagging. I'm not sure if he'll be able to perform, Saturday. You'd better sort him out.' I'd whack the player concerned, only a gentle tap in the midriff, and Taylor would tell him: 'You'd better sit down or he'll kill you.' It was relaxation, it made us laugh, it lightened the load. The routine that brought success to Derby was to do it again, on a grander scale, at Nottingham.

We just went out and won promotion to the First Division in our first season back together!

To win promotion we needed to build a new side. Not all of Taylor's early signings were inspired – but most of them were. I don't know where he was looking when he took a lad called Sean Haselgrave from Stoke, but he should have left him there. I don't know what he'd done for Stoke's midfield but he did nothing for ours. Bargains are not bargains unless they provide something you didn't have already.

But when Taylor brought Peter Withe from Birmingham he had seen something that had eluded everyone else. The big Scouser believed he was good enough for a career at top level, but failed to convince anyone until Taylor moved for him. Withe had even played in South Africa, apparently, trying to make a name for himself there, but he looked destined to become one of the game's angry and disillusioned drifters, complaining that he would have made the grade if only somebody had been bright enough to spot what he could do. Fortunately Taylor was bright enough to recognise Withe's potential. He was capable of playing top-level football, as he proved with us and later at Aston Villa, where he helped them win a European Cup.

Taylor never made any bones about his recruits. He never saw the need to justify them to me, believing they would prove themselves – and his judgement – within a matter of a few games. In any case, why should I ever question the judgement of the pal who told me to go and try to sign Dave Mackay for Derby County?

We also took Larry Lloyd from Coventry – on loan, at first, and then permanently. So permanently, he has stayed in Nottingham ever since, and after years in the pub trade he is now almost as big as the bloody Castle. Whenever I see him I worry that he's about to burst!

I worried when Taylor said we should sign him. Lloyd had

played three times for England at centre-half while with Liverpool. But Liverpool had a reputation for never parting with players who went on to do any good anywhere else. Lloyd had done nothing since leaving Anfield for Coventry. As far as I could see, and as far as people could tell me, he had done two things at Highfield Road – wasted his time and stirred the shit. Now shit-stirrers I could cope with. But I had no time whatsoever for players who wasted theirs.

There is a theory about me that says my intolerance of indiscipline and abuse of talent stems from the fact that my own playing career was cut down in my prime. I have never, knowingly, carried a chip on my shoulder about that. But it might have had something to do with my attitude towards players who failed to realise how lucky they were, how privileged they were to be playing football for an extremely lucrative living. I didn't want a time-wasting, talent-wasting, trouble-making Larry Lloyd plonked on my doorstep. Taylor told me I wouldn't be getting that at all, but instead was signing the best available centre-half in the country, and I believed him. Implicitly.

In any case, it was my job, my side of the partnership, to sort them out and get them to play once they had put a pen to a contract. I had my rows with Lloyd – not least of them a notorious incident in Greece after beating AEK. Everybody was in blazer and trousers for the trip home next morning. Lloyd came down in jeans and top. When I told him to change into his blazer, he refused. I fined him a thousand quid, he said he wouldn't pay, I left him out of the team. By the time he turned up at the ground the following week, intending to stick a transfer request in my hand, I'd taken the week off. He paid his fine, eventually.

Footballers need something tangible to prove they are on the right lines. The competition known as the Anglo-Scottish Cup was frowned upon and scoffed at as a meaningless, valueless

161

trinket. Not by us. We had players who had been nowhere, won nothing. We wanted something to show for our belief that we had the makings of a useful side, capable of winning promotion to the First Division. Winning the Anglo-Scottish Cup back in 1976 gave us as big a boost as the Conservatives would get winning a by-election today. The pundits might not have thought much of the tournament, but they began to wonder: 'Are Cloughie and Taylor going to do it again?'

You bet we were. It was the end of the 1976-77 season, and once again we'd gone abroad without knowing our fate. This time we were all together in Majorca when we heard the news. Another coincidence . . . again we were waiting for a Wolves result. Last time they had beaten Leeds. This time they beat a Bolton side who had only needed a draw to take third place and deny us promotion.

Once again a Clough–Taylor team had triumphed on holiday. We were back in the First Division, back in the big time. We were on our way.

14

GLORY DAYS

I shout my opinion. I yell my contempt. I mean every
word of it. I've got to be a winner or they'll cut
me to shreds.

THE WHEEL HAS TURNED FULL CIRCLE. EIGHTEEN MONTHS AGO MY
Forest team were relegated, back where I found them, a division
adrift of the best. After I quit they had to choose well if they were
to find a manager capable of achieving instant promotion and they
went for the man I recommended – Frank Clark.

No-one was more delighted than I was when Frank repaired

the damage in his first season, re-establishing Forest in the Premiership, the élite group we used to call the First Division. But if he wants to emulate what we did in the late 1970s he'll need to be bloody good. We won the League Championship in our first season up from the Second Division, and then went on to win the European Cup the season after. Frank will remember it well because, as Max Boyce says, he was there. In a way, Frank was a symbol of that instant, unprecedented run of success, that continued with our successful defence of the European Cup a season later. What a signing! What a team! What a manager I must have been!

Frank had joined us a year earlier. A journalist tipped me off, as journalists often tip off managers on transfers. Doug Weatherall, the *Daily Mail*'s man in the North-East, who seems to have spent longer on the patch than the Tyne Bridge, rang me and said: 'Newcastle have dropped a clanger. They've let Frank Clark go on a free transfer. Although he's turned thirty he must have another two or three years in him.'

'Where is he now?' I asked. 'Can I have a word with him?'

Doug explained: 'He's in Doncaster, talking to their manager, Stan Anderson.'

Now, I couldn't have that. Stan Anderson, an ex-playing colleague of mine at Sunderland, signing Frank Clark to play in the Fourth Division? Not if I could help it. Bargains don't come along very often in top-level football. Bargains like Frank Clark, without a fee, don't come along more than once in a lifetime.

I told Doug: 'Get hold of him and tell him Cloughie wants a word. Tell him not to sign for Doncaster or anybody else before he's talked to me.' Journalists can be useful on occasions. They can often get through to people quicker than managers. If I had rung Stan Anderson and told him I wanted a word with Frank before he signed, I can imagine what Stan would have told me: 'You can f**k off.' So Doug did all the donkey-work.

I can't remember, but I do hope he got an exclusive out of the story.

Frank turned up at the City Ground the next day and signed within half an hour. He was thirty-two, but was to make nearly 120 appearances at full-back and one memorable appearance up-front. That was the day I pulled off Peter Withe and sent on Frank as substitute. He turned to me on the touch-line, and asked, with that endearing little lisp of his: 'Where do you want me to play, boss?'

'Bloody well play at centre-forward,' I said. 'I've just pulled Withey off, haven't I? The full-backs are doing brilliantly, so get yourself up-front.' So up he went, and scored his first ever league goal at the age of thirty-two. Tony Woodcock, who was sitting next to me in the dug-out, said: 'You do realise the others will never get a bloody ball from Frank again.' Sure enough, every time Clark got the ball after that he turned with it and ran for goal, oblivious to team-mates either side of him.

'Look at him,' Woodcock shouted. 'Just look at him. One bloody goal in his life and he's after a hat-trick!' We won the match.

I knew Frank could play football. What I didn't know when I signed him, was that he could play the guitar. I don't know whether he still plays it at Forest, these days, but he should. You would be amazed how much a little bit of music can bring people together. It brought our family together when we were kids, singing along while Mam played the piano in the front-room on Sundays. I have a piano in my dining-room at Quarndon. It stands just along the wall from the mangle. I often look at it and wish I could play it. What a pleasure it would be to be able to sit, alone or with company, and perform a beautiful piece of music! Perfectly or modestly, it wouldn't matter. The odd bum note would make no difference. It's the sheer joy of playing that appeals.

I've often threatened to learn, but it's probably too late now. I suppose I never will.

I can still see Frank Clark sitting at the back of the team coach strumming away, singing in a lovely soft voice with his team-mates gathered round and joining in. Country or middle-of-the-road or whatever they called it, I was never quite sure. Taylor used to spin round in his seat and shout: 'Not another one of those bloody songs, Frank!' He didn't mean it. Taylor appreciated Frank's songs as much as any of us. He knew the importance of 'togetherness' in a team. Clark and his guitar entertained us not only throughout the country but across Europe.

One of the biggest grumbles from professional footballers is about the amount of travel they have to do. Most of them hate it, few manage to take it in their stride. Some play cards, others clasp headphones to their ears, and one or two try to watch the telly, which is never easy on a bus. We always took our own food with us, never ones to call off at service stations, cafés or restaurants, because we wanted to get back as quickly as possible. The players had no option, originally, because I was the one who wanted to be home and what I wanted, happened. Eventually the habit became general.

You'd be surprised how quickly the journey home from Wembley passed with a couple of sandwiches, a bottle of orange, and Frank Clark on his guitar. After one of our League Cup finals I was home in my lounge with fish and chips on my knee and the trophy perched on top of the telly by half-past seven. Is this a record?

Wembley is not a place for hanging around when you've done your job. Playing there is a knackering, draining experience. All we wanted was to have a glass or two of champagne in the dressing-room – and then get off home.

Getting to Wembley as often as I did never went to my head. Some people thought it did, but they're the ones who don't know me. I never had time, in management, to sit back and savour exactly what we'd done. It never sank in. We didn't bother with all that pretentious rubbish of hotel banquets, where people you don't like stand up and say what a wonderful person you are and what a wonderful job you've done, when deep down they'd probably like to see the back of you – and the feeling is mutual.

The next few seasons were to break a few records, I know that. Taylor and I put together a team that took football by storm, both at home and abroad. It had a bit of everything and plenty of the most vital elements of all – talent and the ability and determination to make the most of it.

Enter one Kenneth Burns! And against my better judgement in the first place, I have to say. It was Taylor's idea – again. 'We'll sign Kenny Burns,' he said. 'Ideal to play alongside Larry Lloyd. Nobody'll get past those two.'

'Forget it,' I said. 'I don't want trouble-makers, I don't want shit-houses, and I don't want an ugly bastard like Kenny Burns littering up my club. I don't buy thugs.'

Taylor worked on me, bringing all his persuasive powers to bear. He did a complete job on Burns. He had him followed to the greyhound track, his favourite haunt in his days with Birmingham, apparently. I think he had him tracked to the pub, to the ground and back home again – although it didn't necessarily follow in that order. Taylor could hardly have 'screened' Burns more thoroughly if he'd employed MI5.

We liked to be thorough with our signings. We looked into their background and asked people about their character – is he a boozer, a birder, a gambler? That kind of thing. If there was something to be known about a player – something he preferred to hide – you could count on us finding out. Such information can be priceless!

That stupid director at Derby, Jack Kirkland, had asked

what exactly was Taylor's job. The Kenny Burns signing, like the Larry Lloyd signing, and the signing of Garry Birtles for around two thousand quid from Long Eaton – that was Taylor's job. Exactly.

So was our agreement to 'nick' Archie Gemmill for £25,000 from Derby. We threw in a goalkeeper called John Middleton in part-exchange, and we should have let them have half our reserve side as well. I've talked about our 'best' signings – Mackay, McFarland, Todd, etc. – but Gemmill comes high on the list. How we managed to get a player of such courage and talent for so small a price, I'll never know. There were many times when people in football suggested Taylor and I ought to have been arrested – and possibly with good reason – but the Gemmill 'steal' was definitely an imprisonable offence. He was *that* good a player.

As for Burns, a fellow Scot, Taylor found nothing untoward. Oh, we were well aware of his reputation on the field. He kicked and hit people. But off the field – according to Taylor's 'intelligence reports' – nothing. 'He's been as good as gold,' Taylor assured me. 'No problem at the greyhounds, no fighting and never pissed. I think people have given him a false reputation.'

I think nothing of the sort. I think Taylor was doing his job superbly and convincing me how much I needed a footballer I didn't particularly want. It worked – with the proviso that if Burns stirred it, Taylor would answer for him. 'Done,' he agreed. And I thought I had been.

I signed him on a Saturday afternoon. Never forget it. Our rendezvous – far too posh a word for Burnsy – was a service area on the motorway. He lurched into the car-park in a vehicle I was sure had been stolen – I couldn't believe anybody could actually own a car like that! I couldn't see a tax disc on the windscreen and I'm darned certain he had no insurance, either.

'Where are we going?' Burns asked.

'Well, we're going to the ground, eventually, but I have to call at a sweet pea exhibition, first. And you're coming with me.'

Sweet peas are my favourite flowers, with my favourite scent. I was either making a presentation or they were naming a particular variety after me, I'm not sure which, but I'm certain that one scruffy Scotsman was totally bewildered by it all. I'm not sure whether he'd heard of sweet peas before, but now he was faced with thousands of them. To this day I think he was expecting the small round green pea he associated with sausage and chips. He probably thought we were going to a frozen-food depot.

Burns was a bit wild, a rough character. He was startled when I said to him: 'You're going round like a bloody tramp. You've got a car that should get you arrested. You've no tax, probably no insurance, in fact it wouldn't surprise me if you told me you'd never taken a test and never held a licence.'

Kenny Burns didn't take much handling after joining Nottingham Forest. He became an improved person – visibly and actually. I'd heard that he'd been none too kind to his wife. I knew he spent too much time at the dog track, unshaven and dressed scruffily. I told him: 'Get shaved, get yourself a decent coat and get your wife down to the ground occasionally.'

And when he did I made a fuss of her. It was a case of demonstrating decent behaviour to a lad who had come from a rough background and who had few standards, if any at all. It was just like bringing up a child. And it worked. The last time I saw him, strangely enough, was back in a service station car-park. He just clambered out of a mini-bus carrying the non-League team he'd joined. He was munching a sandwich. But he did say, 'Hello.' He was polite.

Burns turned out to be a key signing. He graduated with

honours – not least the Footballer of the Year Award, after only one season with us.

Gemmill, Burns . . . and Peter Shilton. Who could have wished for three better newcomers? Shilton cost me a record £270,000, and he was worth every penny.

Shilton had been wasting his talent, despite making a lot of money. He had moved from Leicester to Stoke, a club that had started to go downhill. I caught up with him at Mansfield, of all places, in some minor match. The England goalkeeper in all his glory – playing in front of a handful of spectators and the odd stray dog at Field Mill. And not a medal to show for his career to date. After I had opened the transfer talk, such as it was, Stoke's chairman at the time warned me: 'You do realise he'll put you in the workhouse. He's earning a fortune, and he'll want at least a ten per cent rise.'

I told him the player who could put me out of work hadn't yet been born. Shilton wasn't going to put me anywhere, apart from at the top of the League and the top of my profession. We knew he would cost us over the years, because he loved money and needed plenty with his interest in horses! But we knew it was worth some hard bargaining to get the best goalkeeper in the business.

One of the stupidities among football directors – and it has applied for as long as I can remember – has been their failure to appreciate the value of the goalkeeper. Even today some will still find it hard to believe the keeper should be paid as much as the full-back or anybody else in the side. A good goalkeeper can save you eighteen points a season. That's like a striker scoring a winning goal once every six games. It can mean the difference between winning a title or qualifying for Europe and missing out. It can mean the difference between being relegated and surviving. Shilton was a class act – and class acts don't come cheap.

As a young player at Middlesbrough I was propelled by a feeling that I couldn't fail, that nothing would stop me, that I would always score goals. That same sensation of supreme confidence began to stir as we set out among the so-called big boys in 1977-78. We didn't take the First Division by surprise, we took it by storm – right from the opening spell of four straight wins, scoring twelve goals with only one going in the opposite direction, past Shilton. The longer the critics kept saying the bubble would burst, the more we inflated it.

'It just can't go on,' they wrote. 'Bollocks!' I thought. After sixteen games we had lost only three, and after that third defeat – ironically at Leeds – we didn't lose again.

Twenty-six league matches without defeat swept us to the Championship at the first time of asking. But there was more, as that cock-eyed Irish comedian would say. We extended that unbeaten sequence through the first sixteen league games of 1978–79, totting up the equivalent of an entire season without losing – forty-two matches. It was a record at the time, it still stands, and I doubt if it will ever be bettered.

We won the Championship with time to spare, clinching it with a goalless draw at Coventry – one of twenty-five clean sheets achieved in 1978-79. Who said Shilton was too expensive? One season away from Stoke, and he already had the first medal of his career. There were to be others, but he wasn't around the day we won our first trophy of the title season.

The pundits still believed that the bubble was going to burst. They didn't give us a hope in hell – not against Liverpool at Wembley, Kenny Dalglish and all. Not in a League Cup Final we had to face without Gemmill and defender David Needham, both cup-tied, and without John McGovern and Colin Barrett, both injured. Peter Shilton just happened to be cup-tied as well and that, as you might imagine, was the clincher for the doom-and-gloom merchants.

The 'bollocks-to-'em' philosophy worked again. When things seemed against us I told the players that it was us versus the world. 'Close ranks, say nowt and let's play. We've enough talent in here to take on anybody.' I wasn't worried about Liverpool. And I wasn't in the least concerned about Shilton's stand-in, even though Chris Woods was young and inexperienced. He was a goalkeeper, wasn't he? He was ambitious. He, like every player, longed to play at Wembley, and if he wanted to be like Peter Shilton, here was his chance.

Age was never a deterrent to me. If Steve Powell could play for Derby against Liverpool at the age of sixteen, why not pick Woods at eighteen? He was two years older – a comparative bloody veteran! He was fine. He had to make a save or two in a 0-0 draw which never threatened the voting for Match of the Season but proved we could cope with Liverpool. In fact, they didn't beat us all season.

We needed a break before the replay at Old Trafford and decided to take the players to Scarborough. Taylor had a particular liking for the east-coast resort, so much so that he had bought an apartment there. He once came to me with a suggestion out of the blue. 'I think I'll take the lads to Scarborough,' he said.

'Smashing,' I replied. 'How long for?'

'Oh, there and back in the day.'

'There and back? Scarborough?' He must have spotted a sceptical look on my face. 'He's at it,' I thought. 'I know he's bloody at it.'

'Do you plan to give them any training?' I asked.

'No,' said Taylor. 'You take them training today. Then a nice little break and a breather in Scarborough and when they get back, they'll be spot on for Saturday.'

When I saw the coach driver, Albert Kershore, two days later, I asked him: 'Scarborough, Albert – the trip go all right?'

'Fine, boss,' he said. 'No sweat whatsoever. The roads were nice and quiet. The only trouble we had was getting the wardrobe out of the coach!'

'Wardrobe? What wardrobe?'

'The one for Mr Taylor's flat, boss.'

Yes, Pete loved Scarborough. And on this occasion it put us in the right frame of mind for the replay. Liverpool folk still dispute the penalty John Robertson stuck past Ray Clemence to win us the Cup. They claim that John O'Hare was outside the area when he was brought down. But how many times have teams had reason to complain about penalties given in Liverpool's favour at Anfield? They didn't like it when one went against them. On the coach journey over the Pennines afterwards, I seem to remember somebody shouting from the back: '. . . anyway, bollocks to 'em.'

But midway through that incredible season I might easily have walked out on the team that won the League Cup to qualify for Europe and then went on to win the League title. I wanted to be the manager of England, I was the 'people's choice', and in the December I thought I'd cracked it.

After all, if it was to be decided on the strength of an interview there was only one candidate. The others were wasting their time. At least, that's the way I saw it.

15

ENGLAND

When the FA get in their stride, they make the
Mafia look like kindergarten material.

THE PEOPLE WHO WORK THEIR WAY UP THE LADDER OF THE FOOTBALL
Association are among the most privileged in the land. They
travel the world – duty-free. Those who refused to make me
England manager at the end of 1977 will never know what they
missed. But they were scared to death of what would have hit
them.

They've bungled a few things in their time. They've dropped

a few clangers. Their biggest mistake of all was in failing to appoint the best man for the top job: me – or me and Taylor, to be strictly accurate.

If form counts for anything in sport, if the strength and influence of an interview means anything in fitting a man to a vacancy, then I should have been installed in the job I longed for – the job the vast majority of the population believed was mine by right.

I went to London in brilliant nick. My Forest team was at the top of the First Division, in the middle of that record run of forty-two unbeaten matches. If the FA's odd-bods wanted to nit-pick and point to my dismal times at Brighton and Leeds, they should also have remembered my record at Derby. After the event, after turning their backs on the best-qualified candidate, they had even less excuse, because I was about to go on and win successive European Cups. That season, I would become the only living manager to win the League Championship with two different clubs. I'd done it at Derby, and I was halfway to doing it at Forest. Nobody had achieved that 'double' since the legendary Herbert Chapman pulled it off with Huddersfield and Arsenal in the 1930s.

I had been 'courted' by Peter Swales – the Manchester City man who was later to become chairman of the International Committee that appointed and then released the ill-fated Graham Taylor. Swales was on his way up the ladder. I met him at the home of my journalist pal Vince Wilson, and a couple of times elsewhere. Swales gave me the impression that, as an ambitious man within the Establishment, he wanted to know as much as he could about the bloke who would eventually get the big job. He left me with the impression that if and when it came to a vote, he would be backing me. I'm certain he didn't, because I only received one vote and I'm told it wasn't his!

After Don Revie quit, Ron Greenwood was put in temporary

charge. Revie had legged it into the desert at the first sight of Arabian 'readies' – what a despicable way that was to chuck in the England job!

The short list included Bobby Robson, who would be appointed some years later, Lawrie McMenemy, who had won the FA Cup with Southampton the year before, and me. Then there were the FA's own 'in-house' contenders – Director of Coaching, Allen Wade, and his sidekick, bloody Charles Hughes. Even now I can't imagine how such a man could be considered as a possible manager of his country. I would have thought twice about letting him drive the team bus or putting him in charge of the kit.

Lawrie had a sound enough background, even though he never played at top level. He had learned his trade as manager at Doncaster and Grimsby before taking over at Southampton and giving the place more to talk about than the coming and going of the *QE2*.

Robert Robson, as I called him, had the best job in the game as manager at Ipswich, where he did so well – although he did miss out when he should have won the League title, the year Aston Villa nicked it. He worked for the best board of directors in football, headed by the Cobbold brothers. They owned a brewery, which was the first thing in their favour – but they also had a gorgeous, laid-back attitude to football that didn't recognise such a word as crisis. I don't think they'd have sacked Robert Robson even if he'd taken them down as far as the Fourth Division. But they didn't have to worry about him, either, because he kept them challenging for the big prizes, here and in Europe.

Funny how all three of us had things in common. All from the North-East, and all with relatively small, unfashionable clubs. But if any of us thought we had a cat-in-hell's chance of landing the England job, we were deluding ourselves. Instead of sending an official to call us for our interview, they should have sent men in white coats to lead us away. The job was cut and dried before a word was spoken. It was Ron Greenwood's – and he wasn't even interviewed!

I was totally comfortable during my interview, even though I never like the formal occasion. I didn't much relish sharing the same room with the likes of the FA chairman, Professor Sir Harold Thompson, now dead and gone. He was an academic, a stroppy, know-all bugger who in my view knew nothing about my game. If he was such a brilliant mathematician, he figured it wrong when the FA got rid of Alf Ramsey. I was wary of the Mad Professor and I could sense that he was wary of me. Sir Matt Busby was there – and there was something reassuring about the sight of him, a wise man who knew our business and would understand football talk. Bert Millichip, now Sir Bert and FA chairman in his umpteenth year, was also there. I think he smouldered at the very sight of me because he thought I had been poking my nose into his business when I had criticised his club, West Bromwich Albion, for failing to provide their manager with a contract. I seem to remember upsetting him too, at some lunch or dinner. There was Swales, the one whose vote I thought was guaranteed, and Dick Wragg, the old blusterer from Bramall Lane. Wragg was forever telling people: 'Pop in and join me for a bit of lunch next time you're in Sheffield' – but I never came across anybody who did. I suppose there were ten or twelve of them in the room at Lancaster Gate, but the others were faceless people I didn't know.

I told them their job would suit me down to the ground, that England had enough good players to win things. I said that I didn't like the horrible shirts Revie and the FA secretary, Ted Croker, had come up with in their dealings with a kit company – garish red white and blue, cheap and nasty. I wanted the team restored to the white shirts that men like Finney and Matthews used to wear. Nothing wrong with tradition if it's good. I also told them I was that keen to get involved in the England set-up, I'd take any job they cared to give me. Now I couldn't have been fairer than that! When I went striding out of the interview, across Lancaster Gate to an hotel where Peter Taylor was waiting, I felt as if I was walking on air.

'How's it gone?' Taylor asked. 'Do you think we've cracked it?'

'I'll tell you one thing, pal,' I said, 'if that job depends on the interview, if interviews mean anything at all, I've pissed it. Can't miss. Assuming it's not bent, of course.'

But it wasn't straight – it was cut and dried for Greenwood. The entire bloody interview process had been a sham and a sop to the public. So much for the body of opinion that might have wanted McMenemy installed. So much for those who would have applauded the appointment of Robson. So much for the opinion polls showing, overwhelmingly, that I was the public's idea of the right man for the job.

They gave it to a manager who couldn't make up his mind which should be the very first name on his team sheet. Ron Greenwood didn't know who was the best goalkeeper in the country. Now I'm telling you, if a manager can't decide on his No. 1 what chance has he got of coming up with the right combination all the way through to No. 11?

Greenwood operated what I regarded as a cop-out system, a kind of rota arrangement to accommodate both Peter Shilton and Liverpool's Ray Clemence. He considered them to be equals. He would pick one of them for one match and the other for the next fixture. I couldn't believe it at the time and now, after years' more experience and time to reflect in my retirement, I find it inconceivable. A manager, whether with Inverness or England, is paid to make up his mind, to decide between players who operate in the same position. To make a judgement. To pick his best team. When Greenwood picked his England line-up he was uncertain about the very first name on the list. That can't be right.

Don't get me wrong – Ron was an accomplished manager, highly respected within the game among fellow-professionals and in Europe. Under his guidance West Ham became known as 'The Academy' because of the stylish football they played. They didn't win much, mind, and I always had the feeling that a team which enjoyed the benefits of players like Bobby Moore, Geoff Hurst and Martin Peters should have delivered a title or two.

Talking of Bobby Moore, the late England captain who held the World Cup above his intelligent blond head in Wembley in 1966, I do blame Greenwood for one thing. Ron wouldn't let me have him! I tried to buy Moore for Derby County. Not a bad successor to Dave Mackay, I thought, but Ron wasn't falling for it. I had already had a word with Bobby – a tap, I suppose – and he gave me enough encouragement to make an official move. I phoned Greenwood and said: 'Any chance of you letting me have Martin Peters?'

I knew what the response would be. 'No chance whatsoever.'

'In that case,' I said to him, 'I'll take Bobby Moore off your hands.'

It was a serious move and Greenwood was ready for it. He thanked me for calling, I think he remarked on my audacity, he told me I'd better look elsewhere, and he wished me a good afternoon. Well, as Taylor suggested when we went in for Mackay: 'You've nothing to lose if you try.'

I was thinking about the England job only a few months ago on holiday in Cala Millor. I thought about what a good candidate I had been, the interview, and the moment I possibly passed up any chance of being appointed. I think it was when I told them: 'I'll do any job you care to give me.'

The memory hit me like a bullet. I remembered the few moments as I stood and turned to make my way out of the room. I think Sir Matt Busby inadvertently cost me the job I'd set my heart on.

'One moment, Brian,' Sir Matt called. 'When you said you would take any job, did you mean it?'

'Of course,' I said, 'any job. Any job at all.'

I'd meant it, not thinking in terms of the bucket-and-sponge job with the 'B' team or anything like that. I'd said it as a way of proving to them that I was enthusiastic about England and eager to get involved. A bit like Sam Longson, years before, the old so-and-sos called my bluff. They gave the top job to Ron Greenwood at a time when he was no longer team manager of his club, having moved aside as general manager a year or two earlier.

They gave me – and Taylor – the task of running the youth side, and although it did appeal to some extent, I'm still convinced it was done to keep the Press and public off their backs. Taylor and I were never slow to poke our noses in when we could smell a chance of promoting ourselves, and we hadn't yet taken over officially before the opportunity came for a spectacular little intervention.

It was in Las Palmas, where the youth side were playing in a tournament that everybody except us seemed to think the Russians were sure to win. A coach called Ken Burton was in charge – at least he thought he was, until Taylor and I stepped in! We'd gone there basically to observe and spend some time on the beach, but when I saw what was happening I couldn't believe my eyes. Talk about amateurish!

I couldn't understand the defeatist atmosphere that had been allowed to develop. We just had to make some contribution before the games, moving in at the last minute to make sure those young players knew they had a chance. Eventually they reached the Final, but even then I still sensed that most people in the party, FA people and suchlike, were quite happy to say: 'We've done well to get this far, but it's the Russians we're playing, remember.' That attitude dominated their thinking, as if to justify their trip even before a ball had been kicked in their biggest match of all. What on earth had they bothered getting on the aeroplane for if they didn't think they could win the tournament? Duty-frees?

Taylor, I remember, was having a quiet drink with a group of journalists, including Bob Cass and Joe Melling. They were 'looking for a line' as usual and were obviously delighted, though surprised, when we arrived.

'What are you two supposed to be doing?'

'We're not involved. Just observing,' said Taylor. I nearly wet myself. An observer, to Taylor, meant a Sunday newspaper!

I had seen the England youth players outside the hotel, standing around on a street corner waiting to be taken to the stadium. They must have stood for a quarter of an hour, while the team coach went round and round the block because the driver couldn't find enough space to park. Things like that got under my skin – you don't treat any athletes that way. I went berserk. 'What the bloody hell is going on?' I said to the lad in charge. 'Get the police, somebody – anybody to make room for the coach to get in to pick up these lads. They've a job to do, there's a match to win.' I lost my rag at the sight of an England team being made to stand around and wait because of inadequate arrangements.

The press lads in the bar had seen and heard everything. Taylor turned to them and announced: 'Gentlemen, I think the observing is complete. I think we are now at work!'

When we boarded the coach the first thing I did was kick off a woman who was already sitting at the front.

'You can't put her off,' somebody in a blazer told me. 'She's the official interpreter.'

I said: 'I don't care who she is, she's got a fag on – get her off my coach.' And off she went.

I got involved with the team, though not in great detail. I

can't remember who was in the side, exactly, but Clive Allen was there and he'd done quite well in earlier games. I think all of them at least went out with the belief that they were entitled to be on the same pitch as the kids from Russia and that, by passing the ball and enjoying a little bit of luck, they might even win.

At half-time the dressing-room door opened and some bloke wandered in with the oranges or something. Never one to tolerate intruders in my dressing-room – some club chairmen have been refused entry – I told him: 'I don't know who you are and I don't know who ever gave permission for you to come in here – but f**k off.'

I was later informed he was a Professor Frank O'Gorman, a surgeon from Sheffield. He must have been the team medic, I suppose. Possibly one man who did manage to have that lunch Dick Wragg used to offer to all and sundry!

I didn't care because I was in my element, in my domain, I was working on my shop floor with sleeves rolled up, and we were in sight of a successful, productive shift. We beat Russia 1-0. It gave me a real boost when somebody said it was the first time the youth side had won anything in donkey's years.

We lasted about a year with the youth team before packing it in and returning our undivided attention to the far more important business of managing Nottingham Forest.

People wonder what kind of an England manager Cloughie would have turned out to be. There's only one answer – a bloody good one. Greenwood hardly pulled up many trees, even though he was acknowledged as a very talented coach. England did nowt in the European Championships and should have done better in the 1982 World Cup. Watching from afar, I couldn't believe the negative selection and approach to our final two matches against West Germany and Spain. Two goalless draws when, with more

Still learning; at only thirty years old, I was the youngest manager in the Football League. Here I help out by driving the Hartlepools coach *Manchester Daily Mail*

At a House of Commons reception after Derby won the League Championship, 1972. Chairman Sam Longson stands between me and the Prime Minister, Harold Wilson; also visible on the extreme right of the picture is the local MP, Phillip Whitehead.

Celebrations after Derby win the First Division title, 1972. (left to right) Alan Durban, Kevin Hector, Roy McFarland and Alan Hinton look happy; Chairman Sam Longson and I less so. *Derby Evening Telegraph*

Chaos at the Baseball Ground after Peter and I walked out in protest against the Directors, October 1973. *Syndication International*

With Peter
Taylor at
Brighton, 1973.
Sunday Mirror

In Tehran, to
discuss the
possibility that I
might become
Iran team
manager. Even
I might have
had trouble
with Ayatollah
Khomeini!
Sunday Mirror

Holidaying in the Scilly Islands, 1972. I had just received the news that Derby had become League champions, after Wolves had beaten Leeds at Molineux.

On a Spanish beach with Nigel and Elizabeth. *Daily Mail*

In the dugout
with Nigel
(left) and
Simon.
*Peter Bolton/
T.V. Times*

The proud
father.
Bildbyran

Leading the teams out with Bill Shankly for the Leeds-Liverpool FA Charity Shield, 1974. I had asked Don Revie to lead Leeds out, but he refused. Not a good omen; and I was to stay only forty-four days.
Sunday Mirror

Training at Scarborough. I don't believe in too much coaching; either a player can do it or he can't.

Clough to lead
England? I want
to see the FA [...]
1977, but the[y]
didn't want m[e].
*Paul
Hunt/Empics*

With Trevor
Francis, the first
£1 million
footballer.
Ray Green

naking
ad elf clear?
enb Thomas
i

The greatest
partnership in
the history of
football. *Roy
Peters/Sportlines*

confidence in ourselves and an aggressive outlook, we should have won them both.

Bobby Robson had a bit of luck after failing to get the team to his first European Championships and seeing his side hammered out of sight in the Finals of the same competition four years later. They struggled through to the later stages of the World Cup in Mexico and in the end they were able to blame Maradona's cheating hand for their elimination. Four years later, however lucky they might have been at first, England were unlucky to lose on penalties in the Semi-Finals.

As for Graham Taylor, England failed in the Europeans and didn't even make it as far as the World Cup, although I believed he had earned the job when he was appointed.

So, would I have made a worse England manager than any of those three, or than Revie before them? Of course not.

It wasn't my record on the field that denied me the job. We would have had one of the most exciting, positive England sides of all time if I'd been in charge. Although I couldn't have guaranteed the success that Sir Alf brought to this country, we would have had a team that at least looked the part in a kit more in keeping with the country's traditions. We would also have had Glenn Hoddle in the side on a regular basis. How could successive England managers have failed to see what Hoddle could have done for the team? His beautiful touch and control, his limitless vision for the exquisite ball nobody else anticipated, his wonderful gift for the telling pass – what more could any manager require? It wasn't what Hoddle couldn't do that worried me – it was the managers who failed to recognise what he could do. They must have been blind or daft – or both. I believe he finished up with fifty-three international caps. That is disgracefully few, an indictment of those who failed to appreciate an outstanding talent.

What chance do you have if you cannot recognise a footballer who is capable of winning matches?

Oh no, the FA didn't reject me because they feared I couldn't pick a winning England team. They didn't reject me because Ron Greenwood had a more impressive record at club level, even though he'd been doing the job far longer than I had. They didn't reject me because I would have made them wait while the team boarded the aircraft first – and then made Professor Thompson and his pals sit at the back because we were already occupying the best seats at the front. To be honest, I would have argued a case for the FA men to travel on a different plane – preferably to a different destination. I never encouraged the practice of directors travelling on my team coach. At Forest, they had their own.

They rejected me because they were scared stiff. They wanted a diplomat, first and foremost, who would not put a word out of place and jeopardise relationships with their opposite numbers from overseas. They did not want a manager who would have given the press boys more fun and more copy than any England manager in history. They did not want an England manager who told the Japanese: 'If you can make watch-sized televisions, it's about time you learned how to grow grass.'

And, sure as hell, they did not want an England manager who was prepared to call the Italians 'cheating bastards', no matter how true that was. Oh no, they didn't want their cosy, pampered existences rumbled and exposed. They didn't want an intruder into their private little duty-free world.

They failed to understand that I would have curbed my language and revelled in the relief from the day-to-day, week-to-week, month-to-month grind of club management, and that I had the talent that would have given them a successful England and kept them on their precious foreign 'holidays' even longer.

When you are a high-profile football manager and a controversial, opinionated individual as I have been, your reputation can work against you. But football and football management *needs* characters. I think it was Rodney Marsh who once described our football as 'a grey game'. It only becomes grey when there are grey people in charge. The FA shied away from me because of my media reputation, when they should have concentrated on my results in the record books.

They turned me down because of what they feared I would bring to the job – not because of the results I'm certain I would have achieved. They were wrong, because I was right for the job. I will always believe it was the worst decision the Football Association ever made. And they will never be able to prove me wrong.

Still, life had its little compensations for the rejected, would-be England manager. He just went away to win the League Championship and a couple of European Cups. And sometimes he reflected on that meaningless charade of an interview at FA headquarters.

And thought: 'Sod 'em.'

16

AT THE PEAK

My wife said to me in bed, 'God, your feet are
cold.' I said, 'You can call me Brian in bed, dear.'

THEY TELL ME PEOPLE HAVE ALWAYS WONDERED HOW I DID IT. THAT FEL-
low professionals and public alike have been fascinated and puzzled
and intrigued by the Clough managerial methods and technique and
would love to know my secret. I've got news for all of them – so
would I. The only explanation I can come up with can be found in
one word: talent.

Let me nail one myth before I go any further. If I have heard it once, I've heard it a hundred times: that Brian Clough ruled by fear. Absolute and utter garbage – I just frightened everybody to death, that's all!

Only joking. Here's a little story that should destroy the popular theory about my management for all time. I'll give them fear!

One morning I picked up the phone in my office and rang through to the dressing-room where I knew a group of young-sters, apprentices, were tidying up. One of them answered the call.

'Hello?'

'I want a cup of tea brought to the office – now,' I told him.

'You can get it yourself,' said the kid.

'Do you know who you are talking to?' I asked him.

'Yes, but do you know who *this* is?'

'Not sure.'

'Then get the bloody tea yourself.'

Hmmm. That young man didn't seem too frightened of his manager. Although others, senior professionals, were usually a bit wary of me – and, yes, on isolated occasions, a bit scared – the emphasis I strived to create, in general terms day to day, was exactly the opposite. Fear was the last thing I wanted. I don't believe you can do anything if there is fear in your heart. You can't run, speak, dance, sing, or screw a nut onto a bolt. When the nerves jangle, the things you want to work don't respond. It is just the same with footballers.

By winning the League Championship in 1977-78 we had qualified for the European Cup. Peter Withe had scored goals to win us promotion and then help us lift the Championship, and he believed he was entitled to have a crack at playing in Europe. He was wrong, that's all. He was no spring chicken and we received what I thought was a generous offer from

Newcastle. It doesn't matter exactly how much, now, but I decided the time was right, the money was adequate – and that Garry Birtles, the ex-carpet-layer brought in from Long Eaton by Taylor, might just have a future at centre-forward. A few of our fans cribbed when I decided to get rid of Withe. Some suggested that I sold him because he'd been doing too well and hogging the publicity. Some idiotic folk were daft enough to think that I had a 'down' on centre-forwards, those who played in the position where I made my name at Middlesbrough. Have you ever heard such tripe?

Others would have you believe that the signing of Trevor Francis was the reason we won the European Cup in 1979. Wrong again! Trevor Francis scored the goal that won the Final, but he was only part of what had already become a cracking good side. And it didn't bother me one iota that I had turned that extremely talented young man into the first £1-million footballer in Britain. Even though I hadn't!

Birmingham City's manager, lovely Jim Smith, insisted that the magical million had to be paid, but I refused on principle. As the negotiations dragged on, early that New Year, I was having trouble with Peter Taylor, who couldn't understand my reluctance to take the transfer beyond that historic threshold.

'Get it bloody paid,' Taylor urged me. 'What's the difference – nine hundred thousand, nine hundred and fifty thousand, nine hundred and ninety thousand? He's the one we need and Smithy's ready to sell. It's not our money, anyway. Get it paid, for Christ's sake!'

I still dug in my heels. I didn't want to pay a million quid. I don't know why, maybe it was some kind of mental block. Fees had never bothered me before and didn't bother me afterwards, but there was something about a million pounds – something in my head that said it would be wrong to saddle any player, even one with Francis's outstanding ability, with that kind of label.

Footballers have enough problems, pleasing managers and fans, without carrying any extra burden.

I finally agreed that we should pay Birmingham £999,999. And possibly a few pence. I had protected my principle, gone as near as damn it to meeting Jim Smith's asking price, and shut Taylor up. And it all made not the slightest bit of difference. When Trevor came over to the City Ground to sign – and inevitably have his leg pulled as I told the Press he could not be guaranteed a place in the team – the headline writers labelled him 'Britain's first million-pound footballer' anyway. Perhaps Taylor had told Jim Smith: 'Bollocks to Cloughie, I'll make sure you get your million,' or maybe he'd paid the extra pound out of his own pocket. If you believe that, you'll believe anything!

Trevor Francis was a bright lad who should have done more with his playing career. How many England caps does he have to show – fifty-two? He should have had many more. There is a train of thought which says that if Trevor had had a touch of Denis Law in his temperament, more of a nasty streak in his character, he would have been one of the true greats of the game. It's a reasonable point – but we are rarely blessed with the perfect combination of talent and temperament, so I'm just grateful that Francis had what he had – and that Nottingham Forest enjoyed the benefit of it for a season or two.

Those who claimed I would not have made a good England manager because so-called 'star' players would not have accepted the way I treated them should talk to Trevor Francis. 'The first million-pound footballer' took the Clough treatment as well as anybody.

I gave him a wonderful début. I stuck him in the third team playing before a crowd of – oh, there must have been at least twenty, plus, I seem to remember, two dogs who were far more engrossed in one another. He didn't mind – about the third team, I mean, not the dogs – and he didn't object when I insisted that he rammed a pair of shin pads down his socks. 'Those legs of yours have cost me a lot of money,' I said. 'From now on you make sure you protect them.' I've never understood managers who allow players to perform without pads and then complain when they have injury problems. My players wore pads and you never heard me cribbing about problems with injuries.

Francis was ineligible for the League Cup Final and the opening rounds of the European Cup. So he brewed the tea – simple as that. Players travelling with the team, but not picked for whatever reason, were expected to muck in and help out. Shift the skip, pass the tie-ups, pass me my sweater – that type of thing. And if you're doing nowt else, you make the bloody tea. All part of the togetherness we created. You could call it 'family', but I'd rather not be compared with Don Revie's Leeds, if that's all right with you. Anyway, Trevor Francis made the tea at the League Cup Final – and if you ask him, I bet he'll say he was only too delighted to do it.

It hadn't been tea the night before that final with Southampton – it had been champagne. I ordered it the moment we checked into our hotel the night prior to the game. I don't know how many bottles, ten maybe, but I do know we finished the lot. Some of the players preferred a beer, some might not have had a drink at all, but I don't think we made it to our beds until turned midnight. We all sat around, enjoying a few drinks, cracking jokes and generally winding down. I'm sure some managers and coaches make the mistake of thinking you have to wind up, or build up to a big game. I often found it far more effective to wind down.

We beat Southampton 3-2 – a smashing match that had one sour note. I had wanted Taylor to accompany me at the front of the Forest team for the walk across the pitch from the tunnel. Alan Hardaker was the boss of the Football League at the time – Secretary, actually, but as much of a dictator as I was – and turned down my request. So I told Taylor to lead out the team on his own. I could just imagine Hardaker sitting there in the Royal Box with a smug expression, thinking he had 'done' Clough at last. The man did plenty of good for football, but he could be a crotchety sod and I just had to have the final say. After the players had been presented with their medals, I grabbed Southampton's manager Lawrie McMenemy by the hand. He didn't know it, but it was the best offer he'd had for ages.

'Where are we going?' he asked.

'You're coming with me and we're going straight up those bloody steps together.'

And up we went – the first managers ever to make that walk up those steps to Wembley's Royal Box. They all do it now, I notice. All official and above-board and part of the scene of celebration in the old stadium. And about time, too. But on that March afternoon in 1979, we were the first. You should have seen the expression on Hardaker's face! If looks could kill . . .

I was in the middle of one of the most satisfying seasons of my career. A League Championship and a League Cup in 1978, the season before, and now the League Cup successfully defended. All in the space of the twelve months that followed the FA's rejection of me as a suitable manager of England. I wonder if any member of that interviewing committee gave a single thought to the possibility that they might just have made a mistake?

Trevor Francis was a prime example of the way I regarded and handled big-name players whose status sometimes scares or inhibits weaker managers. I pulled his leg, I used him as the target for the occasional wisecrack, and so did Taylor. But we never sought to humiliate him. We never humiliated anybody . . . unless, of course, they deserved it!

Trevor was treated like the rest of a squad that had developed the kind of spirit and close understanding I first experienced at Derby. I would have worked in exactly the same way with the England squad, because I don't know of any other. I am a great admirer of talent – and there should be more of it in an international side than at any individual club. I adore watching people with class. Be it Geoffrey Boycott with a bat in his hand, Frank Sinatra holding a mike, or a potter creating a vase from a dollop of clay on his wheel – class should be appreciated, even if it stems from an art form you know nothing about. I couldn't for the life of me understand that ballet at the Bolshoi, but I knew that those taking part were the best in their trade.

I would have had the benefit of the best with England. And they would have had the benefit of the best from me. If any single one of them had refused to toe the line or accept the way I did things – however big a name, however great a star he might have considered himself to be – I'd have kicked him out. And found somebody only too willing and eager to take his place.

The League Cup was nice to have, again. But there was an even bigger prize to be fought for. Fate – or those who carried out the draw in Zurich – decreed that if Nottingham Forest were to win the European Cup in 1979 we were going to have to overcome the biggest hurdle of all in the very first round. We were lumbered with Liverpool, yet again – two games against the defending champions of Europe, with the second leg in that cauldron at Anfield, where very few visitors ever got away with anything. Now, I could not have come up with a more searching examination of my team. I think Professor Sir Harold Thompson must have arranged it.

In those days I operated a system of low basic wages and high incentives. I don't suppose you could work it nowadays, in the era of the £12,000-a-week so-called 'superstar'. In fact, I know you couldn't. But my reasoning was that if you stuck players on massive basic salaries you undermined the very essence of competition. Winning need not matter as much to somebody who could pay off his house anyway.

I put the players on £1,000 appearance money and £2,000 to win the Liverpool tie. I cut the incentives down for the second round! As far as I was concerned Liverpool were the cream, and if we could 'do' them we had a good chance of going all the way. When I put my proposal to the directors, one of them complained: 'Don't you think that's a bit high?'

'Balls,' I said. 'Two £500 payments for playing Liverpool – bearing in mind we should get a full house at our place – and £2,000 a piece for getting through over two legs – you surely won't mind paying that, will you? If we lose you'll be wishing you were in a position to have to pay it.' They agreed.

When I gave Kenny Burns a copy of the incentives he said: 'Hey, we're not getting much for the Semi-Final, are we?'

'No,' I said, 'but have you looked at the first round against Liverpool?'

Burns wasn't skipper but I assumed he was talking for the rest of them when he looked up after checking the figure, smiled and said: 'That'll do us.' Once you had that type of reaction from a player you knew it was enough. And that was management at its best. The club could afford it easily – if we beat Liverpool.

The first leg was at the City Ground, where there was a crowd of more than 38,000 waiting. European competition was new to us, so we just took it in our stride. I told the players we'd won a Championship when nobody fancied us. 'The best way to look at it,' I said, 'is that it gives us a nice break from the League. European games are always a nice little break.' My lot couldn't wait to get started. Young Birtles, so recently fitting carpets for a living, knocked in a fairly simple goal, if any goal is simple in a match and an atmosphere like that. And I can still hear Taylor's voice, late on in that hectic first game. Liverpool, more common in Europe than Dutch cheese, should have killed the game at that stage, with only a few minutes to go. They were only one goal down and the second leg was still to come. But one of them tried to play a dangerous pass that was cut out by Colin Barrett.

We were in Liverpool's half in a trice. I think it was Birtles who crossed it, but I'm not sure who headed it down – possibly Tony Woodcock. I can see Colin Barrett, up there from his full-back position, whacking it into the net. Classic Forest, playing right to the final whistle, as I always told my teams to do: concentrate and stay involved until the referee decides your time is up. Taylor leapt to his feet, shouting: 'That'll do us.' And it did. Hardly time for another half a dozen kicks before the referee ended the match, leaving Liverpool wondering if what they referred to as the Forest 'jinx' was to cost them again. It wasn't a jinx at all. It was talent.

I was never one for overdoing the tactical approach to matches. The European Cup second leg at Liverpool was, I suppose, one of the biggest matches of my career in management – if not *the* biggest. I could imagine most managers going into the most minute detail prior to a game of such importance, but I'm not sure I mentioned Liverpool once in our preparations for that momentous night at Anfield – another instance of the 'Bollocks to 'em' theory. Don Revie used to bore his players rigid with massive dossiers on their opponents – who gets forward down the left, who comes forward for free-kicks, which foot does the keeper prefer for clearances, and all that crap.

I had enough on my plate bothering about my lot, without fretting about the others. In any case, if I had the right players in my squad and if I picked the right team and if they were confident and free from fear – the other lot would be the ones doing the worrying. I knew we were strong in the department that became a Liverpool tradition, started by Bill Shankly and continued by Bob Paisley – defence. We had Peter Shilton in goal, which was as good an insurance policy as it was possible to take out. His strength was his appreciation of angles. His weakness was his love of race horses – especially the ones that cost him money.

Shilton's love of horse racing was well known at the club and elsewhere. He was an 'enthusiastic' gambler and, I believe, bought part ownership of horses from time to time. It wasn't in his contract at Forest but we had a private little agreement that he could take a couple of days off to attend the big race meeting at Cheltenham.

When I appeared on television panels I loved talking about Shilton. I'd say the opposition might outrun Birtles and Woodcock, running back to their own half. They might get through our midfield and, very occasionally, they might get beyond Larry Lloyd and Kenny Burns. But when they'd done all that, once they thought they were in the clear, they'd look up and see a bloody gorilla standing there with shoulders like Mr Universe, and they'd wonder where the goal had gone! Now, as an ex-goalscorer myself, I know that's off-putting. You can lose your nerve. You would be amazed at the number of strikers who went clear on my Forest side, having done what appeared to be the hard part, and then couldn't even hit the target – just because Shilton was there.

His use of angles was a vital element, his size was another and he had the ability to get his body in the way of everything. He wasn't that brilliant in the air, in fact little Les Green, the one with hands as big as shovels whom we signed early in our Derby days, was a better puncher than Shilton. That didn't matter so much, because in all other respects Shilton was, without doubt, the best.

We had a good balance all round. Lloyd and Burns at the centre of defence could scare people – nobody messed with those two. In fact, they used to resent the headlines that were forever coming Shilton's way. Burnsy told him: 'I'm sick to death of reading about you – the other side never gets as far as you because we keep 'em out. You only have two shots a match to save.'

'Ah yes,' said Shilton, 'but they're always two good 'uns.'

Larry Lloyd used to lumber about the place. I got him back in the England side – where he had a nightmare, incidentally – because we used to protect him. We put people around him who made up for what he didn't have. Larry was not the best reader of a game – but Kenny Burns was. Lloyd was an explosive type, so when he blew his top Frank Clark would amble over, tap him on the shoulder, and say: 'The gaffer says you'd better cut it out, or else.'

Lloyd was a bully on the field, but he couldn't bully us because we wouldn't let him get away with it. I used to take the mickey out of him. When he came to sign from Coventry, I had asked him how he felt about the terms I'd offered. He'd stalled and said: 'It hasn't quite gelled with me yet.'

'It hasn't what?' He didn't live it down for at least six months. Every time he missed a header or put a pass wrong, I'd say: 'It's obviously still not bloody gelling with you, is it?' Everybody else in the dressing-room took it up. They absolutely murdered him.

We had the perfect balance across the middle of the pitch as well: John McGovern and Archie Gemmill, with Martin O'Neill and John Robertson out wide. Gemmill made a perfect combination with McGovern, who was lacking in pace but who saw things quickly. We varied it, including others at times, but always bearing in mind that same sense of balance. Then there were Birtles and Woodcock up front. Although Trevor Francis was not eligible to play in the European Cup prior to the Final itself, looking at that lot it's a wonder he ever got in the side at all!

We said very little immediately before the Anfield leg. We'd had a few bottles of wine in the hotel at lunch-time – just to make sure the lads slept well in the afternoon. We were always quiet in the dressing-room. I used to get stripped and into my match gear but I was never on edge, never gave them a sign that I was tense or agitated. 'Just sit down,' I would say, 'take your time and relax.' I remember buying twelve stools at one time, so that the players could all sit with their feet up in the Forest dressing-room.

Different players prepared in different ways in the hour or so before a match. Shilton would be ready twenty minutes before kick-off, immaculate, while others would still be tying up their bootlaces when the bell was signalling them to get out there. Inevitably, there were one or two white faces – and they were the ones I'd go and cuff round the head, nudge in the ribs or say something, anything to try and put a smile on their face. While all this was going on, Robertson was probably hiding in the bog having a fag.

Kenny Burns, meanwhile, didn't give a toss about anybody or anything. He wandered about the dressing-room in exactly the same cocksure frame of mind, whether we were playing Liverpool or Lincoln. I still have a vivid picture of Burnsy, in one match with Liverpool, angrily turning on Kenny Dalglish and pointing a finger at him. That's all he did – pointed a finger. It was reminiscent of Dave Mackay. I think Dalglish finished up on the Kop because we didn't see him again.

I smile, these days, at references to Forest's great tactical triumph, that night at Liverpool. Some folk do get carried away. Some observers manage to convince themselves that complicated, technical things are happening when they're not. Some so-called 'experts' come out with a right load of bullshit.

I never once looked at the likely Liverpool line-up and said: 'This is the way we'll operate, you mark him and you do that.'

The oldest temptation of all, when you're two goals up and going away for the second leg, is to say: 'We'll settle for a clean sheet.' You find you get bombarded, especially at Liverpool. Our feeling was – a feeling, a conviction, a sense that it was the best thing to do, not a flipping 'tactic' – that we'd be better off taking the game to Liverpool and playing in their half. There is nothing worse for defenders than having to run back towards their own goal. As it turned out, we didn't need a goal that night at Anfield, because we occupied Liverpool in their own half for so long that they didn't score either. We got the goalless draw that took us through, but we didn't specifically play for it.

Archie Gemmill was a key figure that night. He took care of Ray Kennedy – that big, powerful Geordie who was so important to Liverpool and who, I was so sorry to hear, is now struggling to overcome Parkinson's disease. It wasn't pre-planned that Gemmill would stick with him and mark him out of the game. But Gemmill's running power would always bring him out on top. He was like a little ferret – in and out, in and out, and he could beat anybody in a sprint. He would run all day and all night and, pound for pound, inch for inch, he could jump as high as anybody I've ever seen.

My players didn't need to be told what to do – they did it as a matter of course. They did the things they knew they could do when we bought them. You don't spend a fortune on a player and then expect to have to teach him how to play, do you?

I dealt in simple terms. I always knew what my players could do, individually and collectively. I was puzzled when Don Revie rang me and asked, in his capacity as England manager: 'How good is Roy McFarland?'

'He's by far the best centre-half in the country,' I replied. 'But why are you asking me?'

He said: 'Well if you don't know, nobody knows. You're his manager.'

Sounds daft and sounds obvious. But it's not. There was me thinking, at the time, that Revie knew everything – and he was asking for my opinion. It stuck in my memory. I knew that to have any chance of success I had to know every strength and weakness of the players at my disposal. If you got enough of it right, grouped together talented players in positions they were familiar and comfortable with, and if you were satisfied they had sufficient will to win, you had a chance.

My management was about giving and receiving respect. Players won't work for managers they don't rate and therefore don't respect. I was lucky to start at such an early age, and lucky that I still had the ability to play a bit. The players I worked with knew I wasn't exactly a dummy.

All I asked of players was that they did their jobs – and that's not an over-simplification. Defenders used to have two things to do – head a ball and tackle. These days some of them actually get forward as well. But heading and tackling – I stuck to those principles right up until the day I retired. One of the reasons Forest were relegated from the Premiership in my final, awful, season was because I had nobody at the back who could head a ball. They weren't too good at tackling either, so it cost me dear.

A winger has to be able to cross a ball. If he can't, then the next best thing is to have a bit of pace. A centre-forward's job is to score goals and if he's none too clever at that, the next best thing is the ability to create them. As for the midfield player – I don't care what other attributes he possesses, but he must have the ability to pass the ball.

We had all those things in our side. A keeper who knew what he was doing, defenders who could head, tackle and scare people, a midfield with pace and know-how and a wonderful talent for delivering the ball where we wanted it, and men up front who would run and work and, hopefully, get us a goal. We might not have scored a goal, but we struck a mighty blow at Anfield that night. The players had earned their three grand apiece by clearing the highest hurdle that would be put before them that season. Psychologically, they knew they had cracked it. If they could beat Liverpool over two legs, they could beat the rest.

And we did. We were to lose only four matches in the 1978-79 season, and the one that brought most disappointment ended that incredible run of forty-two unbeaten matches in the League. We were never given the amount of credit we deserved for that, you know, but maybe it was because we hogged the headlines and the limelight for retaining the League Cup as well as the Charity Shield, finishing runners-up in the First Division – and bringing that European Cup back to Britain.

The more I think of those forty-two games, the more I glance at that silver salver showing every one of them, the more convinced I am that it was an absolutely phenomenal achievement, an almost unbelievable run of results, worthy of its place in football history. I suppose it had to be Liverpool who brought it to an end, didn't it – a 2-0 defeat at Anfield? In view of what we had done to them, a few weeks earlier, they must have savoured every second. But they only got two points. It didn't matter who you beat or how many goals you scored, the prize for victory, then, was still two points. We soon swallowed our disappointment. By the end of the season it didn't matter too much, anyway – not when we were swaggering around with the European Cup in our hands.

We didn't have much trouble beating the Greeks of AEK, or that team called the Grasshoppers, wherever they come from – Zurich, isn't it? Anyway, we swept the pair of them aside to reach the Semi-Finals where, once again, we confounded the whole country and probably the rest of Europe put together. Everybody thought we'd blown it when we conceded three goals to FC Cologne in the first leg at our place. The Germans were probably already booking their hotels in Munich for the Final – their people do have a reputation for taking things for granted! TV interviewer Gary Newbon – oh, how I've taken the piss out of him over the years! – left nobody in any doubt that he thought we were out, there and then.

'Well, Brian, that's it, then,' he said, or words to that effect.

'Absolute crap,' was my response. I probably said 'garbage' – but I'd have meant crap, because, as I tried to explain to those idiots who convinced themselves that a 3-3 draw at home was a disaster, we had another match to play. 'Let's see how valuable Cologne's three away goals turn out to be when we go over there.' As usual, Taylor and I made sure the players were relaxed. No point in filling them with fear and trepidation by saying: 'Watch him, be wary of this one, don't do this but make sure you do that.' We just told our players they were a better team than Cologne.

We had no Archie Gemmill that night, but we did have a side convinced they could win, and eventually we had a goal from Ian Bowyer to prove it. I remember how, late in the game with Cologne bombing us from all angles in search of an equaliser, the ball ran out of play close to the benches. I ran and picked it up, handing it to one of the Cologne players because it was their throw-in. Now, I'm not a lover of the Germans, but in that particular instance I was doing my job. Couldn't be small-minded enough to let the ball run by.

Just as I was doing my job when I left out poor Ian Bowyer for the next match. Bowyer was one of the most genuine pros I ever worked with and he was to become an extremely worthy and valuable captain.

But when you've forked out as near as damn it a million quid for Trevor Francis, you have to find a place for him, occasionally.

17

KEEP SMILING THROUGH

Our squad is so young they don't need a razor.
The only beard they believe in belongs to Father
Christmas. And I don't have the heart to tell them
the truth.

THERE IS A PHOTOGRAPH ON THE WALL OF MY STUDY THAT CAPTURES, in a few seconds of frozen time, the reasons for my success as a football club manager.

The picture shows the moment, just before half-time, when the goal was scored to win Nottingham Forest that first European

Cup against Bobby Houghton's Swedish champions, Malmo, at Munich's Olympic Stadium in 1979. This was in some ways the finest moment, my finest hour – although, hand on heart, I have to confess that winning the First Division Championship gave me a deeper sense of satisfaction and pride.

The ball had been crossed from near the corner flag by the 'scruff', John Robertson, and it was about to be headed into the net by my new star signing, Trevor Francis. The picture captures both ends of my managerial spectrum: featuring one player who had been nursed, cajoled, sometimes bullied, but mostly encouraged to the top of his profession; and another who was a thoroughbred even before he came under our influence.

Some people claim that the development of John Robertson sums up the Brian Clough managerial story – epitomising the method, style and secrets of my technique. That's for others to decide, for I don't believe there has ever been any mystique about the way I have worked. Nevertheless, the tubby little Scotsman provides me with a memory that is still among the most satisfying of my long stint in the game. When I sit in my garden and close my eyes I still see that moment in Munich when Robertson suddenly took control and made his move by the left touch-line. The anticipation, that strange sense that tells you something special is about to happen, caused Taylor to stiffen and grab my arm.

Back to that photograph on my study wall. Robertson is not far from the corner flag, there are half a dozen or more Malmo players in the box, Trevor Francis is hurtling towards the far post, and Robbo sends in the perfect cross. Bump . . . bump . . . bump . . . BUMP! One-nil, pass me the European Cup. Thank you very much.

We would probably all be arrested nowadays, if we had travelled to a football ground the way we journeyed to Munich for that European Cup Final. You're not supposed to have booze on the bus any more. But we had crates of it on ours!

Just beers. A few drinks for the lads on the way if they wanted it and nothing wrong with that, to my mind. Just another instance of the way we created a relaxed mood, rather than have a coachload of uptight footballers worried sick about the ninety minutes coming up. Managers sometimes do forget that it's only a game, after all.

They tell me that during one England trip of recent years the players were treated to an in-flight video of their previous performance – complete with commentary booming throughout the aircraft cabin. Some treat! They must have been bored to tears. If that plane had been struck by lightning on its approach to the airport I wouldn't have been surprised. Somebody had to do something to liven things up.

I livened up our lads when I named the ones I'd chosen for duty. We had three players who needed treatment for injuries of sorts. Frank Clark was a definite non-starter, but there was a chance that Martin O'Neill and Archie Gemmill would play. Had it been left to them, they would have played. They insisted they were fit.

To be fair, when he is faced with the opportunity of playing in a European final, a player could be tempted to lie. I wouldn't only have been tempted, in their position – I would have lied through my teeth. They both said they were OK, but I decided that they were both out. I don't think either of them has forgiven me to this day, but, to be completely frank, we were never the closest of colleagues, even though Gemmill was later to work for me for years as a coach.

My decision to leave out O'Neill was justified to some extent when, a little while later, his hamstring 'went' while he was playing for Northern Ireland. He's a successful manager in his own right these days – he's brought Wycombe into the League, won promotion at the first time of asking, and fully deserved the new contract he signed recently. But when he played for me we often failed to see eye to eye. I looked upon O'Neill as a bit of a smart-arse, and I can't say I was altogether dismayed when he didn't take over from me following my retirement at Forest. I far preferred Frank Clark, and I told the directors so.

As for Gemmill, I know he never forgave me for leaving him out of that final. Knowing him, he would have run and run all night whether he was fully fit or not, but you don't take risks, or shouldn't take risks, in matches of that magnitude, so the decision really made itself.

The Final itself you would call drab, if you weren't calling it bloody awful. The Swedes were not good enough to take us on, and because of our injuries we were never at our best. Just for a few moments we were, though – enough to create and score the only goal.

It was because we were not steeped in European competition and tradition that we did things slightly differently. We honestly regarded it as a break from the League, which was always my priority, anyway. It takes a good manager to win a title over forty-odd matches, but anybody can win a Cup without being that good, just so long as he is lucky. Having said that, I think I won mine because I was that good!

And because Taylor and I worked hard at putting smiles on players' faces. We've been known to take our team to the most austere of training-camps, smack in the middle of nowhere, on pre-season preparations. On the other hand, prior to the 1980 European Cup Semi-Final against Ajax, we took them to the Amsterdam red-light district.

We'd never done it before, but I can't remember any of them shaking their heads when I asked if they fancied going to 'have a look'. I think one of them made sure I had said 'look'. We went there at night, of course, threading our way between the clubs and the sex shops and the live shows where the birds performed. Some of the players were in track suits, others in club sweaters, and as we sauntered towards one establishment 'showing live', Taylor tried to negotiate discount for a block booking. 'Anything off the price for twenty-two of us?' Taylor shouted to the bloke on the door, who then disappeared to the back after asking us to wait 'just a minute.'

When he reappeared, having obviously talked it over with his boss, he told us: 'OK, if you can come back in half an hour.'

'Too late,' said Taylor. 'That's it, deal off, you've had your chance.'

The lads collapsed laughing, I was helpless, Taylor never batted an eyelid or changed his expression. He just waggled his tongue in his cheek in that curious little way of his. And we all wandered off and bought some shrimps and ate them out of the bag.

It wasn't that we tried to do things differently. Even though we had won one European Cup – and earlier that season we had beaten Barcelona over two legs to win the Super Cup as well – we still regarded ourselves as relative newcomers to international club football. In any case, we liked to see a few things and we enjoyed a good laugh. We were a team in every sense of the word.

We had to defy public opinion even to get as far as Amsterdam because in the previous round we had lost 1-0 at home to Dynamo Berlin. Once more, the pundits thought we'd had it – all over, no hope, no chance. Once again, we told everybody they were wrong. Part of the incentive for me was that, as in Cologne, I'd been given an opportunity to sort out the Germans on their own territory. I always loved doing that. It was even more emphatic than last time – we sorted out the Berlin favourites 3-1, no problem, no argument.

It has to be said that although I encouraged an attitude that seemed easy-going to anybody looking in from the outside, no club in England had a more dedicated and committed group of professionals than Nottingham Forest at that time. Carefree in many ways, yes, but we developed little routines. When we found things we liked, we stuck to them. More often than not we used Aer Lingus for our European flights simply because, the first time we hired them, they put on a brand new plane. I think it must have been St Patrick's Day. Whatever the reason, it certainly impressed me, because I'm not the world's most confident flier and need a few drinks before climbing aboard. The sight of an immaculate, gleaming new aircraft filled me with confidence. We also insisted on flying from the East Midlands Airport on our doorstep, which meant we could always get home quicker. We flew in the morning so that we could have breakfast on board – sausage, beans and fried potatoes.

We had beer and champagne as well – doesn't everybody? – and I think John Robertson on occasions sneaked behind the rear seats to have a fag.

As I have said, we sometimes did the unorthodox. The doubters again gave us no chance when we travelled up to Glasgow after a goalless home leg with Celtic in the UEFA Cup – a reasonable assumption, in that the Scots have never been renowned for giving a great deal away. I remembered that the Celtic manager and former player, David Hay, was supposed to have a pub. I talked with our Scottish players, gave the coach driver directions, and announced: 'Right, lads, we're just going to pop into David Hay's pub for half a beer.'

We all trooped in, taking the staff completely by surprise, but they looked after us superbly for more than an hour. One of the biggest problems when you are playing away from home is boredom. Players become bored either sitting in hotels playing cards or practising set-pieces with the manager chuntering on. I'm not sure which is worse. A bored squad of players holed up in an hotel invariably sees one or two of them sneaking out of camp. If my lot wanted a drink – always within reason – I let them. The more you varied the lifestyle, the more they relaxed and enjoyed it.

After a couple of halves or so, it occurred to me that we ought to go and find our hotel and check in. Lunch at two, kip for an hour, and then train on the local golf course. By the time we were back and showered they were serving dinner. Afterwards we had a tired but pleasantly relaxed group of players on our hands, only too ready to take to their beds. Everybody was happy, nobody was moaning or bored. And by the way, we beat Celtic 2-1.

We had no Trevor Francis for the second European Cup Final. He had busted his Achilles' tendon against Crystal Palace four games from the end of the season, so we didn't even take him with us. I think he might just have been a teeny bit miffed. But that's the way it goes, that was my decision, that's management – that's life. We had the likes of Stan Bowles – a lad who liked flying even less than I did and was even known to disappear at the prospect – on the books that season, and we took Charlie George on loan, briefly, from Southampton. They did their bit before I blew them both out, but there was an even more familiar English name waiting for us in Madrid.

Kevin Keegan had made a magnificent career for himself. His achievements at Liverpool and Hamburg were a credit to his total professionalism. I don't know of any individual, in any sport, who made more of his natural talent than Keegan did. He wasn't blessed with intricate ball skills or touch, but he worked at every aspect of his game, like all pros should but not enough of them do, and became an outstanding footballer. Not many Englishmen have been voted 'Man of the Year' in Germany. Keegan was.

But he got a rude awakening at the Bernabéu Stadium. I think he had a space already prepared and waiting for his winner's medal in his trophy cabinet at home. I think the entire Hamburg team had spaces waiting. They were certainly clear favourites. But we were in brilliant nick. Partly because of the place where we had trained – out of town, up in the hills with stunning facilities and a hotel for ourselves. But partly because we had just come back from Majorca. We spent the week prior to the European Cup Final in Cala Millor – doing absolutely bugger-all.

I told the players there would be no training, no formalities. It was a case of get your shorts on and into your flip-flops and down to the beach. And at night have your few drinks – but if you've got a bad head in the morning, don't come complaining to me. We didn't bother with deadlines or whatever they call them, either. The players came and went as they pleased. And if they weren't in till two in the morning they slept till eleven.

These, bear in mind, were professional athletes who had played well in excess of sixty matches already that season and were only a week or so away from the demands of a European Cup Final. The last thing they wanted was physical hard slog or being bored out of their skulls, practising free-kicks. They didn't even want to see a football at that stage. Not for a while, anyway. But I knew that when they next set eyes on one, out on the grass of the Bernabéu Stadium, they would welcome it like a long-lost friend.

Busy doing nothing, soaking up the sunshine and San Miguels in Majorca, was the best preparation any team ever underwent prior to a European final. While we were on the beach, Kevin Keegan and his German team were no doubt 'imprisoned' in a deadly serious training-camp, rehearsing their corner kicks and set pieces for all they were worth. Some do it one way, some prefer another. I know which alternative our players preferred and how much good it did them.

Dear Harry Storer, all those years ago, taught me a basic lesson in football. 'The hardest position in the world to play is centre-forward,' he said. 'Because the hardest thing to do in the game is score a goal.'

I now lean towards the belief that the second most difficult position to play is on the wing. Once they approach the corner flag, as they often do, they are virtually surrounded. If they take the ball one way it's out of play for a goal-kick and if they take it the other way it's out of play for a throw-in. There's a hairy-arsed defender barring their way to the middle and they know they're likely to get kicked. Unless they have a team-mate close by to take a simple little pass, they need the talent to get themselves out of trouble. Not many wingers can do that.

John Robertson could. That night in the stifling heat of the Spanish capital, less than a fortnight after his testimonial game against Leicester, John Robertson enjoyed the highest point of his career. Taylor and I stiffened with expectation on the bench in the Bernabéu Stadium the moment Robbo received the ball on the touch-line, and set off, jinking in and out of the Germans. It was one of those moments – it is difficult to explain why or how – when you just know something special is about to happen. From right outside the box he struck a shot with his right foot – even though he was left-footed. That's how good he felt, that's how much the confidence was oozing from him. From the edge of the penalty box he scored the goal that retained the European Cup for Nottingham Forest.

That night in Madrid the one with the heavy legs and the big backside left Kevin Keegan as flat and limp as a Christmas balloon in spring. It was the first time I experienced sour grapes from Keegan – although they weren't expressed nastily, just out of the depressed feeling that comes with defeat. I bumped into him doing an interview at the airport on our way home and he was complaining about our tactics, saying he was disappointed with the way Forest had played. What he failed to point out was that we had no bloody choice. We'd had no Trevor Francis for a start, so Garry Birtles had been forced to run his balls off up front all on his own. I've never seen a lad cover as much ground, willingly and unselfishly, as Birtles did that night. Honestly, I've never seen a more exhausted footballer than Birtles was afterwards in all my time in the game. On top of that, I'd played eighteen-year-old Gary Mills in Francis's place – not up front but as part of a protective midfield. What's wrong with playing an eighteen-year-old in a European Cup Final if you think he's good enough? Management is about judgement, not the ability to read birth certificates.

In the dying minutes of that final we were really sweating, begging the referee to blow his whistle. My lot were dead on their feet. They were entitled to be after the effort they'd put in, but some unkind people suggested the San Miguels were taking their toll! Hamburg were desperately searching for an equaliser.

Suddenly I spotted Keegan in the right-back position as the ball ran out of play and the referee blew his whistle. Taylor and I leapt to our feet, thinking it was all over, but he'd only blown for a bloody throw-in. We had to sit through another thirty seconds that seemed like thirty minutes, but I looked at Keegan's position, deep in his own half – and, I must say, still wanting the ball – and I knew it was a tribute to the way Kenny Burns had played him. He and Larry Lloyd hadn't scared Keegan, exactly, but he'd not been able to make much of an impression. They had seen him off. No wonder he was disappointed at the way we played.

A group of our players were disappointed when I imposed fines on them before we had even set off home with the biggest trophy a team can win. As I have explained, we had tucked ourselves away in an hotel miles out of Madrid. The players' wives, girlfriends and members of the Forest staff were staying in the city, and after the match several of the players asked if they could go into town and join them.

'Not a prayer,' I told them – and despite their impassioned and heated attempts to persuade me to change my mind I refused. 'We decided to stay in this hotel and that's the way it is. We came here together as a team and we stick together as a team. I don't want any of you pissing off into town or anywhere else. We've won the European Cup together and we'll celebrate together.'

But that group, including O'Neill, Lloyd, Robertson and Burnsy, I seem to remember, made up their own minds to defy my orders. When I found out I was so incensed that I decided to confiscate their winners' medals. Can you imagine the outcry that would have caused back home? I would have had the FA, the League, the players' union, perhaps even the House of Commons gunning for me! After giving it a lot of thought, I opted for fining them a few quid apiece. The principle was the same. And they had to pay up – aye, even John Robertson whose goal had just won the European Cup. You don't bend the rules – even for heroes.

18

THE PARTING OF THE WAYS

When I was admitted to the heart unit, somebody
sent me a 'get well telegram' that said 'we didn't
know you even had one'.

THE NIGHT WE WON OUR FIRST EUROPEAN CUP, IN MUNICH, I COULDN'T
resist digging Taylor in the ribs. 'You do realise where we could
have been today,' I asked, 'don't you?' He knew exactly what I
meant.

Peter Taylor and I had carried Nottingham Forest to heights
they had never imagined – in the face of several previous

attempts to lure us back to our old home at Derby. On more than one occasion, Taylor was keen to go.

Not me. The memories of the good times there lingered on and gave me a warm glow or two on the rare occasions I had time to sit and ponder. But I was never seriously tempted to return to the Baseball Ground. Whenever I mentioned the possibility to Barbara, she would say: 'Never go back while Sam Longson and Stuart Webb are still at the club.'

I did the decent thing, the first time they came for us. I agreed to meet their new chairman, George Hardy, at his home. One of the first subjects he raised was money.

'Try not to be greedy,' he said.

'Me? I've never been greedy in my life.' I had a fair idea what he was up to, the stroke he was trying to pull – he wanted me on the cheap.

Some of the businessmen who come into football are strange creatures. They talk about their love of the game and all that, but more than anything, football gives them notoriety, a platform, publicity, fame on a scale they would never get from being scrap-dealers, property men, haulage contractors or even tycoons. Take the case of Robert Maxwell, if you can stomach the prospect. He was known in certain circles, of course, and he was known even better when he bought national newspapers. But when he had the *Daily Mirror* and Derby County – oh, what a combination that turned out to be! He had an ego bigger than his yacht – perhaps that's why he fell overboard!

Once he had Derby in his empire he had another excuse for plastering his own picture in his own papers. Even television massaged his ego by showing him lumbering all over the Baseball Ground wearing a silly hat and celebrating in front of fans who couldn't stand the man.

Hardy wasn't in that league, but, like most chairmen, he felt he could call the shots and get his own way. As I listened to him chuntering on I was damn sure he felt that all he had to do was to flannel me for a few minutes and I'd come running down the A52 back to Derby, hand in hand with Taylor.

'There is something I'd like to show you,' he said, leading me outside. 'It's my son's coming of age.'

'Oh, smashing. Wish him Happy Birthday from me.'

'This is what I've bought him,' said Hardy as we stood in front of a gleaming sports car. Did he realise what he was saying? Here was a man who wanted me to return to Derby for relative peanuts – and he was showing me a bloody birthday present that must have cost a fortune. He made me feel about as valuable as a second-hand Mini.

I went straight back to Taylor and told him: 'There's no way I'm going back there.'

But Derby were to come for us again, early in 1977, and again Barbara was adamant that I shouldn't go. This time, though, Taylor was dead keen. My only thought was: 'You bastards . . . you've had to come back because you're in the cart.' By then they were even more run down than they had been when we first went there. If it had not been for Arthur Cox taking over in June 1984 and lifting them from the Third Division to the First in successive seasons from 1986, the club we turned into League Champions might not be with us today.

Taylor thought we were going to be with them again, though. Not only did he talk to Derby – he agreed to them setting up a press conference to announce our return! He must have assured Stuart Webb that we were going.

'How about it then, when are we going?' he kept repeating, day after day. It reached the stage where Stuart Dryden became so concerned that he called us together. During a pause in the meeting Taylor put me in a corner and said: 'We should go – the time is right to go.'

'You can do what you like,' I told him. 'But I'm not f**king going anywhere.'

As he walked out of the office Taylor was still mumbling to himself: 'We'll be going, we'll be going.' Peter wouldn't take 'No' for an answer.

I'm sure he had told Webb that he would be able to talk me round. I can imagine Taylor saying to him: 'Don't worry, we'll be there – trust me.' He and Webb were of the same ilk – money-wise, street-wise, look-after-yourself-wise, both excellent at their jobs.

Typically, Taylor would not be there when the shit hit the fan. I went into work at Forest, as usual, and found him dressed up like a dummy out of Burton's window – suit, tie, the lot.

'We're due across at Derby,' he announced.

'Eh? You're bloody pushing it, pal. How many times do I have to tell you – I ain't going to Derby.'

'Well, they've got a press conference arranged, so we've got a problem.'

Note the convenient use of the word 'we', yet again. Taylor had dropped himself in it, but I was the one expected to get us out of it.

'This is daft,' I told him, 'but I'll go over and tell them they're wasting their time.'

I've always said 'Nothing surprises me in football' and, in general terms, that's true. But I had completely underestimated the scale of the event Taylor had allowed Derby to arrange. They were all set up in the boardroom – directors, Press, umpteen camera crews – and the champagne on ice. There were crowds outside as well, because word travels fast in Derby – especially where Brian Clough is concerned.

Webby met me at the door. I said to him: 'Before you take me through, you do realise I'm not coming back here, don't you?' For a second I think he believed I was kidding. But one look at my expression was enough. His face drained to a ghostly white.

'But we've got the cameras here,' he said, and looking over his shoulder I could see the cables trailing in the passage.

'Well, you'd better take me straight to the directors and I'll get it over and done with in two seconds.'

And there they all were. Every one of them shook hands with me. Yes, even Sam Longson. He was no longer chairman but he was there, and I shook his hand. There had been bitterness but it was beginning to fade and, in any case, I was ready to do whatever was necessary to get me in and out of there, double-quick. I hit them with it straight away: 'Gentlemen, before you say or do a thing – I am not coming back to your club.' Stunned silence!

One of them said, eventually: 'Well, you'll have to get us out of the cart. You'll have to explain.' So I met the press boys and muddled through some short statement as best I could, actually apologising for the inconvenience that had been caused to so many people. I even popped my head into the office of Colin Murphy, the stand-in manager, and told him: 'Get yourself a new contract, Col. I'm not coming near the place.' The poor lad was fired not long afterwards, and I seem to recall me insisting to George Hardy that he should treat Murphy fairly and pay him every penny he was due.

Taylor remained at Forest in his shirt and tie, enjoying a gin and tonic while I went and sorted out the mess he and Webby had created between them.

In fact, Taylor did quite nicely by staying with Forest. Soon after joining the club he had borrowed £5,000 from them to help towards buying a house. He sometimes used to borrow money even if he didn't need it – on principle! After I had turned down Derby he beckoned me into his office and said: 'Will you do me a favour, if you're adamant we're not going back?'

'Oh, I'm adamant. I'm going nowhere.'

'In that case, then, will you ask Forest to get rid of that £5,000? We've got to get something out of this.'

'And what do I get out of it?' I asked him.

'I'm sure you'll get "Good-morning" from the directors when you ask them!'

Classic Taylor! Could it be that he became five grand better off on the strength of me saying 'No' to a move I had no intention of making anyway? Now that is nice work if you can get it.

Nothing lasts for ever, and the end of our great partnership was one of the enormous changes that took place in the early years after winning that second European Cup. The double act that some in the game mischievously referred to as the 'Kray twins' had run its course. I was not to know it at the time, but so had a wonderful, brilliant friendship.

It had survived many rows and differences. Football is about opinions and they are bound to differ, occasionally. Taylor regarded the question of which players to buy as his province, his domain, and he resented advice from 'outsiders', or even from colleagues.

He used to enjoy telling me of one director who had more courage than most and was not afraid of standing up to Peter during his time as manager at Burton Albion.

'The trouble with you, Taylor, is that you think you know everything,' the director complained.

'You're dead right. Compared with you I *do* know everything.'

He told that story over and over. But it wasn't a joke with Taylor, it was serious.

At one stage, when Taylor was watching one game a week rather than three or four, the local radio commentator, Colin Slater, was seeing more matches than he was. Slater was a good friend of Geoffrey Macpherson, a Forest director I once described as a bumbling amateur. Macpherson came in one morning and said: 'I have been recommended a centre-forward. I've had a tip-off about a lad who plays for Chester – Ian Rush.'

'Ian Rush can't play at all,' Taylor grumbled after Macpherson had gone out.

'But have you seen him, that's the point,' I said. 'Cover yourself if you haven't. Go and see him.'

I'm certain he didn't bother. I think Ian Rush went on to score a goal or two in a reasonably successful side, didn't he?

Kevin Keegan had similar success at Liverpool, and I suppose I should have signed him on the strength of what I saw one grey, murky night at Scunthorpe. We were at Derby, then.

'Any good?' Taylor asked next morning.

'Aye, it wasn't a bad match and I saw a kid called Keegan.' His name had been whispered around and quite a few of the big clubs were taking a close interest.

'And what did you think?'

'Well,' I said, 'considering he was in a Scunthorpe side that struggled I thought he did quite well.'

'Yeah . . .' said Taylor, none too interested. 'They've all looked at him.'

'Have you bloody looked at him – that's the main thing.'

It wasn't long afterwards that Keegan was transferred to Anfield, even though Bill Shankly himself hadn't seen him play, and we all know what kind of career Keegan had from then on.

Peter set himself up as a supreme judge of talent, and on most occasions it was justified. But he took exception to others suggesting possible targets. It was ironic that his departure from Forest occurred during the same span of time that saw the departures of some of the highly talented individuals he had brought to the club – among them Birtles, Francis, Burns, Shilton and Lloyd.

It was towards the end of the 1982 season – a not too clever season, either, seeing that we finished only twelfth – when he slumped in an easy chair, sighed, and said: 'I think we've shot it.' The royal 'we' yet again. He was on his knees, but 'we' were in trouble.

There were only three games left, and we had just been beaten at home by Manchester United in a run of five games that had brought us only one point. Defeat always got him down. We sat there for ten minutes or so and hardly another word was spoken until he broke the silence: 'I'm going to pack it in. I'm going to retire.'

He was genuinely depressed – not only by the results, but by some of the players he had persuaded me to buy. When I look back on them, he was more than entitled to be depressed – I'm surprised he wasn't downright suicidal! Ian Wallace, the 'poof' Justin Fashanu, and a lad called Peter Ward had between them cost the club a total of around two and a half million quid, which was a hell of a lot of money then, particularly for players who rarely looked like justifying the investment.

'So what do you want me to do?'

'I want you to get me out with a few quid and my Jag.'

There was no point in trying to talk him out of it. He looked all in. He'd clearly had enough. One particular, worrying memory flashed across my mind – the heart attack Taylor had suffered at Derby in 1970, a minor one, but a heart attack all the same. He'd complained of feeling unwell, so I had told him to put his fag out for a start and take some time off. When he came back from a holiday in Majorca he was still worried, so I took him to a specialist friend of mine who put him through extensive tests, diagnosed the slight attack, and wouldn't even allow Peter to drive his car home. Peter was told to take two and a half months off, but after only four or five weeks unsympathetic directors were asking when he was coming back. The men who didn't know the nature of Taylor's job thought they were paying him for nothing.

I remembered, as well, my own little 'flutter', the Christmas prior to Peter's decision to pack it in. I was never completely certain about the detail of my problem, although I suppose I should have had a clue when they whisked me into the coronary section of Derby's Royal Infirmary. There was speculation that suggested another bout of pneumonia. Obviously there were questions about the ticker. But I wasn't kept in for very long, and if you ask my opinion I reckon the problem was either too many brandies over Christmas or too many bad signings over recent months!

I knew that when Taylor went, most of the laughter would go with him – brilliant, spur-of-the-moment humour, like the day we were invited to meet Princess Margaret on a royal visit to Nottingham. It was some charity 'do', and I was intrigued to see her 'fagging it' at one point. When the proceedings reached the formal stage, with everyone standing quietly and virtually to attention, I felt a sudden hefty dig in the ribs. I could only turn and scowl a 'behave yourself' look at Taylor, standing next to me. Bang! In came the elbow again and the whispered instruction: 'Tell her we won the European Cup.' I just started to laugh, people looked puzzled if not annoyed at my apparent bad manners but Taylor kept on: 'Tell her, go on – she'll be interested.' Daft, I know, but I did tell her in the end – and she said 'Good', without giving the impression that she was totally over the moon about it, as Taylor seemed to expect.

Oh yes, I had many fond memories of the times we spent together. Now I was genuinely concerned for the man who had shared so much with me and my family, becoming an 'Uncle' to my children. Here he was in my office, looking a little bit bewildered, considerably fatigued – but not quite exhausted enough to forget that it would be handy if he could keep his company car.

So I went to the board, told them of his decision and, as I have said before, I fought for him like a brother. He wasn't very popular with the directors, who didn't want to pay him threepence. They used to think the assistant manager – when he wasn't away talent spotting – should have been at his desk from nine in the morning till four in the afternoon. They knew Taylor was rarely in before quarter to ten and most days he would 'shoot off' by one o'clock at the latest – with *The Sporting Chronicle* tucked under his arm.

But those directors were wrong and I told them so. Did they really believe Taylor had played no part in winning the Championship and all those cups? They weren't getting away with any cheapskate excuses for not seeing him off with a bob or two in his pocket. I negotiated for him a pay-off in excess of £25,000. And he took his precious Jag, although I think he had flogged it within weeks. He disappeared to Majorca for just about the entire summer – but guess what happened only a few months after he told me we had 'shot it'?

I took a telephone call and there was Peter's familiar voice. 'I'm thinking of coming out of retirement and taking over at Derby,' he announced. 'Any chance of you coming with me?' Taylor, bloody Taylor! But I loved him.

19

MY WAY

Neil Webb won't refuse a contract. He knows that
if he turns me down I'll give him our equivalent of
Chinese water torture. I'll lock him in a room with
our directors.

ONE THING THAT STUCK IN MY CRAW WHEN PETER TAYLOR 'RETIRED'
was the commonly expressed view that I would not be able to manage without him; that Nottingham Forest would be found wanting
in the department he filled so successfully – despite persuading us
to buy the likes of Justin Fashanu!

I gathered good people around me. Ron Fenton became my assistant and was a valuable friend and ally over the next few years. I nicked Alan Hill from Notts County to come and work with me again on the youth and scouting sides of the club. Liam O'Kane was not only a trusted colleague, but a coach who smiled a hell of a lot more than Archie Gemmill.

In the years after Taylor quit we finished third in the League on three occasions, we were twice semi-finalists and once runners-up in the FA Cup, twice League Cup winners and once beaten finalists, and semi-finalists in the UEFA Cup. Oh, and we won the Simod Cup and ZDS Cup, whatever that is. Now that doesn't look to me much like the record of a failure, even though my last season and relegation from the Premiership in 1993 certainly does – and was.

It was bound to be different after Taylor left, but let no-one be in any doubt – some of the teams we built during the following years gave me just as much satisfaction and delight as those of the past, even the one that won the European Cups.

There was no replacing Taylor, of course. Ron Fenton was nothing like Peter. Chalk and cheese. Where Taylor made me laugh, throughout our times together, Ron seemed to find it difficult to smile himself. In fact, he's become a far more relaxed and jovial individual since we both left the City Ground. There were times when I used to say to him on a Monday morning: 'If you were a salesman, with that expression on your face, you couldn't sell water to a man dying of thirst.'

For all that, Ron was a genuine, reliable, honest and loyal working partner who shared with me a great deal of success over eleven seasons after Taylor and I parted company – eleven seasons in which we never finished lower than ninth, apart from that awful, final season of 1992-93.

We might not have won another League title, but we played the kind of football supporters loved to watch and maintained our standards. I detested the sight of players mouthing off at match officials, lashing the ball away in disgust just because a decision had gone against them. Throughout my career in management I not only frowned on players who showed stupidity and childishness of that kind – I fined them for it. It never ceases to amaze me how many managers complain about what they call the over-reaction of referees towards the futile practice of dissent. It's the managers who are as much to blame as the offending players, because the man in charge of the team has the authority and the opportunity to cut it out – at a stroke. It was never a problem to me.

We didn't do too badly with some of the signings and débuts made after Taylor's departure, either. Stuart Pearce, Des Walker, Neil Webb and Lee Chapman were part of a list that doesn't strike me as a roll-call for dummies.

Lee Chapman had come from France. He'd been with Stoke, Plymouth, Arsenal and Sunderland, and had played in Sweden and France before I paid £350,000 for him. Derby thought he was their man – in fact, Robert Maxwell announced as much in his *Daily Mirror* with a sports-page story that said Chapman had as good as signed for Derby and that they had beaten me to it. Some exclusive!

We were in Scotland for some reason, and the agent Dennis Roach was with us when we first heard that Chapman might be on his way back to England.

'I have Chapman's number, if you want it,' said Roach, which was hardly surprising seeing that he had the number of just about every footballer able to draw breath in Britain or throughout the rest of the world!

When I phoned, Chapman said immediately: 'I'd much rather come to Forest than to Derby,' and the deal was done.

It was the best move Chapman ever made. We improved his game to such an extent that he was unrecognisable compared with the player the Highbury fans used to jeer at. He slipped into our style. He improved because we gave him the ball below the level of his forehead. He received it at his feet 90 per cent more than at any time previously in his career. Although he was never a great goal-scorer, he got his quota with us, so I was staggered when he announced he would have to go.

And I do mean Chapman *had* to go. It was not so much a transfer I organised for him – more a favour. He had been badly advised, financially, over his transfer to France, and he suddenly found the Inland Revenue pushing him for their entitled cut from his money.

'I'll get crucified if I let you go now,' I told him. 'You're having your best-ever spell with us.'

'But I've got a big house with a big mortgage and I just don't have the money to pay the tax people,' he said. 'I need a signing-on fee. I have to get away.'

I always liked young Chapman. So I agreed to let him leave even though it was against my better footballing judgement. Howard Wilkinson at Leeds paid £400,000 for him in January 1990. There are occasions when players have to move, in the interests of themselves and their families, and this was one of them.

It was only a few months after that Simod Cup win at Wembley when many good judges – our own John Robertson among them – described that Forest side as being superior, in some ways, to the one that had triumphed in Europe at the start of the decade. There were certainly more players who were comfortable with the ball and able to pass it.

Neil Webb, who arrived at the City Ground in 1985, was one of my most effective signings. Several clubs wanted Webb, Queens Park Rangers and Aston Villa among them, but no-one had a chance once we had met at an hotel in London after a Forest game against Tottenham. At that time, though, people weren't sure where he was likely to be most effective. Was he a striker or a midfield player? He had not established himself as one or the other at Portsmouth.

As I've said before, management is about judgement and the ability to make decisions. In his first full game with us Webb attempted some kind of fancy cross from the touch-line and succeeded only in flipping the ball out of play. So I dragged him off, sending on a substitute instead. I told him that it was hard enough trying to play the ball normally without attempting to chip the bloody thing from that kind of position. 'You've got to remember to keep the ball on the field,' I said.

We taught Webb his game. We taught him how to become a midfield player because, at first, he didn't tackle enough. When I asked him his first job in midfield he spluttered and looked confused, so I told him: 'Your first job is to get the ball, because we can't play without it.' Eventually we got him into the England side – as we did with so many others.

So success followed success. Like the League Cup win in 1990, with a goal from a lad who might not have lived to see the day if I'd caught him right, the night I clouted him in the dressing-room at Derby. Nigel Jemson had as big a head as I have!

His father is a police officer and his mother often wrote to thank me for looking after her son. I think she appreciated the fact that the discipline at my club would do him the world of good. He learned it the painful way.

Our reserve side were winning a match at Derby but were tired, almost on their knees, with ten minutes to go. I sent Jemson on as substitute, with instructions to play on the right and to run the ball to the corner flag at every opportunity. As usual, he wanted the limelight. He started running inside with the ball and being caught in possession, putting a hard-earned victory at risk. When I got to the dressing-room I was blazing.

I repeated to him what my instructions had been and when he spluttered something about thinking he could hit a pass or run for goal, I just said 'Stand up,' – and clouted him.

He never quite managed to convince me he was worthy of an established place in my side, and he didn't convince Trevor Francis, either, after moving to Sheffield Wednesday. Francis has rung me several times to say: 'I can't get anything out of this lad. All he seems to want is to get back to Nottingham.'

It's funny how many players who left Forest wanted to return. Many turned up at matches when they were not on duty for their new clubs. We built that kind of intimate place and an atmosphere in which everybody felt relaxed at at home.

Garry Birtles was another player who left and then came back. We had sold him to Manchester United for a million, but he failed to make the grade at Old Trafford, as so many others have failed there, and he came back for a second spell at the City Ground. Perhaps he had forgotten while he was away that I could never stand moaners.

It was one of those matches you accept against your better judgement, a long haul to the Middle East somewhere, for the guarantee of a few thousand extra pounds for the club coffers. I never liked those jaunts, particularly, but there were times when they had to be done. I was up at five in the morning to drive from home to the City Ground to get the coach to Heathrow and I was feeling delicate. Who doesn't at five in the flamin' morning? Birtles was grumbling under his breath when I arrived, and just wouldn't stop. None of the players was particularly chuffed to be boarding the bus at that time of day but at least, like me, they put a brave face on it, and when they hadn't anything bright or interesting to say they kept their mouths shut.

Not Birtles. He went on and on and on. I warned him several times, but it made no difference. I could hear him still complaining: 'What are we doing here? Why do we have to go all that way?' as the coach headed out of Nottingham towards the motorway. Enough was enough.

'Driver – stop the coach. Somebody's getting off,' I shouted. And everybody fell silent and listened.

'Birtles . . . off!'

'But . . . gaffer . . .'

'Never mind the buts. I'm sick and bloody tired of listening to you whingeing and moaning about something we're all having to put up with. Off!'

'But what do I do from here? How am I supposed to get home?'

'Haven't a clue. You should have thought about that when you were complaining. We know how we're getting to the airport – you make your own arrangements. Find a phone box and call a taxi. Ta-ra.'

We shut the door of the coach and left the million-pound footballer at the side of the road.

I can't stand moaners. I can't stand flying either, and although I adore children I can't stand kids – or anybody for that matter – mucking about while I'm waiting to take off. We were on the plane, waiting, and there seemed to be children all over the place. I was sitting alongside John Lawson, a local journalist and friend, and these nippers kept leaping about and bumping me.

I said to the bloke in front: 'Get your kids under control and make sure you keep them away from me.' But it had no effect whatsoever. He didn't say a word. The kids kept bouncing around, I was getting more and more steamed up, and eventually I could take no more. I leaned forward and clouted the bloke, shouting: 'I've told you once already, get your kids away from me.'

He spoke for the first time. 'They're not my kids. They're nothing to do with me!' I didn't say another word – until that flight, intended for the Middle East, attempted to take off. I am petrified even when things go according to plan. When they don't, I'm not keen on hanging around. That plane set off OK, but somewhere along the runway it began to shudder and slowed down. And stopped. Apparently, after taxiing back and checking it out, the plan was to have another run at it. But not for me, it wasn't.

I called a stewardess and told her: 'Tell your skipper we're getting off.'

'But you can't get off,' she said. 'We won't be opening the door.'

'Tell your skipper that if you won't open the door I will be opening it, because we are leaving this plane. *Now!*'

They opened the door and we got off and eventually went back to Nottingham. I don't know what happened to the match guarantee. I couldn't have cared less. I've never regretted getting off an aircraft in my life. What did upset me a bit was that Birtles was home before us!

It was an isolated incident with him. He was a good pro and never much bother. Which is more than can be said for one of the signings Taylor lumbered me with when he packed it in. Justin Fashanu was a total pain in the neck. I have to say I was surprised to read, in recent years, that he'd been dating the landlady from *Coronation Street*'s Rovers Return – is it Bet Lynch they call her? I'd have thought he'd have been more likely to ask out Jack Duckworth.

We spent a million pounds on Fashanu and it must have been the worst money we ever invested. He'd just scored a well-publicised goal for Norwich against Liverpool that was shown time after time on BBC Television's *Match of the Day* and was voted Goal of the Season. There were times, after we bought him, when he looked as if he would never score again. He managed a pathetic 10 per cent return – three goals from thirty-one league games, plus one appearance as substitute.

Glory days.
John Sumpter

Shaking hands with captain Dave Mackay after Derby win the Second Division trophy, 1969. *Peter Robinson/Empics*

The ITV World Cup panel, 1974. Me on the left, Derek Dougan, Pat Crerand, Brian Moore, Bobby Moncur, Malcolm Allison and Jack Charlton; *London Weekend*

John Robertson scores the only goal in the 1980 European Cup Final to give Forest victory over Hamburg. *Peter Robinson/Empics*

The 1979 European Cup Final: Nottingham Forest 1, Malmo 0. *Peter Robinson/Empics*

Holding hands with Tottenham manager, Terry Venables, before the 1991 FA Cup Final - the only major trophy I never won. *Steve Mitchell/Empics*

March 1993, and I am made a Freeman of the City of Nottingham. I told those attending the ceremony: 'I had a walk along the River Trent today - as you know, it's my normal practice to walk on it.' *Ross Kinnaird/Empics*

With my OBE: some rude people have suggested it was the Order of the Big 'Ead. *J.M.S. Photography*

Collecting money for a Multiple Sclerosis charity walk.
Steve Etherington/ Empics

Showing solidarity with the miners.
Claire Mackintosh/ Empics

Sad day: my last game after more than eighteen years as manager ends in a 2-0 victory for Sheffield United and relegation for Forest.
Bob Thomas

Retirement at Quarndon. Time to take the dog for a walk.

Some players failed to impress me for various reasons. I bought Gary Megson, but didn't play him because I didn't rate him. I didn't think he had the ability to trap a bag of sand. He's gone on to enjoy a good career and I'm delighted for him. I signed John Sheridan and didn't play him either. For a start, we couldn't get him to smile, and for another thing – like little Asa Hartford who was given just three league games before we moved him on – he wasn't our kind of midfield player. Sheridan would play a pass and then stand. We wanted movement in our team – so we moved him on to Sheffield Wednesday. When you make a mistake over a signing the best remedy is always to admit it, as quickly as possible – and get rid, if you can.

That's what happened to Fashanu, but only after a great deal of trouble. He was sent off again and again. I had to bollock him for throwing his boots to the crowd – God knows how many times he thought we were going to provide him with new ones! I once booked him into a nursing home to have an operation on his feet. He had peculiarly shaped big toes and we thought that might be one of the problems, contributing to his awful scoring record. He just didn't turn up for the operation.

Fashanu had a habit of parking his jeep where he shouldn't. I became tired and weary of complaints about his parking-tickets. At one stage we had virtually lost count of the number of unpaid tickets he had totted up from one woman warden – there must have been between twenty and thirty. A police sergeant came to see me and said: 'I'm sorry, Brian, but we are going to have to do him.'

'Don't be sorry,' I said. 'Don't keep warning him. Don't tolerate it a minute longer – put him in gaol.' I pulled Fashanu in and said: 'You must have thirty parking-tickets by now. If you don't get them paid off, the police have received my permission to put you in the nick.' He paid.

The lad was a mixed-up individual. He came to me one

day and announced: 'I've found God.' He rambled on about it, I think he became a born-again Christian or something.

'Found God?' I said to him. 'Good. I should get him to sign a few cheques for you.'

I was getting phone calls telling me Fashanu was frequenting a particular club well known as a meeting place for homosexuals. That in itself didn't bother me too much – it was just that his shiftiness, combined with an articulate image that impressed the impressionable, made it difficult for me to accept Fashanu as genuine and one of us. I called him in and put him to the test.

'Where do you go if you want a loaf of bread?' I asked him.

'A baker's, I suppose.'

'Where do you go if you want a leg of lamb?'

'A butcher's.'

'So why do you keep going to that bloody poofs' club in town?'

He shrugged. He knew what I meant and it wasn't long before I could stand no more of him. He had his own religious teacher, or whatever he called him, and his own masseur. But when he turned up for training with one of them – that was it. I ordered him out of the training-ground, I wanted him off our patch. But he refused to go.

It did cross my mind that he had done a bit of boxing. He had been quite useful at it, by all accounts. I might have been in a bit of danger – but there could be no backing down. If this was to be a confrontation, in front of the rest of the players, there had to be only one winner. Me.

It reached the stage where I threatened him with the police. When he still refused to leave, I phoned them and asked: 'Can you please send one of your men down here to arrest Justin Fashanu?' Soon two of the smallest coppers I have ever seen arrived. I thought Fashanu was going to pick them up and put them in his pocket. He stood his ground, at first, but eventually he was led away, protesting. There was a song and dance about it for a while – players' union indignation and all that – but it soon died down. We managed to get Notts County to take him off our hands, but he didn't survive for very long on the other side of the Trent. He moved on again, this time quietly.

Unlike another alarming incident in Spain, where Ronnie Fenton was in charge. Ron heard a hell of a commotion along the hotel corridor, a sound like a gunshot, at two o'clock in the morning. Colin Lawrence was woken as well, and the pair of them went to investigate at the bedroom Fashanu was sharing with Viv Anderson.

The door was in splinters, with a huge hole right through the middle. They found Viv huddled at the top of his bed, with the sheets up to his neck and his eyes as wide as 'Rochester's'. He must have been still in shock because neither he nor Fashanu – soaking his damaged hands in the wash-basin – said anything for a while. It transpired that Fashanu had been having a nightmare. He had bounced up and down on his bed and then hurled himself clean through the door. Strange boy!

Most of the publicity surrounding Justin Fashanu since then seems to have centred on his private life. I presume he's still visiting the same places when he's in need of a loaf of bread!

No, buying Fashanu was not one of Taylor's better decisions. Of course Peter was missed. Of course there were seasons of indifferent achievement and of course the club should never have lost its status in the top bracket of the game. But it might have been lost altogether, in the mid-1980s.

Unless I had stepped in with a cheque for £35,000, Nottingham Forest could have ceased to operate. The club was broke. Skint, down-and-out, all washed up. It's not easy retrieving big money spent on bad players. Bank interest charges on a three-million-pound stand can be crippling and in our case became desperately serious. A tax bill was overdue, and the tax people had been ready to serve their writ the following day.

Now, I've never been one for chucking my own money around, but Forest had reached such dire straits that it was left to me to get them out of trouble. I rang the Inland Revenue and asked them: 'Would you accept a cheque signed by me?'

'Yes,' I was told, 'we would definitely accept your cheque, but we cannot accept any more promises or cheques from your club.'

So I signed one of mine and kept them alive and kicking. I had dug them out of trouble – only to have to do it again, this time using their assets and on a far bigger scale – scattering the wolves from the door with the £750,000 sale of Peter Davenport to Manchester United.

I was to get my £35,000 back, but I wasn't so bright, or so lucky a few years later, when my chairman Maurice Roworth, who was supposed to be an accountant, came to me with money troubles of his own. I didn't ask him for the exact details, but I had the impression that it was a temporary difficulty – what do they call them, cash-flow problems? – and that it would not be very long before he could reimburse me. I lent him £108,000. I have not been a total prat about money on too many occasions, but this was one of them. Roworth was arrested and eventually sent to prison for fraud, around a million quid adrift. I will never forgive the man for taking my money in such circumstances. If he knew he was going down the pan to the tune of one million pounds, why make it 1.1 million pounds at my expense? I'm not sure precisely how long he served in jail but I'm not convinced it was long enough. I don't suppose I'll ever see that money again.

But amid the problems of the 1980s another young man emerged, not only right out of the Clough mould but straight out of the Clough family. Our Nige made a massive and extremely brave decision. The little fella who had once slept all the way home under my seat on a long-haul flight, decided he would like to come and work for me. Now I'm telling you, it is never easy for a child to work for a parent – but when the gaffer in question is this particular father I know the arrangement was far harder for him than for me.

My attitude was simple, straightforward and to the point: 'You'll make a living if you're good enough, but if you're not, you'll be out.'

I have no greater regard for Nigel than I have for his elder brother, Simon, or his younger sister, Elizabeth. I love them all, dearly, and know that with their 'old man' they, like their mother, have had a great deal to put up with!

I do believe, though, that Nigel – 'the Number 9' or 'the centre-forward', as I referred to him when we were at work – deserves the utmost credit, not only for the way he endured me as his boss, but for the dignified manner in which he has conducted himself. He has won a lot more England caps than me – and I think he should have had just a few more!

After leaving school he had played for AC Hunters, a Sunday League team his brother had organised, which played on a municipal park in Derby. Simon might have made the grade as a player too – who knows? He could play a ball and he could get up and head it. But he had no chance after his bad knee injury – like the one that finished me – in his late teens.

We were all involved with the Hunters. I had no official capacity but I was there, week in week out, supporting them even in the pissing rain. A lot of the Forest lads became involved and even when they were established pros, Nigel included, they would turn up and often run the line.

I used Hunters matches for giving trials to possible signings. There was one occasion when we took a lad from Sweden on a fortnight's trial. His name escapes me, but he was an international at one level or another. He had worked hard in training and played in a couple of practice matches, but the reports from the backroom staff weren't good. 'He can't play,' they told me. 'Well, I'll have to have a look at him,' I said. 'He's come all the way from bloody Sweden. Get him in AC Hunters on Sunday.'

He played, but he didn't shape up. I told them at the ground next day: 'Get him back on the next boat.' Unfortunately, when he got home, he took part in a television interview. Yes, he had met Mr Clough. And, yes, Nottingham was a very nice place. And, yes, he had been very impressed but he had only played in one competitive match – and that was for a team called Hunters.

The lad had said what he said in all innocence. AC Hunters had just slipped out as easily as if he'd been saying AC Milan. You know what the Swedes are like, they speak better flaming English than we do.

The Football League were informed, probably by someone who had seen the television interview. They wrote to us, asking for an explanation as to why a foreign player, brought over for trials, had only been given a game in a Sunday League side unconnected with Forest! They didn't fine us but warned us that it was an unwise practice and not to do it again. I'm not sure which rules we had broken but we did find out that the lad wasn't good enough.

The Hunters' opposition included some real rough diamonds, right villains, occasionally. I think the Sunday League is the hardest league in the business. But as well as the villains, there were some smashing fellas and some nice little teams, and it was a good learning ground for a budding professional.

In fact, Nigel still played for the Hunters on Sundays after playing for the Forest first team the day before! He was an amateur, initially, at the City Ground, so I was able to make sure he was fully occupied at weekends!

Of course there were the leg-pullers and mickey-takers in the Sunday League. Inevitably, Nigel was targeted for more than his share. And one day there was a nasty little incident. Hunters were playing away, although the ground was still fairly local, and when I called into the dressing-room to see the players before the game they were all strangely quiet. Quiet is something that lads of sixteen to nineteen usually are not! I looked at our Simon, and saw that his head was so low it was almost on the floor.

My first thought was that somebody had forgotten the corner flags. At that level of the game you provide your own flags as well as buckets and sponges and if anybody forgets them, all hell breaks loose. I could sense it wasn't the flags, but experience told me summat was up. I wondered if the little lad who saved everybody's valuables in a bag – watches, loose change, etc – had been whipping things again. Then I looked across at Nigel and saw a red patch covering most of his face.

'And what's happened to you?'

He wouldn't say anything, as usual, but one of the other lads chirped up: 'Their goalkeeper's just slung a cup of tea over him.'

I went straight to the other dressing-room and confronted their keeper. 'Have you just thrown tea over my son?'

When he admitted it I decided to prosecute. I cancelled the match and called the police. An inspector arrived with a colleague. 'I don't want any problems,' I said, 'but I do want this lad charging.' We all finished up at the police station and the lad concerned was eventually taken to court and fined. That was one incident where Nigel was picked out because of me. He has always had that cross to bear.

Like most parents we took care in trying to steer them all clear of pitfalls. It was obvious, pretty early in his life, that Nigel was more than useful with a football at his feet. All that practice with Dave Mackay in the old shooting-box under the stand at Derby had paid off. He stayed at school until he got his A levels in French, English Literature and History (at the second attempt), to go with his eight or nine O levels. Barbara wanted him to go to university, Loughborough actually, but his future lay in professional football. He made his début, as an eighteen year old and still an amateur, against Terry Butcher, Ipswich's England centre-half.

Nigel had made it from AC Hunters to the First Division by way of Heanor Town, where he had been noticed by one or two clubs, including Derby. Their manager, Arthur Cox, was eager to sign him, and has never wavered in his admiration for the way my son has played the game and conducted himself. But as Ronnie Fenton kept reminding me: 'You do realise we'll get murdered if your Nige signs for anybody else.'

His first game, or my decision to give in to my staff who had been badgering me for weeks to put him in the first team, produced a quirky little coincidence. It was Boxing Day 1984 – exactly twenty-two years from the very day when I crumpled under that goalkeeper's challenge at Roker Park, to be carried off on a stretcher, my playing career effectively over.

We used to go to work together at the start, sharing the same car. Nigel wasn't allowed his own vehicle for quite a time, because I didn't believe in footballers spending too much time sitting on their backsides. As one who was brought up to jog through Albert Park on the way to Ayresome Park and twenty-six years old before I had my first car, I can't help feeling some wayward modern youngsters would be better advised to do the same. Fat chance – most of them get cars from sponsors nowadays. They don't even need to buy one.

It takes time for any player to become established within a football club. He has to win over his working colleagues, not only with his ability on the training-ground, which is the first hurdle, but in terms of reliability and trustworthiness.

I am absolutely certain that just about everybody in the

Forest dressing-room was suspicious when my lad was thrust into their midst. Their natural reaction would have been: 'Watch it from now on, lads. Anything we say can get straight back to the gaffer.'

I knew Nigel had been accepted the day we were travelling back on the coach from somewhere and I happened to overhear Des Walker. We were giving a lift to one of his mates, whom I saw tap Des on the shoulder, point towards Clough junior and then put his finger to his lips. Walker immediately turned on him and said in a low voice: 'Don't you ever doubt him. He's dead straight. You could tell him anything and it will stick.'

I said nothing, I didn't even let on that I'd heard it, but it made me proud. It was a huge compliment Walker was paying to my son. In fact, the two of them became big mates.

I never became involved in Nigel's contracts when he turned pro. Ron Fenton dealt with them. I never once discussed Nigel's money with him, even when he still lived with us at Quarndon. From the outset I said to Ron: 'His contract is between the pair of you. Don't involve me. You've seen enough of him now, so pay him the going rate. Don't cheat him by underpaying him because he's my son and don't cheat the club by overpaying him for the same reason.'

Honestly, that was the only time I discussed his contract in all the years he worked for me. At the ground I called him 'Clough' or 'Number 9' and he called me 'Boss'. At home, it was 'Dad' and 'Son'. If anything, Nigel was slightly underpaid to start with, according to Ron, but that gave us peace of mind. Once he had established himself he would be able to go and see Ron again, standing up until Fenton invited him to sit down, and say: 'I've been here a couple of years, I'm a regular in the side and I want paying on a par with the rest.' I didn't need to tell him, he would have learned it from the others.

I had no reservations about bringing my own son into

my club because he had virtually lived there since being a nipper. It was second nature to him. He was street-wise and football-wise. He knew when to shut up and when to duck out of the way, because that's how he was brought up.

He kept a low profile. Once he became a pro in his own right and had his own car, he was showered and changed and off before I had time even to get in the bath. Being teetotal as well, he was a popular and reliable taxi-driver, used regularly by the rest of the squad.

When Stuart Pearce first came to the club, from Coventry, he dropped an early clanger with me. It was a little while before Pearce moved from his old home. I have never been too concerned or worried about players living out of town, and I have done what I could to make life more convenient. We would stop the coach to pick them up at various places along the way. Alan Hill pointed out to me one day: 'You keep telling Pearce we'll pick him up at the service station, but he can't bloody drive.'

'Well, get him through his test, then,' I said.

'No,' said Hilly, 'he's been banned.'

It had been worrying Pearce for days. He'd been walking around not daring to tell me his licence had been taken away. All the players knew it, but I was the last to know.

Fines dished out by me were known as 'Red-letter days' – a term first used by John Robertson which stuck. It stemmed from the fact that they came in official envelopes with the red club motif on the front. Nigel received his share. Usually his fines were for late arrival and occasionally I hit him with double. If it was £25 for the others, I took £50 from him. That's the price for being the son as well as the centre-forward!

He won over his team-mates but he had still to win the respect of the opposition. Also, remember, he had to contend with the jeering and sneering of away fans who took delight in yelling things like 'Daddy's boy' the first time he played a poor pass or hit a bad shot. That used to make me squirm in the dug-out. I felt sorry for him whenever it happened – but I never let on. It's a hard life and it's a hard game.

I knew he had to gain the respect of players with other clubs – especially the top-liners. He cracked it one day against Arsenal, Tony Adams in particular.

Adams was a youngster, too. I grew angry at the sight of him crashing into Nigel from the back, time after time. So I called my lad to the touch-line and said: 'The first time you get the chance – cut Adams in half. And, by the way, don't keep me waiting. Meet him full-on and cut him in half.'

Arsenal's manager, George Graham, leapt out of the other dug-out. 'There's no need for that, Brian,' he said.

'Hey,' I told George, 'I've been watching him clatter our centre-forward for the past twenty f**king minutes and he hasn't faced him once yet. Everything's coming in from the back.'

Within minutes our Nige had turned with the ball, approached Adams face on – and gone straight through. Not over the ball but just powered right through the lad, leaving him on the deck wondering what the hell had hit him. I have only seen one other player do it better – Willie Carlin at Derby, and he was even smaller.

That challenge on Adams established Nigel among his fellow pros the length and breadth of the country. Word went round. Nobody messed with him after that. Players categorise others – they either jump or they don't jump. Nigel Clough didn't jump. Tony Adams didn't take another liberty with him, all match. Message received and understood.

Nigel was known as Rip Van Winkle to the rest of the dressing-room, because of his ability to sleep in any circumstances and his reluctance to get out of bed. I enjoyed it when he played a beautiful pass or when he responded to my regular enquiry: 'What number do you wear?'

'Number 9.'

'Well, it's about time you got a goal, then. That's what Number 9s are paid for – to get bloody goals.' It was said to him at work, never at home. To be fair to him, he got his quota of goals, as well as laying on a stack of them. He was Forest's leading scorer for several seasons on the trot.

I was never the best judge of a player but I knew what it took to make one. I knew the requirements. They are not laid down in simple terms, from one to ten or A to Z. If they were, anybody could be a manager. It depends how you look and what you're looking for, because the player who has everything has yet to be born.

Nigel had vision, the ability to see the opportunity for a pass, and the talent to play the ball and to score a goal. His trouble was that he wasn't quick. God gave him a sturdy physique and strong legs like mine but he didn't see fit to give him wings. I'm afraid some people in the game overemphasised his lack of natural pace. They overlooked the fact that he could make up a yard by thinking quicker or seeing things before an opponent.

He also had to possess a stable character, because without it he would have gone under. That applies to all players, but more so to him because of his high-profile, controversial old man. He showed signs of strain after his transfer to Liverpool, because after Graeme Souness left it became perfectly obvious that others at Anfield had begun to doubt my son's ability. Once again, he knew that if he didn't come through it he would go under. He knew the rules. He could have left us before. He could have gone to Bari, where David Platt began his Italian career, but didn't fancy playing abroad at that stage. He could, and perhaps should, have joined Tottenham soon after Terry Venables became manager.

Terry rang me and said: 'I would like to buy your son.

We've got to play football as it should be played at this club and I want Nigel to be part of it. I'll look after him.' I'm sure he would have done. I put it straight to Nigel: 'Would you like to go to Tottenham?'

'No,' he said, 'I'm happy here.' And that was the end of that. I sometimes wonder what might have happened to my son had he gone to White Hart Lane. I think he might just have made it with England a little more often.

He hasn't enjoyed the kind of international career I thought was waiting for him at one stage. It all depended on the composition of the side. With my son you either play to his style or you don't play him at all – there is no in between. That may sound contradictory, coming from me, as I have always argued that either you can play or you can't. But he was a wee bit different. Maybe that was because of the things I encouraged, the way I was repeatedly telling him at work: 'You're not a player unless the ball's at your feet and it sticks. It's got to stick, son.'

Successive England managers, Bobby Robson and Graham Taylor, have got it wrong, the most glaring example being when Robson gave our Nige his first chance with England against Chile at Wembley. It turned out to be no chance at all. Robson played him alongside the lad from Wimbledon, John Fashanu, whose brother had caused me so much trouble at Forest. Fashanu was not only far from fully fit, he wasn't the right type of player to pair with my son anyway – a big, gangly, strong lad, who liked the ball in the air. It was the wrong combination. A bit like my chairman at Brighton, Mike Bamber – God rest him – who put tomato ketchup on everything he ate – even in a bowl of soup. Now Mike should have tried his food without ketchup, just to see what it tasted like. And England should have tried Nigel in the right combination, just to see what it looked like.

Graham Taylor took him to the European Championships in Sweden, but he was the only one in the squad the manager didn't ask to play at some stage. He was later to include Nigel in squads for World Cup qualifiers without putting him in the team. It reached the stage where I was convinced Graham was picking him more as a pal than as a player – somebody bright and intelligent and loyal whom he could talk to and trust.

I talk to him, now, about his football – how he's doing, how he's feeling. But I don't harp on too long about what I think he should do. As a married man not too far short of thirty, he doesn't have to listen quite as intently or as long as he used to. I know when to shut up, these days – when he says: 'Hey, Dad – I've had enough.'

I love him as a son. If you are lucky enough to have one, look for his good points and admire what he contributes. His mother is a total feminist – I think, if she had been around at the time, she would have tied herself to the railings alongside Mrs Pankhurst. Whenever I mention Nigel's football with the slightest hint of criticism, she will tell me: 'Just a minute – it's not *that* important.' I'll say: 'Oh, but it is. He has chosen my profession, my way of life.'

I don't think he will choose football management, though. I'm certain he won't. The main reason ex-players become coaches or managers is because they are not equipped to do any other type of work, unless they've saved enough money to buy a small business. There are a few exceptions, even these days, who go into management out of necessity.

By the time he reaches his early thirties, Nigel should be reasonably wealthy. He already has a shop, anyway – a greetings card shop not far from the Forest ground. When he ends his playing career I think he will make a complete break from the game. Perhaps he will use those qualifications his Mam insisted he had and follow his interest in accountancy.

After his first-team début for Forest against Terry Butcher and Ipswich I asked him for his first impression, the element that struck him most. 'The crowd,' he said. 'The incredible noise.' I had taken that for granted. Familiarity breeds an acceptance of things that newcomers find incredible. Our Nige will miss the roar of the crowd when he eventually calls it a day. We all do. It will all be a fond and distant memory – like the days when he was naughty as a toddler and I sent him to his room and made him look at a photograph of Bob Stokoe!

20

REGRETS, I'VE HAD A FEW

I can't promise to give the team-talk in Welsh but from
now on I shall be taking my holidays in Porthcawl and
I bought a complete set of Harry Secombe albums.

A DECADE AFTER ENGLAND BARRED MY WAY TO INTERNATIONAL MAN-
agement, the Welsh re-opened the door. My ambition to take
over a national side was such that I was prepared to take over
in Malaysia, Mexico or even Outer Mongolia – provided that the
terms and conditions were right.

Seriously, when the Wales job was offered to me on meeting

their FA officials in Birmingham, I nearly snatched their hands off. I accepted and was thrilled to do so. Several misconceptions have been spread around in attempts to find a dark, hidden reason why I never did begin the job.

It is true that a drama was being enacted closer to home. I wanted Alan Hill, who was working for Notts County at the time, to come and work with me again, in charge of Forest's youth recruitment. It is also true that I wanted Hill working alongside me with Wales. I detested Notts County's chairman, Derek Pavis, and he knew it. For years, he was a director at Forest, but he had been voted off the board by shareholders responding to my better judgement. He was to sell his builders' merchants business for several million pounds and took over Notts County.

The simple assumption, wrongly made, was that I used the Welsh offer as a lever to dislodge Hill from Meadow Lane and install him at the City Ground. The switch was made, much to Pavis's annoyance of course, and finished up costing Forest the best part of £20,000 as an out-of-court settlement with our neighbours across the Trent. That was hardly the object of my exercise.

Perhaps time is a healer after all, because when I retired from Forest in 1993 Derek Pavis wrote me a warm, kind and sincere letter talking about 'eighteen years of unrivalled success, the likes of which they will never see again.' I didn't expect it, not from him. That's why I appreciated it such a great deal.

I wanted to be a national team manager. I was ready to do it, too. I had never been more serious about anything in my life. It wasn't England, but it was international management, and I would have made a better gaffer than anybody the Welsh have appointed since. I would have done the job on a part-time basis with Alan Hill, and I believe to this day that I could have done it in tandem with my job at Forest. Although the Welsh invited me to take over full time, I told them their job could be done part time – and it still could, today.

I thought everything was hunky-dory when I informed the Forest chairman, Maurice Roworth. In fact, he seemed to think that the prestige of employing the Welsh manager would be good for Nottingham Forest. But then the doubts crept in. Roworth came back to me and said: 'We're not sure you could do two jobs at once. Your priority has to be with this club' – or words to that effect. What he was really saying was: 'We don't want you to take it. And I'd tell you not to take it – if I dared.'

OK, so I dictated most of what happened at Forest, the way we ran things, the way the club was conducted and went about its business. Not many attempted to argue, but Forest did pay my salary, they were my employers and, between them, they were getting brave enough in the boardroom to raise some resistance to my plan. I discussed the situation at home with Barbara. It was time to give my position some serious thought.

I kept thinking back to the first time a club chairman tried to restrain me – back to Derby, where Sam Longson had pushed me to go on television at every opportunity because it reflected well on the club. And how, when I had become reasonably well known, he did a U-turn. 'You're doing more work for other people than you are doing for this club,' he had told me. 'Cut down on your television stuff.' That, effectively, marked the beginning of the end for Taylor and me at the Baseball Ground.

I couldn't get rid of a sneaking feeling that the Forest directors' reaction to the Welsh offer was the thin end of the wedge. There was no chance of my resigning from the club and telling the Wales people I would go full time, so I reluctantly decided not to go at all. There have been times, since, when I wish I had pushed it to the limit, defied the reservations of the directors, and taken the job part time anyway. Now I will never know what kind of national team manager I would have made. I can only sit and assume that I would have been among the best.

Just think . . . I responded to the doubts of a chairman who eventually went to prison for fraud, taking more than £100,000 of my money with him. What a game, in't it? Wales – thanks for the offer, thanks for the chance England wouldn't give me. I should have taken you up on it.

Months later I did one of the most ill-advised things of my life. Within the space of a few spectacular seconds I turned a night of joy into an occasion of controversy and disgrace that produced a hundred headlines and pitched me into yet another vat of hot water. It became known as 'the night Cloughie belted the fans'.

We had just clobbered Queens Park Rangers 5-2 in the Quarter-Finals of the League Cup. We had played particularly well, Lee Chapman had scored four goals, and we were in the middle of a magnificent sequence of ten successive victories. I was feeling chuffed as I rose from the dug-out to make my customary sedate walk to the mouth of the tunnel, where I always offered a polite 'good night' to the adjacent policeman. Usually I made it to the sanctuary of our dressing-room before the players.

As I got to my feet that night, my path was blocked by fans – thirty or forty, maybe more – leaping about and milling around in what, I was assured later, was a mood of celebration rather than menace. That did not concern me. I was bloody furious that they had 'come over the wall' and that I was having difficulty getting past them. Remember, I had a great relationship with the Forest fans and had been known to impose my influence – not least when I erected a hoarding asking 'No swearing, gentlemen, please' at the popular Trent End of the ground, and they responded. We cut out any foul-mouthed chanting at a stroke.

What happened next was an instinctive reaction. Sometimes

something flashes through the mind without bringing with it a satisfactory reason. I detest seeing fans on the pitch, or on the edges of it, and I simply struck out. I clipped or belted two or three of them who just happened to be nearest to me as I made for the tunnel.

And before you ask, no, I was not the worse for drink. I landed my blows. To put it bluntly, if I'd been pissed I'd have missed!

I still say I was a bit unlucky. I had given permission for Central Television to send a crew to record the goals. At the end of the match the lad on the camera left it running and, of course, he caught me clipping the pitch invaders. I do hope he made a few bob for himself, because his few seconds of film made it all the way round the network. We can smile about it a little now, but at the time it produced a mini-crisis for me. The lads I clobbered became celebrities overnight. We finally kissed and made up on local TV after the immediate dust had died down.

Actually, I only really hit one of them. I clipped two, but one turned and faced me and really copped for it. He wobbled but he didn't go over. I went to the dressing-room clutching my wrist. It hurt like hell and I needed treatment from the physio. At that stage of the evening I had no idea that my barmy outburst had been captured by the eagle eye of the television. I had been led to believe that immediately a match was over a small crew like that would pull the plugs. Even so, I knew there was a fair chance I was in the shit.

I joined Ronnie Fenton in his office and told him: 'I've just hit a couple of supporters who ran on the pitch. I think I've really done it now.' Ron went out for a few minutes and when he came back, a few shades paler, he closed the door and said: 'Dead right. You really *have* done it.' The mood in our dressing-room the following day was a little subdued, but

I'm certain I detected just a hint of a snigger from one or two of them.

I received a lot of letters of support. One was from a Chief Superintendent of Police in Sheffield, who said: 'I've been wanting to do what you did for twenty years.' There was a handwritten note on House of Commons paper from Neil Kinnock, leader of the Labour Party, lending his support and understanding. 'Anyone who has ever seethed at hooliganism and pitch invasion,' he wrote, 'will understand why you did what you did on the spur of the moment.' And there were stacks more of them from ordinary members of the general public, saying that if more kids were given more clips round the lug-holes, the country would have far less hooliganism.

Graham Kelly, Secretary of the Football Association, made a considerate gesture when he phoned me about details of the disciplinary hearing I had to face. 'We'll come to the City Ground,' he said, 'and save you from the hassle of coming to London.' I would have been inundated with journalists and cameras down there. At least, at the Forest ground, I could control things and make sure the Press didn't get where I didn't want them to be. I had received an official warning from the police and the assurance that they were taking no further action. But the media were loving every second.

Before I was called to give my side of the story – I don't recall the names of the men on the commission and I don't want to publicise them in my book, anyway – I sent a message telling the *Sun* photographer to get himself at the back of the ground on the banks of the Trent so that he could have an exclusive picture. I did columns for the *Sun* and I thought it only right that I looked after them. It was a smashing picture, I seem to remember, me sitting on the river bank with a beautiful swan on the water in the background.

Just imagine what one of those odd-bods sitting in judgement would have thought, if he'd known! I'm talking about the one who had the audacity to ask for my 'word of honour' that I wouldn't work for the *Sun* newspaper again.

'Do you realise what you have said?' I asked him. 'Can you repeat it?'

'I want your word of honour you will never work for the *Sun* newspaper again.'

I thought, 'You can go and f**k yourself,' and I told him: 'If the *Sun* knew what you had just said they would slaughter you. You can't dictate who I can work for. They'd crucify you – do you understand what you are saying?'

He said it yet again and then turned to Kelly and said: 'I'm not going to repeat it a fourth time.'

I jumped in: 'You don't have to – I know exactly what you've said and you've no chance.'

They wanted to know the reasons for my behaviour and they asked for assurances that I wouldn't do it again. I suppose that line of inquiry stemmed from the fact that the day after I whacked the fans I was quoted in a *Sun* Page-One exclusive, saying that in the same circumstances I would do the same again. I was still angry and still convinced I had done nothing more than an angry father does to a disobedient son. I finally had to concede, of course, that what I did was wrong and I now regret that it ever happened. I reassured the FA that I would 'try very hard to control myself in future'.

Their response was to clout me with a £5,000 fine. And they banned me from the touch-line although, as it turned out, I was allowed to sit on the bench at Wembley when we beat Luton 3-1 to win the League Cup again. Our Nigel scored two of the goals.

After the FA verdict was announced, I received a letter from the Crystal Palace chairman, Ron Noades. The gist of it, as I remember, was to inform me that the FA had fined me more than the legal maximum for common assault. I didn't reveal Noades's letter at the time, because he would have run the risk of an FA charge as a result. I didn't challenge the fine either, because I had told Graham Kelly: 'Whatever the decision, I shan't appeal.'

I could have done without giving the FA £5,000, because it meant I had to earn almost £10,000 to do it. I could also have done without having to sit in directors' boxes, because I was uncomfortable among them and it led to an incident at Wimbledon where I still believe I was set up. Everybody in football knows I am prone to shouting. Our directors never turned a hair when I began yelling after one particular incident. I was probably complaining about the behaviour of one of Wimbledon's players, because at that particular time their aggressive play – which I call cheating – had reached a peak. Suddenly I felt a hand on my shoulder. I thought it was somebody sitting behind me, one of our lot, so without looking I said: 'And you can piss off as well.' It was a policeman.

'I'm going to have you,' he said.

'Are you? What for?'

'You just told me to piss off.'

'I wasn't to know it was you, I was busy shouting things in the opposite bloody direction.'

'Well, I want to see you anyway,' he said. I genuinely believe he was going to arrest me until Alan Hill talked him out of it. A few minutes later a senior policeman called Wilson came in and shook me by the hand. 'Would you like to watch the rest of the match from the control point?' he asked. 'Come as my guest.'

He was the man in charge, 'The Governor' as all the other police called him. My team got hammered 4-1 and most of the coppers were shouting far louder than I had earlier, every time a Wimbledon goal flew in. They should have been arrested!

Funny how things turn out. Mr Wilson was a Dundee supporter, so after the match I took him to our dressing-room and introduced him to Archie Gemmill. The upshot of it all was that the Nottingham police invited Wimbledon's coppers for a match at our place and I met them all for lunch. It had all begun with a silly incident in which I told a policeman to piss off without even looking. Would you believe it, the first copper to jump out of the mini-van when they arrived was the one who lifted me in the directors' box at Wimbledon?

Another police visit to Nottingham had a strange ending as well. A policeman had written from Ireland to say that a group was coming across and the match they preferred to see was Forest against West Ham. Any chance of twenty of them coming into the dressing-room to meet the players? Of course there was.

On the day of their visit we couldn't find any Bushmills so we drank Bell's whisky out of paper cups. The players signed autographs and chatted and that kind of thing. Just before the police lads were leaving, one of them removed his tie and said to me: 'Would you accept this as a token of our thanks?'

'Yes,' I said, 'and here's mine.'

Months later, I appeared on some television programme wearing the tie the Irishman had given me, and was eventually to receive an official letter asking where I'd got it. It turned out that it was the tie of some élite group – dark blue with a snake emblem. I never found out the nature of the work they did – possibly anti-terrorist – but I kept the tie. And I wear it, occasionally, to this day.

Oh, by the way, I did resign from Nottingham Forest after belting those pitch invaders. Well, at least I offered to resign. But Maurice Roworth was prompt with his written reply:

Dear Brian,

On behalf of my board of directors I am writing to inform you that we are not prepared to accept your resignation and I would be obliged if you could arrange to meet me to discuss an extension to your contract . . .

What a game, in't it?

21

DEATH IN THE AFTERNOON

*We thought we were ninety minutes from Wembley. It
turned out we were five minutes from hell.*

IT STARTED AS JUST ANOTHER, PLEASANT SPRING SATURDAY. THE
fifteenth of April 1989 greeted us with sunshine, the way FA Cup
Semi-Final Saturdays often do. The Forest team coach was alive
with eager chatter, the usual disguise for nervousness among
players approaching the fixture that is the worst one of all to lose.

It ended as one of the grimmest days in modern British

history, certainly the blackest day British sport has ever known. We all recall it now with the mere mention of a single word, the venue of that ill-fated Semi-Final.

Hillsborough.

The coach journey back to Nottingham was made in almost total silence. Supporters' cars, buses and mini-vans – in front of us and behind us on the motorway – offered not one blast of recognition on their horns. We were all in a state of shock, still unable to come to terms with the magnitude of what we had witnessed. But the radio kept reminding us, with the latest update from the scene of disaster we had just left behind. The final, appalling death-toll became ninety-six. How do you comprehend that scores of people had lost their lives simply because they went to watch a football match?

The match had been under way for five or six minutes when it became obvious that a disturbance behind Bruce Grobbelaar's goal was more than a mere skirmish. As fans spilled onto the pitch the referee took the teams off. We were never to return. Only slowly were we made aware that what first appeared to be a disturbance was, in fact, a disaster on a massive scale.

We sat in our dressing-room, not knowing what to do or even what was happening outside. Then somebody popped his head round the door and said: 'They think there are casualties. They think there are people dead.' Our players just looked at one another. Nobody said much. It wasn't long before the full horror of it all began to unfold. Five dead . . . seven . . . ten . . . fourteen.

The police came to say they wanted Kenny Dalglish and me to say a few words over the public-address microphone to try and calm things down. Forest fans, unaware that tragedy had struck, thought that the Liverpool supporters swarming across the pitch towards them had trouble in mind. They thought it was just another outbreak of hooliganism, when all the Liverpool fans were doing was escaping from the area in which people were being crushed to death.

When Kenny and I got out on the pitch there was bedlam and total confusion. Either the microphone wasn't working or there was too much noise for it to be effective. Maybe, in all the confusion, it wasn't even switched on. We were taken to the police control point. It's odd how unimportant things stick in the mind. They took us beneath the stands, through the kitchens, and I can see now all the trays and pies and pasties set out, the stuff they were going to sell at half-time – all untouched. I can still see the icing-sugar on rows of fruit pies. And the chefs still working on refreshments to be sent up to the restaurant and VIP quarters. They were not to know what was happening outside.

Once in the control box, there was little we could do. A few words into the mike about being patient and 'Don't let's have any more trouble', but by then bodies were being carried on improvised stretchers made from advertising boards, and all the spectators were aware of the seriousness of the situation. Any fear of confrontation between rival fans had passed.

Back in the dressing-room I told my players: 'Get in the bath – we're not going out there again.' It's strange, but even in such dire circumstances people with specific duties manage to stick to the set routine. The referee kept saying, 'Just keep calm,' while I was saying, 'Excuse me, but we're going home.' A high-ranking policeman came in and said, 'You can't go yet.' It was even suggested that the match would be restarted – but my players had returned from the bath, changed into their civvies and were ready to leave.

As the death-toll continued to rise, I made my decision. 'We can go any time we like now. There is no way we can play football – it's impossible. And we could be here until nine o'clock tonight.'

Yet another policeman arrived: 'You can't go, Brian.'

'I can go – and I'm going.' And I did. We filed onto our coach and left without permission from anybody. I wondered if there might have been an official comeback later, but of course the seriousness of what had taken place put everything else out of mind. It wasn't a cowardly reaction that persuaded me to leave. It was the realisation that there was nothing we could do, that so many poor people had perished, and that we were just adding to the burden of those trying to help the victims and the distressed. We were in their way.

I have never been one for stopping at an accident. I have never understood people who have to hang around and have a look wherever there is a police car, a fire-engine or an ambulance. If I know there is nothing I can do, no-one I can help, then I clear off and let the emergency services do their jobs.

I'm sure none of the Forest players went out that night, although I didn't check up on them. If they did then they were uncaring. I just went home and never budged. That was where grief hit me – not at the ground where we were caught up in the chaos that inevitably occurs when large-scale tragedy strikes. There was confusion on the news bulletins, anyway. Maybe not confusion but uncertainty. I remember wanting it all to be untrue, to learn – I don't know, by some sort of miracle or mistake – that it hadn't happened. Not so many people dead. The radio or television would flash the latest figure – seventy-eight, eighty-four, and so on.

I thought of parents wondering whether their children had survived. I thought of parents who might not have known their kids had gone to the match in the first place. Then I wanted to share my grief with the people who had died. It was a feeling of complete helplessness, of inadequacy.

I am now going to say something that may sound harsh and I want to make sure I choose the right words. Many mistakes were made at Hillsborough, but I will always remain convinced that those Liverpool fans who died were killed by Liverpool people.

This is my opinion, made not in the heat of the moment or the immediate, angry aftermath, but following all the publicity and the official inquiry. All those lives were lost needlessly. It was such a terrible and avoidable waste.

If all the Liverpool supporters had turned up at the stadium in good time, in orderly manner and each with a ticket, there would have been no Hillsborough disaster. I have a good friend, Kenny Swain, who is a Scouser. He played for me at Forest, he was one of the best pros I ever worked with and he later went into management. His wife Lillian is also from Liverpool, and was friendly with my daughter. I remember her saying: 'It is always the innocent who suffer.' And so it is.

The man who is walking on the pavement, minding his own business when some drunk-driver mows him down. The one who gets his features rearranged by a hoodlum just because he turns round and says: 'Please, don't do that.' Always the innocent.

I'm not accusing Liverpool supporters of being thugs or hoodlums, but it was the innocent who were killed on that dreadful day – killed by others who arrived at the stadium later and in such numbers that mistakes were made. I could still cry to this day when I think of those who had saved their money and bought their tickets and rosettes and arrived at Hillsborough early enough to gain a place near the front of the terrace – not, in fact, the best of places because they were low down and behind the security fences that never offered the clearest of views. Men, women and youngsters who were never to return alive from a match they had prepared for in the right and proper manner.

Of course the police made serious errors of judgement. Of course that gate should not have been opened in circumstances that allowed so many people to converge in the wrong place. Of course they should somehow have been shepherded into a safe section of the Leppings Lane terracing, not one that was already full.

But they should not have been there. Not in such numbers and not, in some cases I'm sure, without tickets.

My sympathy didn't go out to the people who jammed in from the rear of that terrace, or to those who turned up without a ticket. My sympathy went only to the poor people who did everything right, and died for it. And, of course, to their families, who had also to bear the pain.

Lord Justice Taylor's inquiry into the disaster rightly decided that all football grounds should be seated. It was high time, anyway, that English stadiums were brought into the twentieth century and prepared for the twenty-first, in keeping with most of those in the major football-playing nations of Europe and elsewhere.

But fans who turn up late and in vast numbers will still spell danger, even at a ground where everyone is sitting down. I have seen crowd-control measures abroad that I believe should have been introduced at our major arenas for the bigger games long ago – barriers set up hundreds of yards short of the stadium itself, where tickets are checked and imposters turned away.

I am not a psychologist or a policeman, but it seems to me that the one thing that deters the bully, the pitch invader, the one who wants to hate, is fear. They don't like being frightened. Apart from the odd ones who are totally nuts, it does work. Present the bullies with a guy in a helmet holding an Alsatian or armed with a gun or a baton – then they're frightened and will cross over to the other side of the road.

It is not a cure, because I don't believe violence eradicates violence, but it is certainly a deterrent.

The police bore the brunt of the blame after Hillsborough, but I had enormous sympathy with them, because they were so outnumbered. Our police have such a difficult and thankless job to do. I exchanged letters with the one who okayed the opening of the gates. 'I still can't believe it,' he told me. 'I did the same routine I carried out before every match. Went jogging first thing, had breakfast, put my uniform on and went to the ground early.' Then he was caught up in the biggest disaster football in this country had ever seen. Yes, the police made mistakes, but I will forever remain convinced that a major factor was the Liverpool fans who flooded through those gates, after the police had become concerned that if they were not admitted quickly there was a danger of people dying outside the stadium. You need an awful lot of policemen to deal safely with a crisis like that.

And then we had to go to Old Trafford and play the Semi-Final all over again – well, start again, anyway, because we hardly played at all the first time. Somehow, it was like reliving the ordeal once more, although we had to try to forget and attempt to carry on with normal life. But how could anybody be expected to forget the appalling experiences of Hillsborough?

As soon as our coach arrived at Manchester United's ground, it all came flooding back. There were Catholic priests standing on the corner eating pies and waving. But they were not waving in joy, just in recognition. Personally, I was full of apprehension. Possibly we didn't bear our problems as well as we could – we certainly didn't play to anything like our potential and were soundly beaten, 3-1.

The signs in our dressing-room had not been good. Players who were normally relaxed and lively were shuffling uneasily. Hardly a voice was heard. The feeling going through my mind was: 'Not again.' My appetite for the game was not as it should have been, although in normal times I have always enjoyed taking my teams to Old Trafford.

The disaster was not mentioned in our dressing-room that

day. We all shared a sense of purpose – maybe it was more a sense of duty – that we had to put previous events to one side, forget, and get on with it. I felt they had an urge somehow to put right what had happened. They wanted to repay or recover something that had been lost. My team just walked out of that dressing-room with intense expressions on every face and not the slightest sign of a smile. It was not a feeling of dread, more the feeling that 'I'd rather not be doing this, I'd rather be sitting at home.'

Our right full-back, Brian Laws, had the misfortune of putting in an own goal. For some reason, as Laws remained hunched, or kneeling in utter dejection, Liverpool's John Aldridge went across and ruffled his hair. That annoyed me a great deal. Even if it was a gesture of sympathy, which I doubt, it was out of order and unnecessary in the circumstances. I took exception to Aldridge's action and told Laws afterwards: 'How you can accept somebody ruffling your hair when you have just put the ball in your own net is beyond me.' I seem to recall a smile on Aldridge's face as he did it, but it was a long time before any smile returned to mine.

Afterwards Kenny Dalglish said: 'There was only one team who wanted to win out there,' or, 'We wanted to win more than they did,' or words to that effect. I thought his statement was scandalous. If he was suggesting that my team didn't have the stomach for it that day, he might well have been right. But he should not have said it, he ought to have kept his mouth shut. In truth, although it was difficult for us because the vast majority of public support went Liverpool's way, we wanted to get to Wembley just as much as they did.

There were arguments for and against the staging of the Cup Final that year. Those who called for its cancellation did it as a gesture towards the Liverpool fans who had died, and that was a nice thought. The FA trotted out ridiculous protests such as 'cancelling the Cup Final would be setting a precedent.' Garbage. If it is the right thing to do, then set one.

My Forest side, who went on to win their second cup of the season at Wembley – the Simod trophy, to go alongside the League Cup – were to finish third in the old First Division. We should have been able to reflect on a thoroughly successful season, but how could we? That timeless phrase 'Life goes on' remains perfectly true in most instances and most circumstances.

But not for those ninety-six poor people who died needlessly because of what happened at Hillsborough. None of us who were there, that terrible day, will ever manage to forget.

22

GOODBYE, MY FRIEND

I'm not equipped to manage successfully without Peter
Taylor. I am the shop window and he is the goods in
the back.

IT WAS IN OCTOBER BUT IT WAS NOT A MISERABLE DAY. IT WAS NOT
a miserable funeral, either, because – with his family's blessing
– some of the things said at the service for Peter Taylor raised a
smile or two. But it was miserable for me. I felt confused, reeling
with all kinds of emotion.

I had lost a dear friend, and was left reaching out for a

ghost. The damage was irreparable, the differences unresolved. A friendship that had been in some way unique was irretrievable. I had lost my pal. I had lost any chance of ever healing the rift that had been allowed to separate us for seven years.

It was 14 October 1990. The church could have been specially named for the occasion: St Peter's, in the picturesque Nottinghamshire village of Widmerpool, a short walk away from the lovely bungalow where Peter and Lillian had lived. Such had been the intensity of our fall-out and the publicity surrounding it that there had been speculation about whether I would turn up. The thought of all that now seems appalling.

There was never any doubt in my mind that the Clough family should be there. Barbara just turned round and said: 'We're all going,' and that was that. We knew, from the vehicles parked beside the country lanes and in the village itself, that Peter would pack St Peter's. By the time we arrived there was standing room only. Barbara, Elizabeth, Simon, Nigel and I stood at the back. I remember vividly part-way through the service craning my neck and peering towards the front pews. I wanted to be able to see Peter's family: Lillian, his daughter Wendy and his son Philip. They had spent so much time with us over the years. Our children had virtually been brought up together.

News of Peter's death, ten days earlier at the family villa in Majorca, had come as a terrible, devastating shock. You imagine people dying in hospitals, not on holiday and certainly not just along the coast from Cala Millor, the resort that became a legendary haunt for Peter and me and our teams at Derby and Nottingham. I never imagined Peter dying out there. I never imagined him dying at all. I wish he hadn't. I wish he was still around and that we were together and talking the way we used to and going to football matches and telling one another that we'd have done it better if we'd been in charge of the teams we'd just watched.

I walk a great deal in the countryside surrounding my home. I derive great pleasure from watching the seasons change. Spring is my favourite time of year because everything is new. The buds on the trees, the crocuses: but Wordsworth was right when he wrote about the daffodils. There's a row of them on the edge of the cricket field close to my home, and each spring when they come into bloom I think about Peter Taylor. Where there's beauty and freshness and pleasure there shouldn't be anguish and death. No, I never thought of Peter dying at a time when he was enjoying himself, relaxing and lapping up that feeling of contentment that comes from the surroundings you love most.

Oh, how Peter used to enjoy his Spanish holidays! I can see him now, standing on a hotel balcony eating sardines as I walked by. We were on one of our regular trips, end of season, with the Forest players. Wonderful times. I shouted up to him: 'What the hell are you doing?' He yelled back: 'What's it look like? I'm eating sardines. You should get some down you – they're good for you.' I just started to laugh. Not many people would stand in full view scoffing sardines with a fork – straight from the bloody tin. Thank God he still makes me smile! I can't relate some of my memories of Pete because he was a villain – no, that's not kind or even quite right. He was an absolute rogue.

I do so much wish our relationship, close and warm, so special and so successful, hadn't soured. Just a few, brief words on the telephone, I can't even remember what about, were the only ones we exchanged in those seven years prior to his death. I can look back now, indeed, I looked back in that little church in Widmerpool, and say: What a dreadful and needless waste.

Peter's death put everything into perspective. How could a friendship that began back in 1955, when we were players together at Middlesbrough, and blossomed into the first and most successful managerial partnership football had known, how could all that we had gone through and achieved together be ruined by the signing of one player? People inside the game and the public beyond may have remained sceptical about the cause of our split. Surely, they say, two grown men who have known one another, worked with one another for two decades and been close buddies – surely such men could not be driven apart by such a trivial matter as the transfer of a veteran footballer from one club to another?

I must confess that the signing of John Robertson in the summer of 1983 seemed a trivial, inconsequential thing as I stood solemnly in the rear of that crowded church listening to the Reverend James Groate and others saying such kind things about the dear friend who had passed beyond my reach. Seven years of silence was going to last for ever more.

What you must remember is not the transfer itself, but the nature and timing of John Robertson's switch from the City Ground to the Baseball Ground. He was getting on a bit in years and was out of contract, but he was such a classy player, and he had been such an influential part of what Taylor and I had achieved together that I wanted him to stay at Forest for a while longer.

I was out walking the Pennine Way in the Peak District. A children's charity event. Our group included Alan Hill, the club doctor Michael Hutson, and Tony Slater, a police inspector. We had covered about sixty miles, which felt like one hundred and sixty, when we called into a small pub and I phoned home. Barbara told me: 'Everything's fine, but I've got some news for you. John Robertson's gone to Derby.' I was stunned. Although there had been a good deal of speculation about a possible transfer, I could not believe Taylor had carried it out without my knowledge.

I returned to the bar and said to Hilly: 'You wouldn't believe what that shit has done. He's signed Robertson without so much as lifting a phone to let me know. That's it – I'm finished with him. I'll never speak to him again.'

It wasn't the transfer in itself. Robbo was making a few bob, which was fine. It was said he was paid £40,000 – whether he got that much or not I don't know and I don't care. My anger was not aimed at him, it was directed at Taylor, and Pete knew the reason why. I have one or two regrets about our break-up, especially since his death, but I don't have a problem with my conscience and I don't have trouble sleeping. Peter Taylor could not be as close to someone as he was to me for all those years, and expect to get away with the Robertson signing without even giving me a call. Just a courtesy call to say: 'How's the walk going? Glad to hear you've got the club doctor with you – you could need him, silly bugger. Are you carrying oxygen? By the way – I've signed John Robertson.' That would have been classic Taylor. Lead them up the garden path, or the Pennine Way, then hit them with the real reason for the call. He didn't ring and I never forgave him.

Barbara and I have been married thirty-five years. If she bombed me out overnight and then decided to get married again I'd expect her to phone me, just to let me know. I couldn't comprehend how, after a relationship that was warm and close and cemented, Taylor could have gone behind my back.

I said some very colourful things about him in the immediate months following the split. I called him a 'rattlesnake' and a 'snake-in-the-grass' and said, publicly: 'If I was driving along the A52 between Derby and Nottingham and saw Taylor broken down and thumbing a lift, I wouldn't pick him up. I'd run him over.' That was the way I felt for a long, long time. It was a measure of my anger. I felt betrayed, by a man who had been such a friend to me and my family during such an important period of our lives.

It was an astonishing and bitter end to our relationship, but my conscience was untroubled. I didn't instigate it. The things I said were typical Brian Clough, I suppose, but they were not said for effect. I had enough on my plate at Forest. We were doing quite well as the weeks wore on and I thought: 'So Taylor's taken Robertson – so what? Let him get on with it.' I made a decision to wipe him out of my mind. Even when it eventually ended for him at Derby and he walked away having failed as a manager in his own right, I still wasn't tempted to pick up a phone and say: 'Hard luck.'

In church I thought about things like that the night we heard he had died. I just sat quietly at home and thought about everything Pete and I had experienced together. I suppose I just reminisced. I was glad Barbara was there and that my children, to whom Pete had been a favourite uncle, were all living at home at that time. I needed all of them around me.

I still think about Pete a great deal. When I first met him at Middlesbrough he was both an atheist and a communist. There can never have been a goalkeeper who was more of a left-winger! But he soon changed. His philosophy changed in 1971 when he saw a Communist country for himself. We took Derby to Czechoslovakia for a third-round European Cup-tie against Spartak Trnava. It might have been the drab area we travelled through by coach, having flown into Vienna. It might have been the obvious lack of wealth and the fact that we hardly saw a smile on the faces of people who all seemed to be dressed in grey or black. Or it might have been because we had to drive through a 'sheep-dip' on the way to our hotel because the region had been hit by foot-and-mouth disease. Maybe it was a combination of all those things – but Taylor's politics took an immediate turn towards the right long before we flew home. I think he was looking for something that wasn't there, an idealism he had read about but never seen in action before. When we arrived back in England we were barely off the plane at the East Midlands Airport when he said to me: 'It's not bad here, is it?' On the day of his funeral it occurred to me that his atheism had gone out of the window too, seeing that he was having a church service and being buried in the church grounds. I'll bet he hadn't been in a church more than three times in his life.

When I left the church at the end of the service one thing annoyed me. Peter's immediate family had moved to another part of the churchyard for the burial and I was walking down the path towards my car when two TV camera crews approached me and asked: 'Will you do a piece?' Those were the exact words. I think that kind of practice is terrible – I genuinely do. Five minutes after they'd carried Pete's coffin to be buried and I had television people wanting me to 'do a piece'. It all seemed terribly tasteless – I felt like swearing. I had stood in that church and thought of how Peter should have revelled in his retirement. He had used me as a buffer against so many things when we worked together and could have continued to do so.

I was still in work at Forest and we were getting to Wembley finals on a regular basis. He could have come with us, he should have been on our coach or on our train. He should have been a regular at the Forest ground, watching our Nige whom he idolised from a bairn and who gave him so much pride and satisfaction after becoming a professional in his own right.

If only Peter had come to my front door – I'd never have turned him away. That would have done the trick, buried the hatchet, melted the ice. I wish he had just called round for whatever reason. Any excuse would have been fine by me.

Such a notion is pointless, now, and a touch selfish on my part. Since Peter died I have come to realise that I should have been big enough to heal the breach. I should have driven to see him, or telephoned him. At the very least I should have answered or returned one of his calls on the occasions when he tried to get through to me at home. But you don't know people are going to go suddenly. You cannot anticipate them going in the middle of a holiday with loved ones and relatives around them. Not Pete, not in Cala Millor.

Given the benefit of hindsight we can all look back and say: 'I should have done this, and I could have done that.' It takes an event like the death of a friend to make you think in those terms. Whoever said 'Never go to sleep on an argument' was right.

23

NOT MY DAY

Go and ask Bob Stokoe what it meant to win the
Cup. And John Sillett. And Tommy Docherty. They all
won the Cup but where are they now? Out
of bloody work!

I SHOULD HAVE RETIRED AFTER 18 MAY 1991, THE DAY I WITNESSED THE
worst refereeing decision in my forty-odd years in football. The FA
Cup Final, the only one in which I was involved, Nottingham Forest
against Tottenham Hotspur – and Wembley stank to its rafters.

Paul Gascoigne committed two despicable fouls early in the

match. The first was a chest-high challenge with his boot that could easily have seriously injured our midfield player Garry Parker. The second, you will recall, scythed down full-back Gary Charles, but left Gascoigne himself as the real victim with a badly busted knee.

He received not one scrap of sympathy from me. Normally, when a player is injured, I will be prepared to carry him off on my own back. But any sympathy, any understanding or respect I had for Gascoigne disappeared that afternoon. His actions, his sheer irresponsibility did my game so much discredit. I was ashamed to be inside the stadium that day. I can't be exact as to how many people watch the English Cup Final, but I know it is tens of millions worldwide. What must they have thought about our standards of behaviour and standards of refereeing that day?

Some say the referee, Roger Milford, was easy on Gascoigne simply because it was the FA Cup Final – the season's glamorous, showpiece event. Milford himself later hinted that the nature of the occasion influenced his response. Such reasoning is unforgivable: the fact that it was the Cup Final should have made no difference whatsoever. As I sat on the bench at Wembley I wanted to see Milford brandishing a red card over Gascoigne as he was carried off on a stretcher.

My reaction at the time was that he should have been sent off for the first challenge on Parker, never mind the one that led to him being carried off. For such wild behaviour I wished there had been a local by-law prohibiting Gascoigne from playing at Wembley ever again. If we can banish the hooligan in the crowd then why shouldn't we banish the hooligan on the pitch?

As for Milford, here was a referee copping out of his responsibility. I can never understand how people allow occasions to get to them to such an extent that it impairs their ability to do the job. Milford had the ideal opportunity to teach the young man a lesson. Irrespective of what motivates Gazza – big occasions, personal glory or money – someone has to get hold of him and teach him the facts of life.

Despite the fact that Gascoigne has made a lot of money, particularly since joining Lazio in Italy, I look upon him as an unhappy young man. Whether he gets £200 a week or £200,000 does not concern me. All the self-inflicted publicity has not given him a good life. As an outsider – who never tried to sign him, incidentally – I would say his life is a mess.

His talent is absolute. He has strength, vision, the ability to score goals and, to use an old-fashioned term, to dribble. His physique matches those of the centre-halves I used to take on in my playing days! I don't know who taught Pavarotti, nobody knows. When you're born with an exquisite talent you have a responsibility to use it, not abuse it. Gascoigne has abused his own gifts.

I couldn't understand what he was doing at Wembley, running round like a demented bull disturbed by the proverbial red rag. I looked at him and looked at him, and couldn't fathom why Terry Venables was allowing him to behave like that. If I had been Gascoigne's gaffer I would have done my utmost to keep his feet on the ground at all times.

Don't talk to me about difficult players. I used to work with Kenny Burns – the Scotsman reputed to be among the wildest men in football. Burns was no trouble to me, responding to the treatment by playing the best football of his entire career. We helped provide the things which were precious to him – League Championship and European Cup medals. Nobody has managed to do the same for Paul Gascoigne. Ironically, I think his departure from the Final on a stretcher was the decisive moment in Spurs' favour, leaving the FA Cup as the only domestic trophy to elude me. Aye, even though Stuart Pearce put us in front from the free-kick awarded for Gascoigne's foul.

Tottenham became a transformed team, physically stronger

than Forest. I doubt whether Paul Stewart ever had such an influential match in a Spurs shirt. Before we went out that afternoon I thought we would win it. I was less hopeful as the game wore on, but my spirits rose again in the break before we played extra-time. I have been criticised for not stepping forward to talk to my players before they began that decisive additional half-hour. I didn't go simply because they didn't want me.

I knew that the cameras would have been trained on me if I'd stepped forward, so I sent out my coaches. I didn't want the players thinking: 'This is the only trophy he hasn't won. We mustn't blow it now.' I didn't want them freezing after a gruelling ninety minutes and I'm certain they didn't want me telling them what more they could do. At that stage I simply had nothing more to offer them.

When a team is about to enter extra-time in a match as important as a Cup Final – drained both physically and mentally after a gruelling ninety minutes – the last thing they want is a manager wandering among them urging 'one last mighty effort'. I've never understood quite what managers think they can change at that stage, unless they're planning to make a substitution. If he's done his job properly before the game, there is little more a manager can say even at half-time. They've heard it all, they've had their instructions, they're sick of the sight of the opposition who still stand between them and that wonderful cup-winning feeling, and they know exactly what is needed. A goal. We scored one – unfortunately, Des Walker's own goal. That's the way it goes in football, sometimes.

I had walked out of the tunnel, booted and suited, holding Terry Venables' hand for the first few strides. Just a little gesture between rival managers on the one day of the season that is more special than the rest. I walked back without so much as a medal. The FA Cup Final, they say, is the greatest match, the greatest occasion of the football season. Not great enough, apparently, for them to strike a medal for the managers who steer their teams to Wembley. I wrote to the Football Association sometime afterwards, politely asking if I could have a loser's medal. They told me that they only provided medals for the players. I found that an incredible state of affairs. It had taken me forty years to reach an FA Cup Final and I deserved a medal, I should have been entitled to a medal – win or lose. I telephoned Terry Venables – surely the winning manager received a medal? But no, he had nothing to show either, although he did have the Cup itself!

It was wrong. If Sir Bert Millichip was entitled to sit in the Royal Box at Wembley, no doubt after wining and dining in the grand manner to which the chairman of the FA is accustomed, the managers of the Cup Final teams should be afforded the honour of climbing those steps and receiving a medal to commemorate that special day in their careers. Perhaps my enquiries and protests did the trick, because the system has now been changed, to acknowledge that the managers contribute something to football's grand occasion after all.

My own disappointment of Wembley '91 crossed my mind again as I watched Manchester United beating Chelsea in the 1994 final, to win the Premiership and FA Cup double. As player-manager of Chelsea I suppose Glenn Hoddle would have qualified anyway, but it did my heart good to see Alex Ferguson, all smiles and back-slaps, up there receiving his medal just like his players. After all, he had signed and assembled the team that dominated the English game so spectacularly that season. When Fergie glances at his medal from time to time – as I know he will – I hope he gives me a thought.

I got my FA Cup Final medal eventually – no thanks to the FA – to place alongside all the others of which I am intensely proud: the ones I produce whenever my kids talk about my lack of academic qualifications. I spread the medals on the table and say: 'These are my O levels and A levels.' Seeing that Millichip and Co. didn't give me one, I bought one. I borrowed our Nigel's loser's medal and had a replica made. In gold.

I've had replicas made of every single thing I've won but not always in gold – I couldn't always afford it. Miniatures of the League Championship trophy, the European Cup and the League Cup. One of my proudest achievements was the spell of matches spread over the seasons of 1977-78 and 1978-79 in which my Forest team played forty-two First Division fixtures without losing – the equivalent of an entire season without defeat. Despite dominating the Premiership in 1993-94, Manchester United couldn't equal our record, and I have a feeling that nobody ever will. I had two silver salvers commissioned, engraved with details of all the matches, and gave one to my chairman at the time, Stuart Dryden, sadly no longer with us. They cost me £1,500 – a lot of money in those days.

When I won the First Division Championship at Derby, the League sent me a plaque. I had it valued: £4.50. Having won the Second Division Championship, previously, I received a magnificent medal, as big as an old half-crown. I went straight to the jewellers in Derby and had two replicas made, in solid gold with gold chains. One bears the figure 1, the other 2. The first I gave to my Mam and the second I gave to Barbara. Barbara used to wear hers.

Only one thing annoys me about Barbara. She is more intelligent than me which, to be fair, is not too difficult. Academically she is streets ahead, and there are times when I get the impression she is rubbing it in. It irritates me when she answers questions on televised quiz shows before the contestants have time to open their mouths. Well, it seems as quick as that anyway, to someone like me who has yet to come up with his first correct answer watching *Mastermind*. I think not going into education was one of her biggest mistakes. She would have made a superb teacher. When our children had grown up I suggested she 'took a course' in something that would enable her to have another interest outside the house. She told me I didn't have the right temperament for her to do a course, that I would be 'shouting and swearing' and complaining that she was still sitting in another room doing her course work at nine o'clock at night. So she never did the course, but friends introduced her to a scheme for teaching immigrant women to speak English. She does that one day a week and I think it's a nice thing to do.

Over thirty-five years of married life, Barbara has had a terrific influence. She has never been a regular attender of football matches, although she did enjoy the Wembley occasions and came to games more as our son Nigel's playing career developed. But throughout our time together she has brought a vital sense of perspective to a household that could otherwise have been dominated and overwhelmed by football. For instance, on the night I clobbered those fans at the City Ground, she was in bed by the time I returned home. Now that's always a good thing. You don't have to explain until the morning, and by the time you've slept on it the issue does not seem quite so important.

To put it bluntly, she has made it crystal clear that she wanted no part of some of the antics that put my name in the headlines. In fact, after pointing out forcibly that I was wrong on many occasions, constantly accusing me of taking a sledgehammer to crack a nut, she has treated it with disdain.

Barbara has had no time for the escapades in which I am forever finding myself caught up. She has rarely given me any sympathy, and she has been right not to do so. As she put it, I 'lurched from one crisis into another'. She didn't think I matured as quickly as I should, and on occasions when I made the front pages of some newspapers she refused to have them in the house.

She has shunned publicity almost completely. I was once asked to become the subject of that wonderful old radio programme *Desert Island Discs*. I suggested they asked Barbara instead. First, she would have been a far more interesting subject, and second, she would have chosen a wider range of music. I would have been happy on my island with just one Sinatra album. They were silly not to invite her.

When I was a regular face and voice on television, assailing the nation with my opinions on everything that moved, people – particularly women – I'm sure used to wonder: 'How on earth does his wife live with that?' I can tell them how she did it – brilliantly! When I am at my most pompous or arrogant or rudest – and believe me, I reached pinnacles of rudeness – she has a highly tuned knack of assuming an expression of intolerance while turning and looking the other way.

Coming from Middlesbrough, where we were permanently cold as kids, I developed an obsession for wanting to lie in warm sunshine. As soon as we had a few bob I took the family to Spain at every opportunity. Late as usual, rushing into Palma airport, I was told by the girl on the desk: 'The flight is closed.'

'I don't care whether the flight is closed or not – I'm getting on it. We've got three kids and I have to get back.'

'All right, then,' she said, 'I'll open that gate and your plane's over there.'

There were two queues of people shuffling towards two planes. We were at the back – Simon with a case, Barbara with a case, me with two cases and Nigel and Elizabeth with bits of hand luggage. As we headed for the plane I heard the bloke in front nattering away in a cockney accent, so I tapped him on the shoulder and asked: 'What time does this get into East Midlands?'

'Don't know about you, pal, but we're going to bleedin' Luton.'

I turned in near panic, only to see Barbara in her classic Jack Benny pose, standing hand against her cheek, looking the other way as if she had nothing whatsoever to do with me.

I know, now, that I should have retired after the 1991 FA Cup Final. Gascoigne left on a stretcher, but I could have gone with my head held high after watching my team play its last match for me on the grandest occasion of them all. In fact, I had decided – well, virtually decided, to call it a day, but I was talked out of it by my family, believe it or not. And I was confused in my own mind. On the day I genuinely thought we could win the FA Cup and that defeat, coming as it did in extra-time as a result of Des Walker's own goal, put me right on the floor.

It is amazing what a good holiday can do in terms of recharging wonky batteries and rekindling the spirits. Although I had made up my mind, near-as-dammit, to retire after the Cup Final, most of the family eventually thought I might prefer to have another season. My eldest son, Simon, was the only one who said: 'Yes, finish now.' The holiday came in between, and after another spell in Cala Millor I felt in better nick and ready for the new season. I was going to win 'the lot' again. I think pride got the better of me. I had two years of my contract left after Wembley, and with a year still remaining the chairman extended it for a further twelve months. I was loathe to sign it, but I said to Ron Fenton, Archie Gemmill, Alan Hill and Liam O'Kane: 'I'll help you get new contracts, so that if they sack you, you can then get yourselves a few bob.' It is important for a manager to look after his staff.

The team was never going to be quite the same again, although we finished eighth in the old First Division and went to another League Cup Final, or Rumbelows Cup as it was called, only to be beaten by Manchester United. There was an unpleasant allegation in the television programme *World in Action* that I put thousands of Rumbelows Cup Final tickets on to the black market – suffice it to say, that little matter is destined for the courts.

As the 1992–93 season unfolded I knew that retirement was drawing nearer with every match. I also knew in my heart that in deciding to carry on after the FA Cup Final I had made a mistake. A manager who has won League titles with two different clubs, and two European Cups, should not end his career watching his team sliding to relegation. It was the wrong kind of finish, the wrong epitaph.

24

GOING DOWN

*If the BBC ran a Crap Decision of the Month
competition on* Match of the Day *I'd walk it.*

I WILL NEVER LIVE DOWN THE SHAME OR COMPLETELY OVERCOME THE
anguish of the 1992-93 season – forty-two Premiership matches
that saw Nottingham Forest relegated. My eighteenth season in
charge turned out to be my last, the worst of my career. It is right
that I should carry the blame for what, in footballing terms, was a
disaster, because it was my fault.

Forest should not have been subjected to such humiliation.

But the club became the victim of my personal stubbornness, my supreme but misplaced optimism. While the whole country looked on, I was the one standing there, saying over and over again: 'This can't happen to me.'

To be fair, for much of the season everybody – and I do mean everybody – managers, players, directors, journalists and fans – was telling me we were far too good to go down. And until those final, fateful few matches it never entered my mind that we might. There were many contributory circumstances but, looking back, it was my approach and my judgement that were mostly to blame.

Who could have foreseen the problems that lay ahead when, in the Sunday opening game, we beat Liverpool at the City Ground in front of 20,038 spectators? One goal from Teddy Sheringham was enough. Strange how Sheringham was to start the problems that eventually swept Forest out of the élite division of English football. He was to play only two more matches for the club before I decided to let him go to Tottenham.

My mistake was not in selling Sheringham, it was my failure to replace him. Sheringham's ball control wasn't all that hot. At the time I believed that Lee Glover, a brave young man who had overcome serious injuries, was just as good and would see us through.

I had bought Sheringham from Millwall in July 1991, after he rejected late approaches from Tottenham and Chelsea. Thirty-eight League and Cup goals that season represented good value for money, even at £2 million. But he wanted to leave us. He came in and told me he'd like to go back to London.

Old habits die hard with yours truly. I've always followed my tried and trusted instincts and that's what I did, eventually, with Sheringham. If people want to go back to where they've come from, then that is where they're going to be happiest. Sheringham was living what I considered to be a false life. He had separated from his girlfriend, and was seeing his bairn at weekends, occasionally bringing the lad to the ground. There were problems when he was returned to his mother, and I could well understand why. She gave an interview in which she talked about the difficulties of restoring the child to a more modest lifestyle after gifts had been showered upon him by her ex-boyfriend.

So Sheringham was not as happy and contented as he should have been, despite slipping quickly into the Nottingham social scene. Why not? He's quite a handsome young man. But apparently Londoners miss London, a place where I would not have worked if they had given me ten thousand quid a week.

I think someone at Spurs had 'tapped' him, which was inevitable and fair enough, but it just built up from there. At a football club there is only one thing worse than having a player who doesn't want to play for you and that is having one who just can't play. The ones who can't play at least tend to put their lot in – the ones who can play but don't have their hearts in it, you need to sort out straight away.

The Sheringham problem first came to light on a pre-season tour of Ireland. I had stayed behind, and my assistant, Ronnie Fenton, was approached by Sheringham, who had heard a rumour that Tottenham had put in a bid for him. Fenton said he knew nothing about it, and was shocked when Sheringham told him: 'Well, I'm not in any mood to play tonight.' Fenton responded, quite rightly, by telling him that if he didn't fancy playing against Shamrock Rovers somebody else would take his place. And that's the way it was, after Sheringham repeated: 'I don't fancy playing.'

When the team returned from Ireland the newspapers were speculating about a Sheringham transfer to Tottenham, the team he had supported as a boy. I told Fenton and the rest of my staff:

'He's going nowhere until we're ready.' It wasn't long, though, before we heard from Graham Smith – an agent working with Frank McLintock, former captain of Arsenal – who said that he was acting on behalf of Tottenham. Smith offered £2 million for Sheringham, the same figure Forest had paid Millwall. When Ron Fenton told me of the offer my first response was: 'He's not going anywhere.' Smith called again a week or so later, and was again told: 'No chance.'

Not wanting to hang on to a disgruntled player, I was beginning to waver, although Ron was constantly reminding me of our policy: 'We never sell before we buy.' I knew Sheringham was due a £100,000 signing-on fee for each year of his three-year contract. I told Fenton that we would let him go to Tottenham for £2.1 million.

As far as I was concerned, when Teddy Sheringham signed for Tottenham we received our money back. He was paid his £100,000, and all was legitimate and legal. The next thing we hear, months later, is that there's all hell let loose at Tottenham in the so-called clash of personalities between Terry Venables and his new boss, Alan Sugar. Their quarrel ended in the High Court. Not for the first time, my name finished up in banner headlines.

I still cannot understand why my name should have been thrown into a squabble which was Tottenham business and nobody else's. Sugar is not as sweet as his name. In the High Court, he alleged that Venables had said something about £50,000 in cash and 'Cloughie liking a bung'. Terry denied it. It has since been accepted that the notorious £50,000 in the Sheringham case was paid to Frank McLintock and Graham Smith for their professional services as agents working on behalf of Tottenham Hotspur. It is said the money was paid in cash, I don't know. What I do know is that it was not paid to me – not in fivers, not in a plastic carrier bag, not in a lay-by or a motorway service station. Not in any shape or form. Not at all.

It annoys me intensely that things can be said by Sugar or anybody else in the High Court and I have no redress. Like MPs in the House of Commons, people speaking in the High Court are immune. They can stand up and say 'Brian Clough's a poof' or 'you're a thief', and there's nothing we can do about it. I only wish Sugar would repeat his allegations out in the open, away from the protection of the courtroom. I'd love to sue that man!

I was delighted to see, a few months ago, that Terry Venables was officially exonerated. In fact, I don't think an official announcement was necessary. The FA had shown their support of Venables by appointing him as England Coach while the Spurs business was still under investigation. You can't get much more supportive than that. They showed a great deal of faith, which is rare for that organisation. If others had done the same Terry might still have been at White Hart Lane.

Rather than making fortunes out of transfers, I think I have missed out. Some managers, they tell me, have it in their contracts that they receive a percentage of transfer profits. I signed my own son, Nigel, for Nottingham Forest, and he didn't cost them a penny in fees. Ron Fenton and, to a lesser extent, Liam O'Kane – a coach still working with the club – signed a lad called Roy Keane from Irish club Cobh Rangers for £20,000. Within weeks of Fenton and me leaving Forest Roy Keane and my son were sold, to Manchester United and Liverpool respectively, for a combined £6 million.

To the best of my knowledge Fenton and I never had one penny out of either of those deals – not a single penny. That also applies to Sheringham going to Tottenham, a winger going to Rotherham, a full-back moving to Doncaster, any transfer you wish to name. Asking me what it's like to make money out of transfers is like asking: 'What's it like to have VD?' I don't know, I've never had it.

Other transfers became factors in that awful season. Des Walker, the defender we'd helped become a regular international in the England side, had organized for himself a contract that allowed him to leave Forest 'for a song' once he exercised his entitlement to a transfer abroad. We had recruited Walker – another player signed for nowt – as a fifteen year old. No big signing-on fees in those days – you spent the first few years cleaning boots and sweeping out the dressing-rooms and swilling out the bogs. It's changed slightly nowadays, but not too much.

Three years before he left, Walker – a charming young man – had approached me wanting 'rich pickings' – nothing wrong with that. He said: 'I want to buy my mother a house and one for my brother, and I can't do that on the wages you are paying me.' He was out of contract, in the England side, and he knew he had the opportunity of a transfer abroad. The land of opportunity was open to him, he wanted a few bob more, and his performances warranted it. The rules are that if a player is out of contract the club has no control and no option but to offer him at least the same to keep him. Obviously, with players you need, you have to offer more than they had been getting. Otherwise it is their prerogative to say: 'Get stuffed – I can go round the corner and get more money at another club.'

I told Walker that although we'd signed him for nothing as a youngster and he was now an established international player I couldn't bust Nottingham Forest just for his benefit. Eventually he came back with his agent, Dennis Roach, and slapped a three-year proposal in front of me. It represented a fortune in basic wages, but the element that stuck in everyone's craw was a clause stipulating that at the end of the contract he could be bought by a foreign club for £1.5 million. Such is modern football today!

Roach pulled no punches. He is a shrewd operator and knew that if we were determined to hold on to Walker, they had us well and truly by the short-and-curlies. Roach told us: 'Unless that clause is included in a new contract you won't have Des Walker. If you accept it then you have him for another three years.' Simple as that. I agreed, and we held on to Walker for three more years, knowing we would receive only £1.5 million when he left. He helped us get to Wembley four times in his three seasons, so we considered it to be good business, eventually.

Even so, when he left for Italy and joined Sampdoria, he left an awful hole in the Forest defence. I had hoped Darren Wassall would succeed him, but he hopped it as well, moving to neighbouring Derby County for £600,000 the same summer. He too was out of contract and said he wanted a change. In all honesty what he said made a lot of sense. He needed to get on the first rung of the housing ladder, but his wage at Forest was so bad it was embarrassing – around £250 a week with extra if he played in the first team. That was our wage structure, our level. His opportunities had been rare, not only because Walker had stood in his way, but because the lad himself seemed to be injury-prone – something that bugged him at Derby as well. I remember how he once went jogging pre-season to give himself a start and finished up with blistered feet that turned septic. He was out of action for three months! At the time he was asking for his new deal I didn't think Wassall's record or potential warranted the contract he required. The bid from Derby suited him, because it meant he would be that much closer to his parents' home in Birmingham. It suited us too, so away he went.

By the time we had played three games of that dreadful season we had lost three players: Walker, Wassall and the one who scored the winner in that opening game against Liverpool, Sheringham. Injuries restricted Wassall for the rest of that season, allowing him to take part in only half Derby's league games. Nor was the rest of the season exactly to provide a bed of roses for Des Walker, either. I must say this about Des – and it's not a criticism, it is an opinion he will respect – Italian football was not for him. Indeed, before he left, I warned him to his face: 'The money you'll make is one thing and it will probably set you up for life. I hope it does, 'cos I think there will be a price to pay. You are not suited to Italy. Your pace will help you, but I'm afraid it won't be enough.' I was right – he was back in England, with Sheffield Wednesday, after one season in the so-called Promised Land. Over the years at Forest our noisiest supporters at the Trent End of the City Ground had a favourite chant: 'You'll never beat Des Walker.' It broke out every time he won a race for the ball – and he nearly always did get there first. Mind you, in his last season with us, we conceded an alarming number of goals – like Liverpool did last season, another club which built their team on clean sheets, just as I did. So somebody was beating Des Walker the season he left.

I knew the Italians would find him out. They discovered they could turn him quite easily. Their game is played with such exact precision, with players running off defenders and receiving the ball right at their feet – none of the long stuff that enabled Des's extraordinary pace to make him a hero. Why, he ended up playing at left-back for Sampdoria – on the one occasion I asked him to do a full-back's job for me he sulked for a month!

If I saw him now Des would acknowledge the warnings and advice I offered him and probably describe his short stay in Italy as 'an experience'. He would say: 'I'm back in the Premiership, I might not be in the England side but you never know, there could be more caps to come. I had a terrible time in Italy, but at least I made a few bob more than you offered me.' If he has bought houses for his mother and his brother out of the proceeds, perhaps it wasn't such a mistake.

Only just into the season, then, and we were three players short. And what I wasn't to know was that my captain, Stuart

Pearce, would hardly play for me all season. And I do mean all season.

I'd had trouble with Pearce before the season even started. It is my opinion that the problem – involving money and the demand for more, as most player-problems do – festered throughout the season.

At the beginning of that season Pearce had three years remaining of a five-year contract that had been drawn up by his agent, Dennis Roach. I remember Ron Fenton shaking hands with Pearce when the contract was signed and saying bitterly: 'We've got you now for another five years.' Pearce had replied: 'It's only money, Ron.' To which Fenton had responded: 'That's usually the case, isn't it?' But only two years later Pearce wanted his contract changed.

A few weeks before the season started Pearce came to see me. 'The contract I signed two years ago is now out of date,' he said. 'I think I will be the captain of England this year and I deserve more than I'm getting.' He, Ron and I sat down together. 'What are you looking for?' I asked.

He said: 'I want everything doubled – everything in my contract doubled.'

Bearing in mind he was already on four grand a week, I said I thought that was a bit daft. 'I'll pay you a bit more, but you're not getting double.' They were hardly protracted talks. Pearce simply said: 'Well, that's what I'm looking for,' and then got up and walked out. People may be staggered to hear of such demands, but here we have not an isolated case but one typical of modern football at the highest level.

The matter was left for a couple of weeks. I went off to Spain for the holiday I normally used as preparation for the start of a new season. While I was away Ron went to see the chairman, Fred Reacher, and told him he thought Pearce should be offered some increase because, although I had agreed that he deserved 'a bit more', no offer had yet been made. The rules are that if you don't do it before the season starts, you can't change the contract before the following year. Pearce was called in and told that although I was away the new terms would need to be agreed quickly. According to Ron's version of events, Pearce then asked: 'What are you prepared to offer?'

It is important to remember that each year he was due a £100,000 signing-on fee as part of the contract as it stood. Ron made him an offer and later telephoned me with the details. 'I've offered him another £100,000,' he said. 'And what did he say to that?' I asked. When Ron said: 'He's turned it down,' I couldn't believe what I was hearing.

'What?' I said. 'That's ridiculous! Another £100,000 – £60,000 after tax – and he can have that in his hand within weeks? And he's turned it down? I don't believe it.'

But I was miles wide of the mark. I hadn't fully appreciated what Ron had said. That dawned on him, as well, because he rang me some time later and said: 'I think you've got it slightly wrong. I offered him £100,000 *every year* for the rest of his contract.'

'You mean you've offered him £300,000 extra over three years,' I said, 'bumping up his signing-on fee to £600,000 – and he's turned that down?'

When Ron said: 'That's exactly what's happened,' I decided the matter was getting out of all proportion.

Ronnie told Pearce he'd have to wait until 'the gaffer' came back, but warned him he risked not having a deal done by the start of the season. But Pearce had gone into everything. Apparently he'd been to the PFA – the players' union – and been given an extra week's dispensation. We were dealing, here, with a thirty year old who had been a credit to himself and to Forest since I bought him from Coventry for £200,000 in the summer of '85. He'd played more than three hundred games for me and scored more than fifty goals: a worthy and valuable skipper who had established himself in the national side. But there are limits, even for a footballer valued as highly as I valued Stuart Pearce, and I was not about to be held to ransom.

When I got back I pulled Pearce in and said: 'You are being greedy.'

'I don't think I am,' he replied, and the conversation went to and fro, getting nowhere, until I reached the stage at which I could stand it no longer. Inevitably, it finished like this: 'Get out – you're not having another penny.'

After we were relegated, Archie Gemmill turned to me and said: 'There's one player who's really let you down this year.'

'Who's that?' I asked.

'Pearce,' he replied.

Stuart Pearce's heart no longer seemed to be in the club after he failed to get his way with the contract. He had a lot of trouble with injuries that season, and there were times when we thought he was swinging the lead. He wasn't, because he needed an operation on his troublesome groin in the new year and played only once between January and the end of the season in May. But he wasn't with us, either. Neil Webb, whom I'd bought back from Manchester United, was also injured and missed a lot of matches, but he would call into the dressing-room at half-past two and say: 'Good luck, let's get three points.' That was normal procedure – we always had a great dressing-room at Forest. Even when the odds were against us, we could get together and pull things round.

While Webb and others called in and did their best to keep spirits high, Pearce hardly showed his face on match days when he was out of the side. Sometimes I wasn't even sure he came to the matches at all. I always knew where I could find him during the week, though – on the treatment table. His attitude surprised me. I was conscious that the dressing-room missed his moral and physical strength. He had been their example – the one who went out onto the pitch at three o'clock and put in absolutely everything until twenty to five.

I even broke my own rules, letting Stuart join the England squad at a time when we thought he was well on the way to recovery from his damaged groin. Groin injuries are dodgy things. An extra week taking it easy can avoid another six weeks out of action. My philosophy always was that if a player was not fit enough for our club he wasn't fit enough for international duty. In Pearce's case, I took into account the fact that he was England's captain. I told Lawrie McMenemy that Pearce wasn't fit but that I would allow him to join the squad, providing he took things easy. He had been doing a little bit on the training-ground with us, but not full-out by any means.

Graham Taylor was made well aware of Pearce's limitations, I'm sure, but Pearce reported pain in his groin again after the England lot ended one training session doing somersaults. Taylor wasn't to blame, those kind of physical jerks are nothing out of the ordinary – something used to break the boredom. Whether Pearce was wise to join in is another question. When he returned to Forest, injured again, I asked him: 'What were you doing f**king somersaults for?'

'We were all doing them,' he replied. 'I've done them all my life.' But with a groin injury? Sometimes you do assume that a footballer is bright enough to avoid unnecessary risks. Anyway, Stuart's groin had gone again, so we nursed him again – morning, afternoon and night.

Another occasion was a classic. When the Forest physio, Graham Lyas, told me that Pearce's groin had gone yet again, I stormed across to the medical room. 'How come this time?' I asked him. Only twenty-four hours had passed since he had declared himself fit for a reserves game. Pearce, who has stables, told me that one of his horses had got out. He had been jumping over the barbed wire to catch it, when he tripped, injuring his groin again. 'Couldn't you have just let the f**king horse go?' I groaned.

It will surprise many people to learn that I never considered Stuart Pearce to be a particularly good defender. Terry Venables soon decided he wasn't England's best left-back, probably working out, as I did, that when he faces a winger who plays as a winger, he tends to get murdered. He was a good header of the ball, powerful and brave, and scored goals. But he couldn't tackle. When his heart was in the club he was an inspiration, whose enthusiasm and courage and will to win rubbed off positively on the others in the team. But I still feel his heart hadn't been in it, not totally, from the start of that last season.

By Christmas you can usually tell, from your position in the table, what kind of season is in store. We were on the bottom and in trouble. All managers can make excuses for relegation, to such an extent that they can bore the backside off anybody. We had a goalkeeper, Mark Crossley, whom I stood by through thick and thin, despite erratic performances. He handed the only goal to the opposition in an FA Cup tie at Portsmouth, and I later discovered he'd been arrested for some violent offence in the early morning. Our central defence paired Carl Tiler, a lad for whom I had paid £1.5 million to Barnsley, and Steve Chettle, a local youngster totally committed to the club and a pal of Pearce. Tiler didn't develop as I hoped he would. Though Chettle became a regular in the side at Forest and won England Under-21 caps, he will always have limitations at top level. He and Tiler needed Pearce at his best and most committed.

I have always taken problems and setbacks in my stride, but things went badly against us in that last season. I had a record in management second to none, but it was tarnished by that one terrible finale. It was my fault, overall, because I was the one responsible for spending all the money. A million and a half on a centre-half who wasn't up to it at the time; in excess of a million, before that, on the Irishman, Kingsley Black, who was a good squad player but who never justified his fee. Later we bought Robert Rosario for £400,000 – game but limited – and before that I forked out £800,000 to bring back Neil Webb from Old Trafford, but he was never properly fit.

The confidence of the young players dipped. Scot Gemmill's goals dried up. My son Nigel had a thin time too. Only Roy Keane was doing his stuff regularly. Eventually everybody was affected.

I always believed, until it was mathematically beyond us, that we would avoid relegation, but I resisted the temptation to buy our way out of trouble. I was aware that between £3 million and £5 million was required for the improvements to the City Ground to comply with the Taylor Report. I am an optimist, not a pessimist, and I believed that we would put together a string of results to get us out of trouble. It was misplaced optimism. I was wrong. I should have done more about it. I should have bought a centre-half and a centre-forward. I almost did buy Stan Colleymore from Southend. It gives me no pleasure or satisfaction to reveal that I could have signed him and saved Forest half a million pounds!

We were playing Southampton at The Dell on 24 March 1993, the evening before the Thursday transfer deadline. We had been interested in Colleymore for a long time, but all along the line they had insisted that they wanted £2 million for him. I said it was too much – the lad had not done enough to warrant that kind of fee. Before the game Ronnie Fenton told me that we could get him for £1.5 million. 'Let's get the Southampton match out of the way first,' I said, 'it's more important.' We won 2-1, and those goals by Our Nige and Roy Keane effectively killed the Colleymore deal.

On the coach journey home we talked about completing the signing the next day, but I eventually told Ron and the staff: 'We're going to be all right as we are.' That victory at The Dell, following a 1-1 draw with Leeds the previous weekend, had restored my optimism. I believed that we were about to produce the string of results that would see us to safety again.

The reality of relegation only hit home when it actually happened – 1 May 1993, the day we were officially eliminated from the Premiership. Sheffield United, themselves familiar with the struggle for survival, were our visitors at the City Ground and brought thousands of their fans. Together with the good people of Nottingham, they produced Forest's biggest home crowd of the season – 26,752. The match held another slight curiosity, of course, coming five days after the announcement of my intention to retire. There were no ifs or buts – we had to win to stay up. There had been stages where we had games in hand on others, but the way we were playing, that was as useful as a colander for carrying water. It was now or never, muck or nettles, shit or bust. And I cried . . .

Sheffield United scored a goal in each half, to condemn us to relegation. I had never been a manager who followed the modern trend of standing throughout matches – I preferred to sit in the dug-out with my colleagues. For some reason I climbed off the bench some time before the end of that match and just stood. Watching – yes – but thinking, mostly. Thinking about what might have been, what might have been done to save Forest and our loyal supporters from the depression that was about to descend on their ground. Suddenly, after the second goal went in, Sheffield United's supporters, those lovely people from Yorkshire, set up the chant: 'Brian Clough, Brian Clough, Brian Clough . . .' The Forest fans joined in so that, standing there in the old familiar green sweatshirt, I was singled out as the centre of attention for more than 26,000 people. I didn't deserve it. Not the sincerity, the warmth, the concern or the sympathy – not on that occasion. Not on the very day that our worst fears had been realised. The stadium was awash with mixed emotions. Sadness for the club and, I suppose, gratitude towards me for the good days and the enormous achievements that had gone before. The gratitude wasn't misplaced or unappreciated – it was mistimed, that's all. Relegation day is not an occasion for thanksgiving.

Those moments said a great deal for the much maligned football supporters in this country. There was kindness in the air from the United fans, when we might have anticipated sarcasm. There was kindness from the Forest lot too, when we might have expected anger and abuse. They were emotional moments that brought tears as well as a sense of shame to the one wearing the green top whose team was to finish bottom. Shame that lingers with me even now. Shame that will probably never let go.

Everything went through my mind backstage that evening, as I sat with colleagues and friends and a beer or two. The feelings of responsibility for it all seemed to beg a fundamental reaction from me. But what more could be done? What more could be said? Everybody knew beforehand that I was packing it in, that I was already on my way. I felt a little comfort when my grandchildren – Stephen and Susannah – clambered on my knee, oblivious, bless them, to one of the blackest days in the life of their Grandad.

There was one league match remaining, the game at Ipswich on 8 May, where the whole of Suffolk seemed to have turned out to pay tribute to the bloke who'd been relegated the week before. I was mobbed on my way into the ground. The local police presented me with a cake – I've always been a keen supporter of the police in this country, and I like to think that was just their way of acknowledging my support down the years. Another defeat, this time 2-1. The last goal my son was to score for Nottingham

Forest in the Premiership was a second-half penalty at Portman Road.

Overall, the feeling brought about by relegation was one of complete and utter desolation. I'd felt it when I learned my playing career was finished at the age of twenty-nine back in 1964. But this was a different kind of desolation, if that's possible – a feeling of emptiness, of personal let-down and failure and a persistent, nagging question, that pounded and pounded in my head: 'How had it all come down to this?'

Every time I look at the beautiful roses in the gardens around my home in the Derbyshire village of Quarndon, I feel mixed emotions. I adore the scent and the colours of summer – but I am reminded of the Forest flower that wilted.

Those roses will provide a constant reminder of relegation, of the most shameful season in all my years in management, a season that concluded with my retirement from football altogether. They are so vigorous and so strong, because of all the horse muck my ex-captain kindly sends me from his stables. If only we could have relied on Pearce's strength and vigour throughout that season. If only I'd done a better job as manager . . . but then I've always been quick to tell those who churn out 'if only' excuses that if only my Aunt Mary had had balls she'd have been my Uncle Albert.

Pearce looked like leaving Nottingham Forest after we were relegated. Many in the game expected him to move on but he landed himself a lucrative new contract and, to his credit, knuckled down to lead them back to the Premiership at the first attempt. Having achieved that, I can see him remaining loyal to Forest for the rest of his career.

25

THE DAY THEY CLOSED THE BOOK

*I'm going to sit and wallow in the sheer tranquillity
of life beyond management.*

IT SHOULD NOT HAVE ENDED LIKE THAT. MY EIGHTEEN-YEAR CAREER
with Nottingham Forest and forty-one years in professional football
should not have closed in such a sad, squalid, badly handled fashion. I brought brilliant sunshine to the game and should have been
allowed to walk away beneath clear skies, not under heavy, dark
clouds of confusion.

The threat of relegation, soon to become horrible reality,

was bad enough. It was the worst season of my entire life, because it was to be my first season of failure. A year like that is difficult enough to endure for a younger man. At fifty-eight, the pain lingers far longer. Retirement had been on my mind for weeks. I had discussed it with my family and my staff. I had the right to announce it when and where I chose. Nobody should have taken that privilege away from me.

It still hurts inside and I still shed the occasional tear when I recall the way in which Brian Clough's contribution to English football was ended. The day they closed the book.

I telephoned Ronnie Fenton on the Monday morning, 26 April 1993. The previous day, the *Sunday People* had carried a story featuring allegations from Forest director Chris Wootton, who had claimed there had been some sort of *coup* to sack me. He alleged that my drinking had undermined my ability to manage, suggesting I had been legless well before lunch-time.

'I want to see the chairman,' I told Ronnie. 'I want the bastard Wootton sorted out – now! There are pressmen milling around my house. I'll have to get out of Quarndon – can we meet at your place?'

Ron drove over and picked me up and we returned to his home to join the chairman, Fred Reacher. The purpose of the meeting was to discuss Wootton's allegations – nothing else. I wanted to know what the chairman was going to do about him.

I have to confess that during the course of our talks, which lasted less than an hour, I did say to the chairman: 'You do know I'm going to retire at the end of the season?' I think he was a bit surprised and so was Ronnie because, although they were well aware I was contemplating retirement, I had not specified that I would be going at the end of that season. Fred sat back in his chair and said: 'Well, I suspected as much, but I didn't know when.'

Still, the business of the day was Wootton and I told Reacher: 'I want that scumbag kicked out of our club.'

'He's suspended,' Reacher told us. 'There will be an extra-ordinary meeting where he can be removed.'

I wasn't interested in the formalities that might have been necessary: shareholders' votes, official meetings and all that. All I knew was that I had to get Wootton off my patch. I could never have sat in the same room as him after what he had done. To his eternal credit, Fred Reacher assured me he would stand up in court, if necessary, to refute Wootton's allegations. I appreciated that. What I didn't twig was that the chairman was about to jump the gun. It was bad judgement on my part and it was to cause all kinds of anguish within the family.

I should have spotted it the moment I mentioned retiring. After that, Reacher became fidgety and couldn't wait to get out of Ronnie's house. He told us he had to get back to the ground for a meeting with Paul White, the club secretary, and a press conference to make the announcement about Wootton. Ron and I believed that he was going to tell the media of Wootton's suspension, nothing more. When he left, Reacher said nothing about announcing my intention to retire. Nor should he – it was a private conversation between him, Ronnie and me. My retirement was my business, and I anticipated making it public within a few days – certainly not in the immediate aftermath of Wootton's nasty little episode.

I don't know what went through Reacher's mind, but no way did I suspect he was about to face the Press and blurt out the lot. Maybe he panicked or just got carried away, but after revealing that Wootton had been banned he slipped it out that 'Brian will be retiring at the end of the season.' Bloody charming!

Suddenly Wootton was small fry. The story about him didn't matter one jot. In fact, I'm not sure it made a paragraph in the 'nationals' the following morning.

I still had no inkling of what was about to happen even after returning home from Ronnie's house to Quarndon. I had agreed to meet John Sadler, the *Sun*'s sports columnist, who has been writing my stuff for years. He wanted to know about the Wootton situation, but by the time he arrived he already had wind of Reacher's announcement at the press conference.

'I'm saying nowt about the details of Wootton's garbage in the *People*,' I told him. 'He's been suspended and that'll do for now.'

'Forget Wootton,' John said. 'What about your retirement, for Christ's sake? I think my office might just be expecting a piece. Ready when you are, you can start as soon as you like.'

'Retirement? Who's said owt about retirement?'

'Fred Reacher has. There's been a press conference at the ground, he's talked about Wootton's suspension and he also just happened to mention that you're packing it in at the end of the season. In view of yesterday's Sunday papers you couldn't have timed it worse.'

I couldn't believe what John was saying. I could a few minutes later, though, when Barbara rushed into the lounge and said: 'What on earth is going on? What have you done now? I've just heard on the one o'clock news that you're retiring at the end of the season. How could you announce it like this? You know we've talked about it for ages, but how could you put it out today of all days – twenty-four hours after all that stuff from Wootton? You have invited everybody to put two and two together. You must be mad.'

'But I haven't announced anything,' I said. 'We talked about Wootton this morning. That's what the press conference was for. Fred said nothing about blabbing my retirement. He's jumped the bloody gun.'

I had been stupid. Once I mentioned my retirement plan to Reacher I should have said: 'But don't you go mentioning that to anybody. And I mean *anybody*. I'll announce it in good time and in the proper way. Just you deal with that bugger Wootton.'

To say Reacher's 'revelation' caused consternation in my household would be the understatement of the decade. Barbara was livid, and so were my children. They knew of my intention to get out of the game. They knew I'd had enough. They knew it was taking its toll. We are a family and important issues are discussed.

Now my lovely wife doesn't 'go public' very often. She hates publicity, and who can blame her after being married to me for thirty-odd years? But she went public on this. She and the 'children' got together and issued a statement, making it clear that my retirement had been planned for some time and deploring the timing of Reacher's announcement. Hell hath no fury like a woman whose husband has just had his thunder stolen!

It was a total botch-job by Reacher, but I hold no grudge because, knowing the man as I do – and liking him – I am perfectly certain there was no malice intended in his premature announcement of my decision to go. His action was not premeditated, even though it inevitably left an impression that I resigned rather than retired. I had been thinking about retirement for the previous four years!

The season that was just ending had nothing of my so-called illustrious past about it. It had been an absolute nightmare. I kept reminding myself I should have gone two seasons before. There is a time to do certain things and a time not to. There is a time to sell players and a time to buy. There is a time to go on holiday and a time to stay put. There is a time when you need friends and a time when you think – perhaps foolishly – that you can keep going without their advice.

During that final, awful season, each time I looked at myself in the shaving-mirror I said: 'You should have gone, old pal. You missed the right time to call it a day.'

I sometimes think now – and maybe I'm kidding myself

– that if I'd got out after the Cup Final I could have had a period of time out of the game and then come back in some capacity. But pride is beginning to take over and point me in the opposite direction. I am enjoying the release from the pressure and tension, pottering around the house and garden, walking the dog, putting on my dicky bow and attending dinners where they are not expecting me to make a speech. Oh yes, I should have done it years ago.

Whenever I considered retirement, the phrase 'I've had enough' kept crossing my mind. The newspapers started to mention it. Some began fearing for my health – that sort of thing. For years, during his first spell on BBC Radio, Terry Wogan used to get me to work in the mornings. I'd often be seen, driving along the A52, laughing my socks off. The sun was out, the Merc was running like a dream, Wogan was making me giggle – who could fail to look forward to a day's work at a football club on mornings such as those?

The problem now wasn't that I had lost interest. It was just that there wasn't too much cause for laughter. It's harder to smile when your team is at the bottom of the table. Memories helped me through – my OBE at Buckingham Palace, for example. The Queen asked me about the state of English football and I told her: 'It's healthier than ever, Ma'am.'

'Oh, good,' she said, and I'm sure she meant it.

My honorary MA degree from Nottingham University and the 'Freedom of the City' take pride of place, too. Recognition by others, beyond the game, public tributes, tell you that it's not all been controversy and upset. You've made a mark, a worthwhile contribution.

I have two gorgeous daughters-in-law, Simon's wife, Susan, and Nigel's wife, Margaret, and three grandchildren I nickname 'Jackie Coogan', 'Oh Susannah' and 'Walter' – who happens to be a little girl. We see them regularly because they all live near by. If I get grumpy occasionally, Barbara reminds me: 'You do realise how lucky you are, don't you? Your children and the grandchildren could be living in Bournemouth.' That's all it takes to make me realise how lucky I am – particularly as I wouldn't get on a train or drive down the motorway if you paid me a fortune. Now I don't wish to make out my grandchildren as being any better than anybody else's, but they just happen to be attractive, well-behaved, nice grandchildren – and they quite like me. All that was a comfort during my last season.

Even as we became more entrenched at the foot of the Premiership I continued to believe that the sun would start shining, that our fortunes would turn for the better. I never lost my ability to make a decision but I know now that I should have bought a defender and somebody up front to get us a goal. The generation gap was not a problem either, although some people think older managers can lose contact and a little respect the longer they go on. The Clough reputation did not appear to show any cracks. At least, everything seemed to be normal on the surface. But gradually, as we remained at the bottom and the pressure increased, everybody started wondering why I was carrying on – especially after so long in the game.

I'll tell you what keeps a manager going – the chance of three points. When the team wins, it quietens all the dissenting voices – from directors, spectators, friends, relatives and journalists. I wasn't getting enough points to keep me going, and for the first time in my career, I found it hard. I kept thinking of what Don Howe had once said: 'The manager motivates the team, but who motivates the motivator?' In the end, it all proved too much.

I don't have too many regrets in my life but one is that I wish I'd had more time to enjoy my success. Maybe, at Derby and at Forest, we had too much too soon. It was one successful season after another, and I don't think I ever took the full extent of holidays to which I was entitled in my contracts. At

Forest, no sooner were we promoted than we won the League Championship. No sooner had we won the European Cup than we were winning it again. Semi-finals and finals, with Taylor and after Taylor – Wembley, Wembley, Wembley.

Only now, for the first time it seems, can I sit back and say: 'Cloughie, you did your bit, made your mark and gave a lot of people a lot of pleasure.' It was pretty good while it lasted.

Geoffrey Boycott, good old Geoffrey, telephoned Barbara when Forest had clinched promotion to the Premiership at the first attempt last season, and said their immediate return reflected well on me. That was a nice thought, but I couldn't think in those terms. I am grateful to Frank Clark for taking them back without delay. I am glad that I recommended him as my successor. I spent a third of my life at Nottingham Forest and it would have saddened me to see them linger out of the top division.

Unfortunately, I still cannot get rid of the taste of relegation. It is not the acid taste that comes from eating too much and then bending over to cut daffodils. It is a nasty taste of failure. In some ways I would have liked Ronnie Fenton to take over when I retired, but the directors finally appointed the man I suggested years before. Frank Clark faces huge expectations this season. This is when he has to carry the cross and the burden of succeeding me. We must cross our fingers and hold our breath and hope he succeeds. Because it couldn't happen to a nicer man.

As I have explained, I resisted making contact with Forest after retiring. I didn't want to hinder Frank's work, and although I have had a natter or two with Alan Hill, Archie Gemmill and my smashing, loyal secretary, Carole Washington, I made it my business to keep well clear of the place. Little Carole looked after me for ten or eleven years, bless her. Imagine being a secretary with me as her boss for all that time!

I have never seen a baby born. I have never seen the umbilical cord and I don't wish to. I had no desire to see either of my sons or my daughter enter the world. Similarly, I did not want to see the rebirth of Nottingham Forest. I hope the personal ties I formed there remain intact. I gave them a team to remember and built them a stadium that will last a hundred years. I won them trophies and sat the directors in the Royal Box at Wembley. When I left, apart from paying up my contract, they presented me with a beautiful silver rosebowl.

On 23 August this year, I watched our Nigel in action in a Liverpool shirt for the first time. I had resisted the temptation to go to Liverpool, or watch him elsewhere during the entire first season of my retirement. Apart from wanting to cut myself off from the game for a reasonable period, I just didn't want the hassle and attention I knew I would get if I turned up at Anfield – or to any ground for that matter.

So it was not until the second week of the current season that I decided to get off my backside and go to Coventry with Ron Fenton and Colin Lawrence to see my lad playing for the club who had paid more than £2 million for his talents. I'd like to say I enjoyed the experience. And I probably would have if I'd been watching him in the Liverpool first team rather than their reserves. I know I am biased but he really is better than that.

My son Nigel had left soon after me, although there must have been times he wondered why he chose Liverpool. He must also be wishing he had taken up Ronnie Fenton's offer of a new contract, but he resisted signing, preferring, he said, to know what his old man was going to do first. He delayed and delayed and didn't sign a new contract. But Roy Keane did. The Irish lad Ronnie Fenton had found playing for Cobh Rangers and signed for £20,000 signed a new contract all right. And what a good judge he was!

When Forest sold him to Manchester United for £3.75 million, Keane himself picked up £650,000 as a kind of golden handshake. They called it a loyalty bonus, but how could it have been for loyalty – he'd hardly been at the club five bloody minutes? My son, sold to Liverpool for more than £2 million, left without a penny from Forest. Now you may say he deserved nothing, that he was well paid during his time there – obscenely well paid according to his sister, our Elizabeth, who believes footballers are vastly over-rewarded for their efforts. Fine.

But there is something wrong with a system that allows a youngster to pick up £650,000 from a club after only three years, when another receives nowt after almost ten years. Just because one of them signed a contract.

No, 1993 was not the best of years for the Clough family.

EPILOGUE: THE NEXT CHALLENGE

MANY WILD ACCUSATIONS HAVE BEEN MADE ABOUT ME IN CONNECTION with the football manager's constant companion – drink. If I had consumed as much alcohol as the lurid tales suggest then I would have been dead years ago.

Let me attempt to put things in some kind of perspective.

I do drink too much. In the eyes of a teetotaller I drink far too much, but then to a non-drinker one half of beer is more than enough. My problem – if that is not too strong a word – is that booze is part of the managerial scene, part and parcel of my business.

Providing you are working for a club of reasonable means

– and apart from Hartlepools I always did – drink is readily available. It is always there if you want it. It is provided and it is free. If you want to regard it as such, it's a bit like working in an off-licence where the owner says: 'Help yourself whenever you like.'

You have a drink with the chairman. The occasional journalist may be invited to join you. Friends and colleagues, particularly after a match, will sit and share a glass of champagne or whatever takes their fancy, and by the time Monday comes around, the empties have been cleared and the stocks replenished. No different from the boardrooms of major companies or the hospitality suites at television studios. Drink is prevalent in professional football clubs – plentiful, customary and fashionable.

You drink to celebrate a victory. I have had more to celebrate down the years than most of my contemporaries. Sometimes you drink to soften the blow of a defeat, to drown your sorrows if things have not gone well. But my record shows that drink has not impaired my judgement or ability. My drinking was not the cause of Forest's relegation from the Premiership. The reasons for that shameful episode are chronicled elsewhere in this book.

Because of its availability, if you are not very careful, drink becomes a habit that is extremely difficult to break. Mine has become a habit which, according to family and friends, needs curbing – preferably cutting out all together. I regard it as my next challenge.

Whatever life has put in my way, I have met the challenges head on and I have overcome them. Who thought little, run-down Derby County could be turned into League Champions? I did it.

Who thought that Dave Mackay could be persuaded to reject his home-town club, Hearts, and join some young upstart manager who told him he was about to do great things with a dilapidated outfit in the East Midlands? I did it.

Who thought any manager could bounce back from getting

the bullet after just forty-four days with a great club, to go on and prove that he was among the best managers of all time? I did it.

Who thought that what was done at Derby could be repeated and even improved on at Nottingham Forest? I did it.

Who thought that after winning one European Cup, we could follow it up the very next season by retaining the trophy – placing the name of Forest alongside those of the all-time greats: Real Madrid, Benfica, Ajax, Bayern Munich, Liverpool, Inter and AC Milan? I did it.

Who thought that a brash, self-opinionated young footballer whose career was cut down in its prime would go on to forge an even more impressive and lasting name for himself as a brash, self-opinionated and highly successful manager? I did it.

There have been times when I have allowed my drinking to take a hold. There are also times when I steer clear of it for weeks, sometimes months on end. I have reached the moment for me to take a grip on the habit, to address it and make sure it never again gets out of hand. I honestly do not see my liking for a drink as a major problem in my life, although I am aware that my family do worry there are times when I should be more careful and protective towards my own health.

They are right, of course. Like all the other obstacles, all the other challenges in my life, I will face it, tackle it and bring it under my control so that no-one need concern themselves about me. Like all the others I have faced in the past, my next challenge will be beaten.

Whatever steps are necessary to set my family and friends at ease, I will take them. No-one is going to be able to brand Brian Clough as a drinker who lost control and could not conquer his habit. I will beat it . . .

Even if I have to put myself through the mangle.

STATISTICS

PLAYING CAREER

MIDDLESBROUGH

AMATEUR: November 1951. PROFESSIONAL: May 1952
DEBUT: v Barnsley, Ayresome Park, 17 September 1955

		LEAGUE		FA CUP		FL CUP		TOTAL	
		App	Goals	App	Goals	App	Goals	App	Goals
Div 2	1955-56	9	3					9	3
Div 2	1956-57	41	38	3	2			44	40
Div 2	1957-58	40	40	2	2			42	42
Div 2	1958-59	42	43	1	0			43	43
Div 2	1959-60	41	39	1	1			42	40
Div 2	1960-61	40	34	1	0	1	2	42	36
		213	197	8	5	1	2	222	204

NB. 1960-61 was the first season of the Football League Cup.

SUNDERLAND

Signed from Middlesbrough July 1961, £42,000
DEBUT: v Walsall, Fellows Park, August 1961

		LEAGUE		FA CUP		FL CUP		TOTAL	
		App	Goals	App	Goals	App	Goals	App	Goals
Div 2	1961-62	34	29	4	0	5	5	43	34
Div 2	1962-63	24	24			4	4	28	28
Div 2	1963-64								
Div 1	1964-65	3	1					3	1
		61	54	4	0	9	9	74	63

NB. Injured v Bury, Roker Park, 26 December 1962.
Did not play in 1963-64.

CLUB TOTAL

	LEAGUE	FA CUP	FL CUP	TOTAL
App	274	12	10	**296**
Goals	251	5	11	**267**

TESTIMONIAL: Sunderland v Newcastle Select XI,
Roker Park, 27 October 1966. ATTENDANCE: 31,828

CLUB SCORING FEATS: MIDDLESBROUGH

5	v	Brighton	(h)		23.08.58
4	v	Huddersfield	(h)		22.04.57
	v	Doncaster	(h)		11.09.57
	v	Ipswich	(h)		23.11.57
	v	Swansea	(h)		21.03.59
	v	Plymouth	(h)		05.09.59
3	v	Nottingham Forest	(a)		10.11.56
	v	Grimsby	(h)		07.04.58
	v	Scunthorpe	(h)		08.11.58
	v	Brighton	(a)		20.12.58
	v	Scunthorpe	(a)		28.02.59
	v	Charlton	(h)		19.09.59
	v	Bristol Rovers	(h)		21.11.59
	v	Stoke	(a)		12.12.59
	v	Bristol City	(h)		13.02.60
	v	Charlton	(a)		22.10.60
	v	Portsmouth	(a)		28.01.61

SUNDERLAND

3	v	Bury	(h)		27.09.61
	v	Walsall	(h)	(FL Cup)	04.10.61
	v	Plymouth	(h)		28.10.61
	v	Swansea	(h)		09.12.61
	v	Huddersfield	(h)		24.03.62
	v	Southampton	(a)		22.09.62
	v	Grimsby	(h)		03.11.62

FIRST LEAGUE GOAL: Middlesbrough v Leicester City,
Ayresome Park, 08.10.55
LAST LEAGUE GOAL: Sunderland v Leeds United, Roker Park, 05.09.64

REPRESENTATIVE HONOURS

ENGLAND

17.10.59	v	Wales	(Ninian Park)
28.10.59	v	Sweden	(Wembley)

ENGLAND B

06.02.57	v	Scotland	(St Andrews, Birmingham)	1 goal

ENGLAND UNDER 23

26.02.57	v	Scotland	(Ibrox Park, Glasgow)	
19.05.57	v	Bulgaria	(Sofia)	
23.04.58	v	Wales	(The Racecourse, Wrexham)	1 goal

FOOTBALL LEAGUE

08.10.58	v	Scottish League	(Ibrox Park, Glasgow)	1 goal
23.09.59	v	Irish League	(Windsor Park, Belfast)	5 goals

FA XI

30.10.57	v	The Army	(Old Trafford, Manchester)	5 goals

MANAGEMENT CAREER:
MATCHES PLAYED UNDER BRIAN CLOUGH

HARTLEPOOLS UNITED — October 1965 to May 1967

		P	W	D	L	F	A	PTS	Position
Div 4	1965-66	33	13	6	14	48	49	32	18th
Div 4	1966-67	46	22	7	17	66	64	51	8th

DERBY COUNTY — June 1967 to October 1973

		P	W	D	L	F	A	PTS	Position
Div 2	1967-68	42	13	10	19	71	78	36	18th
Div 2	1968-69	42	26	11	5	65	32	63	1st
Div 1	1969-70	42	22	9	11	64	37	53	4th
Div 1	1970-71	42	16	10	16	56	54	42	9th
Div 1	1971-72	42	24	10	8	69	33	58	1st
Div 1	1972-73	42	19	8	15	56	54	46	7th
Div 1	1973-74	12	6	3	3	16	10	15	–

BRIGHTON AND HOVE ALBION — November 1973 to July 1974

		P	W	D	L	F	A	PTS	Position
Div 3	1973-74	32	12	8	12	39	42	32	19th

LEEDS UNITED — July 1974 to September 1974

		P	W	D	L	F	A	PTS	Position
Div 1	1974-75	6	1	2	3	4	8	4	–

NOTTINGHAM FOREST

January 1975 to May 1993

		P	W	D	L	F	A	PTS	Position
Div 2	1974-75	17	3	8	6	16	23	14	7th
Div 2	1975-76	42	17	12	13	55	40	46	8th
Div 2	1976-77	42	21	10	11	77	43	52	3rd
Div 1	1977-78	42	25	14	3	69	24	64	1st
Div 1	1978-79	42	21	18	3	61	26	60	2nd
Div 1	1979-80	42	20	8	14	63	43	48	5th
Div 1	1980-81	42	19	12	11	62	44	50	7th
Div 1	1981-82	42	15	12	15	42	48	57	12th
Div 1	1982-83	42	20	9	13	62	50	69	5th
Div 1	1983-84	42	22	8	12	76	45	74	3rd
Div 1	1984-85	42	19	6	17	56	48	64	9th
Div 1	1985-86	42	19	11	12	69	53	68	8th
Div 1	1986-87	42	18	11	13	64	51	65	8th
Div 1	1987-88	40	20	13	7	67	39	73	3rd
Div 1	1988-89	38	17	13	8	64	43	64	3rd
Div 1	1989-90	38	15	9	14	55	47	54	9th
Div 1	1990-91	38	14	12	12	65	50	54	8th
Div 1	1991-92	42	16	11	15	60	58	59	8th
Prem L	1992-93	42	10	10	22	41	62	40	22nd

LEAGUE MATCHES UNDER CLOUGH

PLAYED	1,140
WON	505
DRAWN	291
LOST	344
GOALS FOR	1,678
GOALS AGAINST	1,298

HONOURS

DERBY COUNTY

1967-68	FL Cup semi-final
1968-69	Division 2 champions
1970-71	Watney Cup winners
1971-72	League champions; Texaco Cup winners
1972-73	European Cup semi-finalists

NOTTINGHAM FOREST

1976-77	Division 2 promotion; Anglo-Scottish Cup winners
1977-78	League champions; League Cup winners
1978-79	European Cup winners; League Cup winners; League runners-up
1979-80	European Cup winners; European Super Cup winners; World Club championship finalists; League Cup finalists
1980-81	European Super Cup finalists; World Club championship finalists
1983-84	UEFA Cup semi-finalists
1887-88	Mercantile Credit Trophy winners
1988-89	League Cup winners; Simod Cup winners
1989-90	League Cup winners
1990-91	FA Cup finalists
1991-92	Zenith Data Systems Cup winners; League Cup finalists

Between November 1977 and December 1978, Nottingham Forest completed 42 First Division matches without defeat.

INDEX